University of Cologne Forum »Ethnicity as a Political Resource« (ed.)
Ethnicity as a Political Resource.
Conceptualizations across Disciplines,
Regions, and Periods

UNIVERSITY OF COLOGNE FORUM
»ETHNICITY AS A POLITICAL RESOURCE« (ED.)
Ethnicity as a Political Resource
Conceptualizations across Disciplines,
Regions, and Periods

[transcript]

The Uoc Forum »Ethnicity as a Political Resource« is an interdisciplinary body of researchers promoting inter-institutional and international scientific exchange. It is part of the Institutional Strategy of the University of Cologne within the framework of the German Excellence Initiative.
The members are: Sarah Albiez-Wieck, Anja Becker, Mario Krämer, Albert Manke, Michaela Pelican, Antonio Sáez-Arance, Tobias Schwarz, Sofie Steinberger, and Thomas Widlok.

Bibliographic information published by the Deutsche Nationalbibliothek
The Deutsche Nationalbibliothek lists this publication in the Deutsche Nationalbibliografie; detailed bibliographic data are available in the Internet at http://dnb.d-nb.de

© 2015 transcript Verlag, Bielefeld

All rights reserved. No part of this book may be reprinted or reproduced or utilized in any form or by any electronic, mechanical, or other means, now known or hereafter invented, including photocopying and recording, or in any information storage or retrieval system, without permission in writing from the publisher.

Cover layout: Kordula Röckenhaus, Bielefeld
Printed in Germany
Print-ISBN 978-3-8376-3013-8
PDF-ISBN 978-3-8394-3013-2

Contents

Preface of the editors | 7

ETHNICITY AS A POLITICAL RESOURCE IN DIFFERENT ACADEMIC DISCIPLINES

Introduction: Ethnicity as a political resource viewed by scholars from different academic disciplines
Anja Katharina Becker | 11

Ethnicity from an anthropological perspective
Christoph Antweiler | 25

More than meets the eye
Analytical frameworks beyond race and ethnicity
Frederik Holst | 39

The universal and the particular
Contrasting nomothetic and idiographic comparisons
Tobias Schwarz | 57

Rethinking 'race' from Asian perspectives
Yasuko Takezawa | 75

Ethnicity as social deixis
Thomas Widlok | 85

ETHNICITY AS A POLITICAL RESOURCE IN DIFFERENT REGIONS OF THE WORLD

Introduction: Ethnicity as a political resource in different regions of the world
Mario Krämer | 99

Politicizing ethnicity – ethnicizing politics
Comparisons and entanglements
Christian Büschges | 107

The contestation over the indigenous in Africa
The Ethiopian example
Dereje Feyissa/Meron Zeleke | 117

Ethnicity as a political resource
Indigenous rights movements in Africa
Michaela Pelican | 135

Ethnicity or nationality?
Minority policy and ethnic conflict in contemporary China
Li Xi Yuan | 151

ETHNICITY AS A POLITICAL RESOURCE ACROSS DIFFERENT HISTORICAL PERIODS

Introduction: Ethnicity as a political resource across different historical periods
Sarah Albiez-Wieck | 171

Ethnicity in history
Wolfgang Gabbert | 183

Political uses of ethnicity in early medieval Europe
Walter Pohl | 201

The work of race in colonial Peru
Rachel Sarah O'Toole | 209

Araucanos or 'Mapuches'?
Prejudice vs. recognition in the Chilean media and academia
Antonio Sáez-Arance | 221

Chinese in the Cuban revolution
An ethnically marked political mobilization?
Albert Manke | 237

Authors | 253

Preface of the editors

Ethnicity as a political resource is a seminal subject in numerous disciplines. Studies on ethnic formations, indigeneity, autochthony, international migration, nationalism, multiculturalism, and racism often approach this topic from a particular disciplinary point of view. However, while much research has been conducted on the formation of ethnicity and its impact on political mobilization in different regions across the globe, the question of whether these political uses of ethnicity are comparable remains unresolved. The same can be said for historical processes of negotiation of collective identities, and the question of whether they should be considered as examples of the use of ethnicity as a political resource. In this regard, the role of both European and non-European forms of colonial expansion is still subject to debate.

The University of Cologne Forum 'Ethnicity as a Political Resource: Perspectives from Africa, Latin America, Asia, and Europe' (UoC Forum 'Ethnicity') is an interdisciplinary body of researchers promoting inter-institutional and international scientific exchange. Its members are the editors of this volume. They are researchers from the Department of Cultural and Social Anthropology, the Department of Iberian and Latin American History, the Department of African Studies, and the Global South Studies Center within the University of Cologne.

The UoC Forum 'Ethnicity' is part of the Institutional Strategy of the University of Cologne within the framework of the German Excellence Initiative. Its objective is to strengthen the interdisciplinary and international dialogue on the formation of ethnic identities and their use as a political resource, applying a diachronic and comparative perspective.

In April 2014, the UoC Forum 'Ethnicity' organized an international conference on 'Conceptualizing Ethnicity as a Political Resource – across Disciplines, Regions, and Periods'. Our aim was to establish a novel base for research on ethnicity – bringing together scholars who might not usually meet to start a new conversation. This conference was the starting point of our endeavor to bridge the gaps within ethnicity research and to bring together views and perspectives from different fields, research topics, and historical foci. In this conference, we attempted to conceptualize ethnicity as a political resource by addressing it from three interrelated angles: How is it viewed by scholars from different academic disciplines? What forms does it take in various regions of the world? And how can it be investigated with specific reference to distinct historical periods? We invited scholars from diverse scientific backgrounds and global regions to interact in three consecutive roundtable discussions, and to jointly develop a comprehensive approach to ethnicity as a political resource.

The great interest in the conference and its success led us to the idea of a joint publication in order to make our debates accessible to a broader public. We believe this publication makes a substantial contribution towards new approaches in the study of ethnicity, and represents the start of an unprecedented conversation between scholars from different disciplinary, regional, and historical backgrounds.

We thank the institutions who helped us to realize this new and exciting endeavor, the University of Cologne for funding the UoC Forum 'Ethnicity', its activities, and the present volume. We appreciate the inspiring discussions with the participants of the conference that significantly influenced the making of this publication. Our special thanks go to the contributors to this book and to Sofie Steinberger for the coordination and patiently holding all the threads together.

University of Cologne Forum 'Ethnicity as a Political Resource':

Directors:
Michaela Pelican (Department of Cultural and Social Anthropology)
Albert Manke (Department of Iberian and Latin American History)

Members:
Sarah Albiez-Wieck (Department of Iberian and Latin American History)
Anja Becker (Department of Cultural and Social Anthropology)
Mario Krämer (Department of Cultural and Social Anthropology)
Antonio Sáez-Arance (Department of Iberian and Latin American History)
Tobias Schwarz (Global South Studies Center)
Sofie Steinberger (Department of Iberian and Latin American History)
Thomas Widlok (Department of African Studies)

Ethnicity as a political resource
in different academic disciplines

Introduction: Ethnicity as a political resource viewed by scholars from different academic disciplines

ANJA KATHARINA BECKER

Ethnicity as a political resource is a seminal subject in numerous disciplines, such as social and cultural anthropology, history, political science, sociology, psychology, cognitive science, and biology. Studies on ethnic formation, indigeneity, autochthony, nationalism, social movements, and transnational mobility often approach these topics from a particular disciplinary point of view. While most researchers agree on the significance of research on ethnic identities and their use as socio-political resources, the various disciplinary approaches to conceptualizing and understanding these phenomena have not yet been discussed within an interdisciplinary framework. In this section, different authors attempt to pinpoint crucial similarities and differences: Are we all talking about the same things when we use specific terms? What are the underlying paradigms behind the concept of ethnicity and related notions in different disciplines? Furthermore, the authors highlight the distinct methodological approaches used in specific fields and discuss how we can most effectively conceptualize and compare various scales and scopes of research. The aim of this section is to start a cross-disciplinary dialogue, to identify gaps, to compare results, and to plan future orientations.

In the following, I will address the major divergences and convergences in the study of ethnicity, and highlight debates and differences in terms of methodologies, concepts and discourses related to the study of ethnicity, to provide a condensed overview of the relevant debates and to point out central complexities and challenges.

MAIN DIVERGENCES AND CONVERGENCES IN THE STUDY OF ETHNICITY

The literature on ethnicity is quite fragmented and compartmentalized. On the one hand, there is some separation between ethnicity, race, and nationhood, i.e. they are sometimes seen as separate fields of study, and not all research perspectives handle them together. On the other hand, the literature is also fragmented along disciplinary lines. There is relatively little cross-fertilization between work in sociology, anthropology, political science, and history, and still less between these and other disciplines such as archaeology, linguistics, economics, and the humanities. Finally, the literature is fragmented along regional lines, too: comparative work is scarce, and there is often little awareness of cross-regional variation in understandings and configurations of ethnicity (Hale 2004: 458; Brubaker 2009: 22). The fact of this three-dimensional fragmentation is a good reason to scrutinize the different approaches to the topic of ethnicity within the various fields.

Anthropological consideration of ethnicity has its origins in the research of the first generation of urban anthropologists working in Africa. Seminal work such as J. Clyde Mitchell's (1957) study of the Kalela Dance in Rhodesia (now Zambia) and Epstein's (1958) monograph, *Politics in Urban African Community* challenged the assumption that detribalization was the inevitable outcome of the movement of rural dwellers to cities. Much of this early work wrestled with the conceptual differences between 'tribe' and 'ethnic group' and resulted in the delineation of three distinct theoretical approaches to the study of ethnicity. The *primordialist approach*, which prevailed until the 1960s, argues that ethnic identity is the result of deep-rooted attachments to group and culture. The *instrumentalist approach* focuses on ethnicity as a political strategy that is pursued for pragmatic interests. And the *situational approach*, emerging from the theoretical work of Barth (1969), emphasizes the fluidity and contingency of ethnic identity which is constructed in specific historical and social contexts (Banks 1996). The latter approach remains the dominant paradigm in anthropological theory to this day (cp. more on this in Antweiler's chapter in this section).

Political science approaches the topic of ethnicity from both an empirical and a normative perspective. As for the former, constructivist assumptions dominate studies of ethnogenesis and changing configurations of ethnic identities, whereas primordialist assumptions dominate theories that are concerned with the effects of ethnic identity on some political or economic outcome (Chandra 2012). As for the latter, the central question is one of determining the sociopolitical implications of ethnic movements for the liberal state. Classical liberals such as

Rawls (1971), Dworkin (1977), and Kymlicka (1996) emphasize the rights enjoyed by ethnic minority groups in contrast to social majorities, and they argue that society must, first and foremost, accommodate and safeguard the plurality of ethnic identities. Communitarian thinkers like Sandel (1982), MacIntyre (2007), and Taylor (1994), on the other hand, argue that the concerns of the social majority may, under certain circumstances, trump the interests of minorities, and they hold that the function of the state is not primarily one of protecting social pluralism, but rather one of promoting the collective interests of society as a whole. In general, however, it should be noted that normative political theory often simply assumes the nature of ethnicity and nationalism as given, with less emphasis placed on the constructedness of social groups and more on the social and political consequences of group claims. In contrast, constructivist social theory accounts tend to reject any solitary notion of groups, emphasize the complex and cross-cutting identities at play in the postmodern world, and articulate the consequences of a more fluid (and contested) politics of identity and representation (May et al. 2004: 5–8). These debates, which also link in with anthropological discussions of culture and ethnicity, thus highlight the complex, and at times constructed and contradictory interconnections between identity claims, their political mobilization, and their social and political consequences. Along with related discussions in cultural studies, feminist studies, and some strands of political philosophy, these debates also explore issues to do with postmodernity, postcoloniality and globalization, and their influence upon articulations of ethnicity, racisms, gender identities, and other forms of social and cultural identity and politics in the postmodern world (cp. Said 1978; Benhabib 1992; Hall 2000). A detailed treatise on the notion of ethnicity in history is featured in Section C of this volume. In this chapter, Takezawa concerns herself with the notion of race from a historical perspective, especially with how race became a globalized concept in the course of colonialization.

Cognitive scientists address the social and mental processes that sustain the interpretation of the social world in ethnic terms. Drawing on experimental findings regarding a general disposition toward essentialist modes of thinking (Medin/Ortony 1989, Gelman/Wellman 1991, Rothbart/Taylor 1992), Hirschfeld (1996) and Gil-White (2001) posit a deep-seated cognitive disposition toward perceiving human beings as members of 'natural kinds' with inherited and immutable 'essences'. Experiments with three- and four-year-olds show that humans have a dedicated cognitive device for partitioning the social world into 'intrinsic kinds' based on 'shared essences'. (Hirschfeld 1996) This provides the cognitive foundations for what Hirschfeld calls "folk sociology" (ibid: 20), which he characterizes as the "commonsense [...] social ontology that picks out the 'natural' kinds of people that exist in the world" (ibid: 20). Hirschfeld emphasizes the worldwide presence of a deep classificatory logic underlying what are on the surface strikingly different systems of racial, ethnic, and national classification. Kurzban et al. (2001) argue, however, that this kind of classificatory encoding is only a contingent byproduct of more fundamental cognitive processes evolved to detect coalitional affiliations and alliances. If ethnic categories are "easy to think" (Hirschfeld 1996: 10), this does not mean that they are universally active or salient. Cognitive perspectives suggest that one way to study the varying salience of ethnicity is to study not only the content of ethnic representations but also the distribution of such representations within a population, their accessibility, their relative salience once activated, and the relative ease with which they 'slot' into or 'interlock' with other key cultural representations (Sperber 1985; DiMaggio 1997). What cognitive perspectives suggest, in short, is that ethnicities are one way of making sense of the world that is grounded in more fundamental cognitive facts; they are ways of understanding and identifying oneself, interpreting one's problems and predicaments, and identifying one's interests.

METHODOLOGICAL DIFFERENCES AND DEBATES IN THE RESEARCH ON ETHNICITY

The issue of methodology with respect to the topic of ethnicity can be illustrated on the basis of two significant dichotomies: the quantitative vs. qualitative dichotomy (including the dichotomy of large-scale studies vs. case studies), and the etic vs. emic dichotomy (cp. also introduction to Section C). Furthermore, there is considerable debate about the question of whether research on ethnicity should be based on comparative studies, or whether this endeavor is an implausible or even impossible one.

Qualitative and quantitative methods are still widely considered in the research methods literature to belong to two distinct research traditions (Creswell 2003: 18). Qualitative research commonly consists in the collection and analysis of material that seeks to uncover meaning and to promote the understanding of the experiences of the research subjects. By contrast, quantitative research is about the collection and analysis of numerical data – the social facts. Each of the two research processes is associated with specific research techniques: Qualitative research methods include, for example, ethnographic case studies, interviews, and observation. Quantitative methods, on the other hand, comprise questionnaires, surveys, and statistics, as well as computer-assisted analytical techniques. This dichotomy is rooted in the basic assumption that both types of method are connected to different, and potentially incompatible epistemological positions, i.e. different conceptions of what knowledge is, what science is, and of how we come to know things. From an epistemological point of view, qualitative research is often thought to value subjective and personal meanings, while quantitative research is construed in terms of testing theories and making predictions in an objective and value-free way. It implies a clear separation of the researcher from the research process and its objects, including people. This dichotomy can be summarized in the following table.

Table 1: The Traditional Dichotomy between Quantitative and Qualitative Methodologies

Quantitative Methods	Qualitative Methods
Search for general laws of behavior, empirical regularities, with a view to making theoretical generalizations	Search for meanings in specific social/cultural contexts, with only limited possibilities for theoretical generalization
doption of the natural science paradigm (where objectivity is valued)	Rejection of the natural science paradigm (subjectivity is valued)
Attempt to create or to simulate experimental situations	Attempt to observe reality in natural settings
Explanation = prediction of events, behavior, attitudes ("statistical causality")	Explanation = understanding, interpreting reasons for observable behavior; sense given to actions ("historical causality")
Use of large-scale study samples and random sampling	Use of small-scale sample groups; case studies; purposive sampling
Analysis of data based on deduction	Analysis of data based on induction or grounded theory
Use of survey instruments with predetermined response categories based on predetermined theoretical frameworks (e.g. questionnaires)	Use of open-ended research instruments (semi-structured interviews, life histories, focus groups, observation, etc.) from which theoretical categories (may) emerge
Numbers (measurement)	Words ("thick description")

Source: Damaris 2001: 3.

This strict dichotomy is undercut by an approach that is commonly labeled the mixed-methods approach. It can be defined as the combination of quantitative and qualitative research methods and approaches based on pragmatic knowledge claims (Bryman 1984; Johnson/Onwuegbuzie 2004). Mixed-methods research is a complementary, inclusive, and expansive form of research rather than a restrictive form of research (Johnson/Onwuegbuzie 2004). Among the strategies used in mixed-methods research are sequential, concurrent, and transformative procedures (Creswell 2003). Johnson and Onwuegbuzie (2004) claim that the problems associated with a single-method study can be reduced by the mixed use of quantitative and qualitative methods in a single study, since the strengths of both methodologies can be incorporated within the same research. Mixed-methods approaches are becoming ever more popular in interdisciplinary projects on ethnicity, as well as in the social sciences and humanities (cp. Brubaker 2009, Wimmer 2013, and Holst in this chapter) It should be noted, however, that the mixed-methods approach has garnered its fair share of criticism: due to their different epistemological foundations both approaches are much more difficult to reconcile than is admitted by proponents of such integrative accounts (Creswell 2003).

The distinction between the emic and etic approaches was initially proposed by Pike (1954) and adapted to develop typologies for cross-cultural comparison derived from field data (Sanday 1979). Etic and emic researchers proceed from divergent assumptions about culture based on their own constructs. Etic researchers tend to segregate common components of culture and test hypotheses. They attempt to identify universal aspects of human behavior and universal processes that transcend cultural differences or to produce new theories that can be utilized across cultures (Fukuyama 1990). In other words, this approach assumes that all cultures can be compared in terms of generalizable phenomena. In contrast, the emic approach attempts to identify culture-specific aspects of concepts and behavior, which cannot be comparable across all cultures. The endeavor of cultural anthropologists who seek to understand culture from the native's point of view (Malinowski 1922) is the main foundation of the emic approach. In the field of cross-cultural research, the emic approach involves examining one culture at a time to evaluate how insiders or participants interpret a phenomenon. The criteria for evaluating behaviors relate to the insiders, and the structure is discovered by the researchers. Despite these differences, Morris et al. (1999) argue that the etic and emic approaches are complementary and that researchers ought to use both perspectives in order to remain objective without sacrificing a deeper understanding from the insider's perspective.

At the core of both dichotomies – that is, quantitative vs. qualitative, etic vs. emic – is the question of whether ethnic groups or ethnic phenomena are, ultimately, comparable. Is it possible to develop a set of concepts, terms and categories that are relevant across different cultures, countries, and even continents? This is a contentious issue. While some researchers advocate working towards standardized instruments and categories for use across diverse settings (Aspinall 2007), others argue that processes of ethnogenesis are so historically and geographically specific that such harmonization is impossible (Favell 2001). This tension relates to the fundamental epistemological question of how research should steer a course between identifying the similarities across, and the differences between, the settings under investigation (Livingston 2003). Here, proponents of both qualitative and emic approaches tend to favor the assumption of incomparability, while proponents of the quantitative and etic approaches opt for comparability.

A major objection against international comparative designs is that they too easily assume an essentialist conceptualization of ethnicity. Echoing objections against the primordialist approach, it is suggested that cross-cultural large-scale studies treat ethnic group identities as natural and fixed and seek explanations largely in genetic or cultural factors (Ellison 2005). Understandings of ethnic identity that emphasize its contingent, contested and fluid nature may sit uneasily with cross-national comparative research. At best, it is argued, studies that seek to compare the experiences and outcomes of migrant/minority groups across national settings offer little in the way of analytical purchase; and at worst, they privilege genetic or culturalist accounts (since they might implicitly assume an ethnic 'essence' that is independent of time or place). However, recent work has argued that comparative research can be useful precisely because there is a need to take social context seriously, and because it allows an exploration of how the significance of ethnic identities varies over time and place (for an extensive discussion on comparative methodologies with an emphasis on comparison within emic approaches, cp. Schwarz in this section).

RELATED CONCEPTS AND DISCOURSES

To understand many of the discussions and debates within the contributions of this volume, it is vital to distinguish and briefly present some of the basic concepts closely related to ethnicity.

There are different approaches in contemporary literature towards the conceptualization of phenomena related to the overall topic of ethnicity. The first approach seeks to establish universal etic parameters to delineate ethnic groups. However, many theorists acknowledge the difficulties involved in providing a universal definition of ethnicity that fits all different groups in various settings and historical contexts (for a constructivist critique, cp. Holst in this section). Consequently, other approaches – which will be addressed in the following – focus on the particular relations of individuals and/or groups to political, legal, and geographic as well as social and emotional contexts.

The second approach takes into account criteria such as emotional attachments and sentiments of belonging, and emphasizes the fluidity and flexibility of ethnic identities (for a case study on multiple ethnic identities in Namibia, cp. Widlok, this section). In this context, notable core concepts are ethnic identity and belonging. Much of the research on ethnic identity has been based on the study of group identity by social psychologists (e.g. Tajfel/Turner 1986). From this perspective, ethnic identity is an aspect of social identity, defined by Tajfel as "that part of an individual's self-concept which derives from [his] knowledge of [his] membership of a social group (or groups) together with the value and emotional significance attached to that membership" (1981: 255). Recently, the use of identity as a term in ethnicity studies has been increasingly criticized. Critics state that the term is a slippery and overburdened concept (Brubaker 2009) but also that it says too little (Anthias 2002). In the critics' view, the term tends to suggest mutually exclusive identities, and that identity is a possessive property of individuals. As an alternative concept, the notion of belonging is favored by many. Pfaff-Czarnecka highlights its advantage, as "identity is a categorical concept while belonging combines categorisation with social relating" (2013: 6). 'Belonging', as an analytical term, can enable us to ask questions about *what* a person belongs to, rather than, as with identity, *who* an individual *is*, or who and what they *identify with* (which are in fact two different questions). Certainly, the use of identification maybe entailed in the notion of belonging as well as in the notion of identity. But more than identification, belonging actually not only entails issues about attributions and claims (as does identity), but also allows us to address more clearly questions about the actual spaces and places where people are accepted as members or feel accepted, as well as broader questions about social inclusion and forms of violence and subordination entailed in processes of boundary-making (Anthias 2013).

The third approach focuses on relationships with political and legal institutions such as states. Here, the main concepts are nationality and citizenship, which are analytically separate. McCrone and Kiely define the difference as follows: "nationality and citizenship actually belong to different spheres of meaning and activity. The former is in essence a cultural concept which binds people on the basis of shared identity – in Benedict Anderson's apt phrase as an 'imagined community' – while citizenship is a political concept deriving from people's relationship to the state. In other words, nation-ness and state-ness need not be, and increasingly are not, aligned" (2000: 25). However, despite the fact that we can clearly distinguish the two concepts, there are also theoretical grounds for expecting the obvious confusion of sense of self as a citizen and sense of national identity that is expressed in many historical and biographical accounts. Furthermore, both concepts are, historically speaking, closely intertwined since they not only emerged simultaneously in Enlightenment political discourse, but were also conceived as two sides of the same coin: a socio-political community of equal citizens unified by a shared nationhood (cp. Gellner 1995). However, as we will see in the next approach, the link between citizenship and nationality is not as close as one might think – as becomes clear for example when former immigrants become naturalized citizens without being considered part of the nation by their fellow citizens.

The fourth approach concentrates on the geographical linkage of groups. The most relevant concepts are autochthony and indigeneity. Both terms go back to classical Greek history and have similar etymological meanings. Autochthony refers to self and soil. 'Indigenous' literally means 'born inside', with the connotation in classical Greek of being 'born inside the house'. Thus, both notions inspire similar discourses: on the one hand, the need to safeguard 'ancestral lands' against 'strangers' who 'soil' this patrimony; on the other hand, the right of first-comers to special protection against later immigrants (Ceuppens/Geschiere 2005). Nonetheless, both terms have followed separate trajectories, with different repercussions for issues of belonging today. Over the past decades, the notion of indigenous peoples has acquired a new lease of life with truly global dimensions, especially since the founding of the United Nations Working Group on Indigenous Populations (1982), representing groups from all six continents (Hodgson 2002). Around the same time, autochthony became a key notion in debates on multiculturalism and immigration in several parts of Europe. The spread of the notion into Western contexts is of particular interest. Most Westerners think of indigenous peoples as 'others' who live in far-flung regions and whose cultures can only survive if they receive special protection, but the epithet autochthon is claimed by important groups in the West itself. This term thus highlights the prominence that the obsession with belonging and the exclusion of strangers have assumed in day-to-day politics worldwide, in the North as much as in the South (Geschiere 2009; Pelican 2009). Concepts like indigeneity and autochthony approach the realm of ethnicity through the political, legal, and public discourses on nationality, citizenship, and belonging (cp. Feyissa/Zeleke, Section B, for more on the concept of indigeneity).

Of course, the various approaches and views that I have outlined are often combined and can complement each other. It must also be noted that intersectional categories like class, gender, and power, which have not been discussed here in greater detail, are important analytical instruments, too (cp. for example O'Toole in this volume).

In the following, five authors will delineate their approaches to the issue of ethnicity and related questions from the perspectives of anthropology, political science, and cognitive science.

CONTRIBUTIONS

Christoph Antweiler is a cultural anthropologist with a background in cognitive and evolutionary theory. In his contribution, he undertakes the challenging project of defining the key concepts used in interdisciplinary discourses on ethnicity. Starting from an anthropological perspective, he gives both a historic and a systematic account of the meanings and usage of terms such as 'identity', 'collective identity', 'ethnicity', 'collective group', and 'ethnic group'. Finally, he addresses the question of whether there are plausible alternatives to be found to the established terminology, and he points out two promising approaches in psychology and sociology.

Frederik Holst has a multidisciplinary background in communication studies, political science, and South East Asian studies. In his contribution, he focuses on the conceptual use of ethnicity and race and considers alternative notions. He proposes a shift from studies on ethnicity to research on ethnicization. He proposes a processual approach: (1) Many conflict issues should not be framed along the lines of identity group categories, but would be better examined along the lines of more complex categories such as class, gender, or state power. (2) He proposes the concept of 'ethnicized' groups instead of 'ethnic' groups. Ethnicization does not reinforce static notions of group identity and belonging, but helps to disentangle the manifold ways in which race and ethnicity have become rooted in various societies. Speaking of ethnicized rather than ethnic groups underlines a fundamentally different approach when describing identity-group formation processes. Instead of ascribing features to homogenous groups, ethniczation emphasizes the constructedness, the politics involved in, and the processes that lead to group formations.

Tobias Schwarz's background is in cultural studies. He deals with an important methodological question – how can we compare research findings on ethnicity? In his contribution, he draws on research on naturalization from political and anthropological scientists to juxtapose large-scale quantitative studies and (mostly) qualitative single-case studies. Using the classification of 'nomothetic' and 'idiographic' as a way to pinpoint the major differences in comparative research by political scientists and anthropologists, he highlights how deductive comparative research that tries to generate universal terminology out of specific emic vocabulary can lead to essentialization, but he also highlights how an inductive comparative perspective can help to find new insights and an overall more detailed understanding of the subject matter.

Yasuko Takezawa is an expert on Asian-American studies whose main research interests are nationalism, the politics of history, and national identity. In her contribution, she argues that the concept of race is an indispensable analytical resource for understanding social phenomena of oppression, marginalization, and resistance against socio-political hegemony. She distinguishes between three aspects of the various phenomena constituting the idea of race: 'race' in the lower-case sense, 'Race' in the upper-case sense, and 'race as resistance'. While 'race' in the lower-case sense refers to differences observed in particular societies understood as inherited over generations, 'Race' in the upper-case sense uncovers cases where race is used as a pseudo-biological construct. Finally, 'race as resistance' indicates a discursive strategy to expose existing racial discrimination.

Thomas Widlok is a cultural anthropologist with a strong focus on linguistics. In his contribution, he analyses emic individual attributions of ethnic identity. He advances the thesis that ethnicity has to be understood first and foremost as a way of referencing ethnic status. In this context, he holds that ethnic referencing is deictic in nature; that is, that the meaning of ethnic terms is dependent on how they are used in different circumstances. The main advantages of importing the notion of deixis to ethnicity studies are, among others, a better understanding of how, when, and why persons switch between ethnic and alternative modes of referencing; and the establishment of a single framework within which universal and culturally relative aspects of ethnic reference can be analyzed.

REFERENCES

Anderson, Benedict (1991): Imagined Communities: Reflections on the Origin and Spread of Nationalism, London: Verso.
Anthias, Floya (2002): "Where do I belong? Narrating collective identity and translocational positionality." Ethnicities 2/4, pp. 491–514.
—— (2013): Identity and Belonging: conceptualisations and political framings, Cologne: Kompetenznetz Lateinamerika - Ethnicity, Citizenship, Belonging, KLA Working Paper Series 8.

Asal, Victor/Shellmann, Stephen/Howard, Ttiffany (2010): "Methodological Developments in Nationalism, Ethnicity, and Migration Research." In: Robert A. Denemark (ed.): The International Studies Encyclopedia: Blackwell Publishing.

Aspinall, Peter (2007): "Approaches to developing an improved cross-national understanding of concepts and terms relating to ethnicity and race." In: International Sociology 22, pp. 41–70.

Banks, Marcus (1996): Ethnicity: Anthropological Constructions, New York: Routledge.

Barth, Frederik (1969): Ethnic Groups and Boundaries, Boston: Brown and Company.

Benhabib, Seyla (1992): Situating the Self. Gender, Community and Postmodernism in Contemporary Ethics, London: Routledge.

Betancourt, Hector/Lopez Steven Regeser (1993): "The Study of Culture, Ethnicity, and Race in American Psychology." In: American Psychologist 54, pp. 629–637.

Brubaker, Rogers (2009): "Ethnicity, Race, and Nationalism." In: Annual Review of Sociology 35, pp. 21–42.

Bryman, Alan (1984): "The debate about quantitative and qualitative research: a question of method or epistemology?" In: The British Journal of Sociology 35, pp. 75–92.

Ceuppens, Bambi/Geschiere Peter (2005): "Autochthony: local or global? New modes in the struggle over citizenship and belonging in Africa and Europe." In: Annual Review of Anthropology 34, pp. 385–407.

Chandra, Kanchan (2012): Constructivist Theories of Ethnic Politics, Oxford: Oxford University Press.

Creswell, John (2003): Research Design: Qualitative, Quantitative, and Mixed Methods Approaches, London: Sage Publications.

Damaris, Rose (2001): "Revisiting Feminist Research Methodologies." In: Women Canada Research 22, pp. 2–18.

DiMaggio, Paul (1997): "Culture and cognition." In: Annual Review of Sociology 23/1, pp. 263–87.

Dworkin,Ronald (1977):TakingRightsSeriously,Cambridge:HarvardUniversityPress.

Ellison, George (2005): "'Population profiling' and public health risk: when and how should we use race/ethnicity?"In:Critical Public Health 15/1,pp.65–74.

Epstein, Arnold (1958): Politics in an Urban African Community, Manchester: Manchester University Press.

Favell, Adrian (2001): "Integration policy and integration research in Europe: a review and critique." In: Alexander Aleinikoff/Douglas Klusmeyer (eds.),

Citizenship today: global perspectives and practices, Washington DC: Brookings Institute, pp. 349–399.

Fukuyama, Mary (1990): "Taking a universal approach to multicultural counseling." In: Counselor Education and Supervision 30/1, pp. 6–17.

Gellner, Ernest (1995): Nations and Nationalism, Ithaca: Cornell University Press.

Gelman, Susan/Wellman, Henry (1991): "Insides and essences: early understandings of the non-obvious." In: Cognition 38, pp. 213–44.

Geschiere, Peter (2009): The Perils of Belonging: Autochthony, Citizenship, and Exclusion in Africa and Europe, Chicago: University of Chicago Press.

Gil-White, Francisco (2001): "Are ethnic groups biological 'species' to the human brain?: Essentialism in our cognition of some social categories." In: Current Anthropology 42/4, pp. 515–54.

Hall, Stuart (2000): "The Multicultural Question. In: Pavis papers in social and cultural research, pp. 1–26.

Hale, Henry (2004): "Explaining Ethnicity." In: Comparative Political Studies 37, pp. 447–469.

Hirschfeld, Laurence (1996): Race in the Making: Cognition, Culture and the Child's Construction of Human Kinds, Cambridge, MA: MIT Press.

Hodgson, Dorothy (2002): "Introduction: Comparative Perspectives on the Indigenous Rights Movement in Africa and the Americas." In: American Anthropologist 104/4, pp. 1037–1049.

Johnson, R. Burke/Onwuegbuzie, Anthony (2004): "Mixed methods research: A research paradigm whose time has come." In: Educational Researcher 33/7, pp. 14–26.

Kurzban, Robert/Tooby, John/Cosmides, Leda (2001): "Can race be erased? Coalitional computation and social categorization." In: Proceedings of the National Academy of Sciences of the United States of America 98/26, pp. 15387–15392.

Kymlicka, Will (1996): Contemporary Political Philosophy. An Introduction, New York: Oxford University Press.

Livingstone, Sonia (2003): "On the challenges of cross-national comparative media research." In: European Journal of Communication 18, pp. 477–500.

MacIntyre, Alasdair (2007): After Virtue, Notre Dame: Notre Dame University Press.

Malinowski, Bronislaw (1922): Argonauts of the western Pacific, London: Routledge.

May, Stephen/Tariq Modood/Squires Judith (2004): Ethnicity, nationalism and minority rights, Cambridge, UK: Cambridge University Press.

McCrone, David/Kiely, Richard (2000): "Nationalism and Citizenship." In: Sociology 34, pp. 19–34.

Medin, Douglas/Ortony Andrew (1989): "Psychological essentialism." In: Stella Vosniadou/Andrew Ortony (eds.), Similarity and Analogical Reasoning, New York: Cambridge University Press, pp. 179–95.

Morris, Michael/Leung, Kwok/Ames, Daniel/Lickel, Brian (1999): "Views from inside and outside: Integrating emic and etic insights about culture and justice judgment." In: Academy of Management Review 24/4, pp. 781–796.

Mitchell, Clyde (1957): The Aspects of social relationships among urban Africans in Northern Rhodesia, Manchester: Manchester University Press.

Pelican, Michaela (2009): "Complexities of indigeneity and autochthony: An African example." In: American Ethnologist 36, pp. 52–65.

Pfaff-Czarnecka, Joanna (2013): "Multiple Belonging and the Challenges to Biographic Navigation." In: MMG Working Paper 13/5.

Pike, Kenneth (1954). Language in relation to a united theory of the structure of human behavior, Glendale: Summer Institute of Linguistics.

Rawls, John (1971): A Theory of Justice, Cambridge: Harvard University Press.

Rothbart, Myron/Taylor, Marjorie (1992): "Category labels and social reality: do we view social categories as natural kinds?" In: Gun Semin/Klaus Fiedler (eds.), Language, Interaction and Social Cognition, London:Sage, pp.11–36.

Said, Edward (1978): Orientalism, New York: Vintage Books.

Sanday, Peggy Reeves (1979): "The ethnographic paradigm(s)." In: Administrative Science Quarterly 24/4, pp. 527–38.

Sandel, Michael (1982): Liberalism and the Limits of Justice, New York: Oxford University Press.

Sperber, Dan (1985): "Anthropology and psychology: towards an epidemiology of representations." In: Man 20, pp. 73–89.

Tajfel, Henri (1981): Human groups and social categories, Cambridge, England: Cambridge University Press.

Tajfel, Henri/Turner, John (1986): "The social identity theory of intergroup behavior." In: Stephen Worchel/William Austin (eds.), Psychology of intergroup relations, Chicago: Nelson-Hall, pp. 7–24.

Taylor, Charles (1994): Multiculturalism. Examining the Politics of Recognition, Princeton: Princeton University Press.

Wimmer, Andreas (2013): Ethnic boundary making. Institutions, power, networks, Oxford: Oxford Univ. Press.

Ethnicity from an anthropological perspective

CHRISTOPH ANTWEILER

Among the main questions discussed in relation to ethnicity, viewed from an interdisciplinary angle, are the following: Is ethnicity a specific *cultural* form of identity, or merely a variant of collective identity? Is ethnicity a phenomenon of all human societies, or primarily a trait of small-scale societies? Is ethnicity of less importance in *functionally* differentiated modern societies? How much relevance should be given to ethnicity in an emerging cosmopolitan or plural world society? Should there be rights based explicitly on *collectives* and *ethnic* identities?

COLLECTIVE AND PERSONAL IDENTITY IN A GLOBALIZED WORLD

Whereas the term 'identity' was already popular in the early 20th century, 'ethnicity' and 'ethnic identity' have only become buzzwords since the 1960s (Glazer/Moynihan 1963; Niethammer 2000; Wikan 2002). Since the 1980s, the notion of collective identity has become a globally common 'currency' of interest politics (Baumann/Gingrich 2004; Cornell/Hartmann 2006, Schlee/Zenker 2009). Claims for economic or political participation began to be made with reference to to culture or tradition rather than by invoking e.g. poverty or basic needs. In a similar manner, when arguing for the exclusion of people from contested resources, the reference shifted from race to culture. The (explicit) allusion to corporeal features receded, but the dominant perspectives on human collectives basically remain categorical and essentialistic.

The specific global formation of collective identity today progresses approximately thus: (a) personal subjectivity is to a certain extent experienced via collective identity; (b) reference to collective identity is the principal means by which to fight for rights, resources and/or recognition; and (c) ethnicized versions of collective identity are appropriated in postcolonial contexts, especially by leaders of ethno-nationalist governments and representatives of indigenous minorities (e.g. Breidenbach/Nyiri 2009; Radtke 2011).

Identity, whether personal or collective, is about staying (partially) the same in the context of others. Thus, identity is always related to difference and demarcation. In both personal as well as collective identity dynamics, both inclusion and exclusion, and often also discrimination, are principally implied. Ethnicity is an aspect or variant of collective identity. Concepts of collective identity were first developed mainly in sociology (cp. e.g. Krappmann 2010; Eickelpasch/Rademacher 2013; Keupp et al. 2013). Collective identity is about perceived or experienced consistency and continuity in human collectives. Human cultures can survive trans-generationally only in the form of collectives. But as a cognitive and emotive phenomenon identity is always related to individual consciousness. The question 'Who are we?' is related to the question 'Who am I?', and *vice versa* (Eriksen 1973; for overviews cp. Leary/Tangney 2012; Schwartz et al. 2012). Thus, as a research topic, collective identity should always be conceptually embedded in personal identity. The connection between both emerges from the questions 'to whom do I (factually) belong?' and 'to whom do I feel I belong?'.

Increasingly, identities, be they personal or collective, have to be negotiated. In view of the multiplicity of options, more and more 'identity work' has to be done (Keupp et al. 2013). For the individual, negotiation with oneself as well as with others includes emotional issues. A central question is the extent to which identity remains subjective and internal, or else is shown openly, thus becoming quasi-objective (Taylor 1977).

The main disciplines to which ethnicity is relevant are sociology, cultural anthropology and cultural studies, social psychology, political science, and the evolutionary sciences[1]. The main disciplinary divergences I see are between cultural anthropology and (a) sociology, (b) cultural studies and (c) evolutionary sciences. This paper is focused on ethnicity as it is approached and discussed in cultural anthropology (social anthropology, anthropologie culturale) today.[2] On the one hand, cultural anthropology is the discipline most often consulted if ethnicity is scientifically reflected. On the other hand, many anthropologists are

---

1   Sociobiology, evolutionary psychology, evolutionary ecology and paleo-anthropology.
2   On the history of the concept, which I cannot cover here, cp. e.g. Heinz 1993, and core texts in Hutchinson/Smith 1996.

among the most serious critics of the concept, especially as it is used in the wider public sphere, e.g. by the media as well as by representatives of ethnic groups.

THE ANTHROPOLOGICAL PERSPECTIVE ON ETHNICITY

The core of ethnicity is the consciousness and feeling of individuals that they are members of a 'We'-group, and their behavioral actions in light of this feeling. Ethnicity is a socially grown collective identity, which assumes a common history and origin as well as shared traditions, and claims to define a culture as different from (all) others. The main anchors and motivating forces for this identity seem to be those of a common language and/or religion (Smith 2003).

Anthropology offers several explanations of the meaning and function of ethnicity. In the following, I want to highlight the primodialist and the constructivist approaches.

The primordialist anthropological approach stresses the continuity of ethnicities: it explains ethnicity with reference to a factual shared history and common origin of the respective collective as an ethnic group (e.g. Naroll 1964).

Others criticize these assumptions and argue that ethnicity is always dynamic and historically specific. Here, ethnicity is conceptualized in a functional or utilitarian way. Ethnicity is interpreted as a result of human interests, political manipulation, and maneuvering by individual or collective actors.[3] It is assumed that ethnicity usually has some individual benefit or social function. Human actors use cultural differences and boundaries between collectives as a resource to achieve specific aims versus competing actors. These aims are not always political, but are often economic (Comaroff/Comaroff 2009). Leaders of human collectives such as ethnic groups use references to ethnicity to achieve conformity among members and to motivate for solidaric action. The collective appears as an ethnic group. In this process, specific current values, norms, and practices are selectively stressed, and specific traditions or aspects of the group's factual history are selected from the historic consciousness or collective memory. Often such alleged 'historic' traits or traditions are in fact created (cp. e.g. Bernard Lewis 1987 on 'invented history').

The constructivist anthropological approach assumes that ethnicity is about boundaries. The principal source of this approach is the classic work of Fredrick

---

3 It is also called 'situationalism', as differences due to social situations are invoked; and 'instrumentalism' due to an assumed strategic using of identity.

Barth (1988 [1969]).[4] Barth and his followers focus on cognitive and symbolic boundaries between collectives, rather than on actual cultural traits or differences. Thus, anthropologists studying ethnicity are more focused on boundary-making, i.e. processes of categorization and the construction of boundaries. The boundary ('We/They') is more relevant than the specifics defining the collective's way of life, such as norms, values, religion, or practices ('cultural stuff'). In contrast to the assumptions of primordialists, the shared way of life among the members of a collective is *not* seen as the basis of cultural boundaries, but as an effect of them. This implies that boundaries are dynamic and that membership may be fluid. Despite the functional importance of cultural boundaries, members of respective collectives can move to another collective.

A further implication refers to the relation between inter-cultural contacts and cultural similarities. The contact and exchange between members of different collectives does not automatically lead to a cultural convergence (i.e. assimilation). Because of the positive functionality of boundaries, contact often results in differences being stressed (Bateson 1985). Typically, groups which interact (e.g. through trade or partner exchange) converge in their ways of life but diverge in their internally shared conceptions of what 'We' and 'They' are (dissimilation). The respective boundary is usually conceptualized as a sharp, dividing, and unambiguous line. Most often, this contrast-intensifying perspective is associated with a worldview centered on the own collective and portraying it in a positive light. The concept might be called a concentric dualism. The high esteem in which the own group is held is combined with an explicitly negative attitude towards other collectives ('Us/Them'), most often neighboring groups. The own group, even if it is a large collective of thousands of people, is perceived as a kinship unit. This ethnocentrism takes the form of a syndrome, as it not only consists of concepts, but also includes feelings, attitudes, and practices.

HOW TO RECOGNIZE ETHNICITIES EMPIRICALLY?

Ethnicity is not confined to cognition, emotion, or consciousness and related behaviors, but also includes all the other material and behavioral aspects of collectives. How do anthropologists recognize ethnicity, when observing in the field, transcribing interviews, analyzing survey data, or looking at written or

---

4   The idea has forerunners in the work of the Manchester School in Central Africa and Edmund Leach's early work on the Kachin in Burma (1954).

other archival records? Identity is first and foremost an individual issue. Thus, to recognize ethnicity, we must link collective identity with individuals and their actions, because cultures do not talk (cp. Radtke 2011)! We need to combine an emic approach using 'naturalistic' data, such as e.g. linguistic and cognitive information, with an etic approach using experimental and laboratory data as well as documentary studies. This combined approach is required because of the basic characteristics of identity. Like individual identity, ethnicity is primarily a cognitive-*cum*-emotional and behavioral phenomenon. To recognize psychic aspects empirically we should seek words and idioms indicating emic sentiments and concepts (e.g. ethnonyms, 'Our land', 'We/They'; 'Us/Them'). To discern behavioral effects we should document e.g. marriage preferences, preferred trade partners, and ethnic work specialization. To find out about the institutional ramifications of ethnicity we should look for state-generated statistics, censuses, and other measures of statal ethnicism. Material traces may be found e.g. in building arrangements, symbols, and patterns of ethnic residential segregation.

POST-BARTHIAN APPROACHES

Recent approaches build on Barth's classic insights (1998 [1969]), his earlier and later empirical studies and refinements (1959; 1966; 1983; 1994; 2002), and critiques of these (Gronhaug et al. 1991; Vermeulen/Govers 1994; Pascht et al. 1999; Bailey 2001; Poutignat/Streiff-Fenart 2008; Guibernau/Rex 2010). Recent works are critical of the focus on boundaries and on ethnic groups as units (Banks 1996; Sökefeld 1999; 2007; Fenton 2010; Jenkins 2014). One post-Barthian shift in anthropological ethnicity research refers to the traits used in the process of othering by the actors. The criteria for differentiation from others often do not derive from members of these groups but are attributed to them by other people or other collectives. These other groups – e.g. colonial powers or the national state – provide terms, criteria, and categories for and about collective groups (e.g. through censuses) (Eriksen 2010). In this vein, there is a sharpened focus in research on religion, power, and economy as factors forming ethnicities, and on systems of ethnic stratification as well as economic segmentation and specialization according to ethnicity.

Another shift is a renewed reflection on the concepts of ethnic groups. Today we can empirically show that in large societal systems there may be ethnicized categories without ethnic groups (Brubaker 2004). This is especially the case in complex, culturally diverse or pluralistic societies. Consequently, ethnic groups cannot be conceptualized as quasi-natural units of social life. This implies that if we find ethnic groups empirically, their existence as social and acting units has to be *explained* instead of simply being assumed.

BEYOND CULTURE PROPER: MAIN DISCIPLINARY DIVERGENCES

The constructivist approach to ethnicity is the dominant one, and has its merits (Wimmer 2010). Boundaries are accepted as a major aspect of ethnicity (Orywal 1986; Wallmann 1986; Orywal/Hackstein 1993). A central contested point, however, is the existence and relevance of *cultural difference*. A broad consensus since Fredrik Barth's work is the idea that boundaries are more relevant and more persistent than differences within the 'cultural stuff'. One divergence among scientists pertains to the importance of these ethnic boundaries. Whereas cultural studies tend to speak of 'cultural landscapes', cultural anthropology, along with biological anthropology and political science, tends to stress the existence and permanent importance of cultural boundaries. Permanent importance is not to be equated with stability. Most cultural anthropologists and evolutionary scientists tend to regard ethnic groups as a universal phenomenon in human societies, and both stress the functional usefulness of boundaries. But whereas cultural anthropology stresses their constructed, instrumental and changing character, evolutionary scientists point to *primordial* continuities, and to the fact that these cultural constructions are *constrained* in several ways.

In terms of offering explanations, there are also problems for any constructivist approach. Constructivist theories of ethnicity fail to explain (a) the universality of ethnicity and ethnocentrism (Berreby 2005), (b) the fact that ethnicity is experienced and perceived by most persons as being primordial (Van den Berghe 1987), and (c) the fact that kinship is the most effective idiom in ethnic groups as well as in nationalism (Anderson 1996; Smith 2003; Malešević 2013). Why are ethnic sentiments far easier to generate with the imagination of 'family' than with references to collectives at higher levels of scale? To explain such observations we need to incorporate theories from anthropology and cultural studies and their insights into human nature. Humans have certain cognitive, emotive and behavioral inclinations, which were formed during the evolution of humanity. Humans spent most of their evolutionary history within small-scale collectives. Small groups functioned as their "cultural survival vehicles" (Pagel 2012). Thus, kin-selection, and other theories and insights from fields such as evolutionary anthropology, evolutionary ecology, human sociobiology, and evolutionary psychology, are relevant. This point seems to be accepted by only a minority of social scientists and anthropologists (e.g. Meyer 2010; Fox 2011; Antweiler 2012b).

Another dispute is located within the social sciences. The divergence is between anthropologists studying smaller social units on the one hand, and other social scientists, especially sociologists, focused on large-scale modern national societies. Cultural anthropologists tend to view ethnicity as an aspect of the general identity of human collectives at different scales (from 180 members of a village in New Guinea to about 1.2 billion Han-Chinese). Sociologists consider ethnicity as a notion common to 'traditional' societies; one which is not suited to modern – that is, functionally specialized – mass societies. Whereas cultural anthropologists tend to call for special rights for migrants or ethnic minority groups or indigenous peoples, sociologists stress the general rights of individual citizens of states, or what could be called 'cosmopolitan human rights'.

Laymen, the mass media, and especially leaders and advocates of ethnic groups often tend to use an essentialistic concept of ethnicity (similar to that of old-fashioned anthropology) as a cultural weapon. The perception is one of clearly bounded ethnic communities with a collectively shared We-consciousness. An especially severe problem emerges from the public use – in the media and often also by representatives of the collectives themselves – is that ethnicity is increasingly simply equated with culture as a way of life. This perspective assumes that ethnic groups are natural quasi-units and portrays ethnicities as congruent with ethnic groups.

HOW TO EXPLAIN ETHNICITY AND GAPS IN SOCIAL SCIENCE EXPLANATIONS?

We should seek explanations at several levels; both more specifically and more generally. To explain more specific and constructive aspects of ethnicity, we have to look at strategies, tactics, and interests, and the realities of the specific socio-cultural setting. In the context of construction, we should also not forget emotional factors. For the more primordial and universal aspects of ethnicity (e.g. categorical thinking, in-/exclusionary behavior, emotive forces) we also have to include our evolutionary past and compare our psychic and behavioral tendencies with those of other primates. For example, ordering and categorizing things and social partners is not specifically human, but naming categories and discussing relations among them is (cp. examples in Schlee/Zenker 2009).

These different, and not necessarily competing, levels of explanation can be illustrated with arguments about the *functionality of boundaries*. Anthropological and sociological variants of functionalism explain ethnic boundaries by their utility for political and economic co-ordination and fostering social coherence in human collectives vs. other collectives. Evolutionary accounts (Pagel 2012; Tomasello 2014) argue for a deeper functionality related to natural selection. The specific quality of ethnicity is due to one human specifity: the faculty to *intentionally* cooperate with groups of relatives *and even with non-relatives*. Group formation and the erection of social boundaries allow groups to combine kin altruism and reciprocal altruism with a further form of altruism only found among humans. This is altruism towards people with similar interests, but who are not relatives. Such an altruism includes even people not personally known but who are nevertheless *trusted* by virtue of their being members of one's 'We'-group with its instituted rules and norms of cooperation. Cooperation and group formation are related to both individual interests and anticipated group size. Decision-making and utilitarian considerations are also relevant to the notion of identity, and thus rational choice theory approaches (sidelined by most anthropologists) should be revisited (Banton 2014).

ARE THERE ALTERNATIVE TERMS OR CONCEPTS?

We should look for alternatives not only to the term 'ethnicity', but also to 'ethnic group'. In this line of thought we could revisit the concept of *ethnos* in classical Soviet anthropology. *Ethnos* combines the assumption of an objectively existing ethnic group with biotic continuity (though not necessarily closed) with the subjective dimension of identity (Bromlej 1974; cp. Tishkov 1992 for a critical assessment). The main alternative terms for ethnicity are 'ethnic identity', 'cultural identity', and 'collective identity' (if they are not used as a mere synonym for ethnicity). Despite different uses and definitions, ethnic identity' mostly refers to the individual, experiential dimension of 'ethnicity; 'cultural identity' stresses the locally and historically grown specifics of identity, and 'collective identity' covers the idea that this identity does not pertain only to ethnic collectives, but is a general phenomenon, also found among other types of collectives (e.g. nations).

One conceptual alternative might be to focus on an integral element of ethnicity: dualistic thinking; with psychology being the main relevant discipline. The argument would be that such binary thinking is a general necessity for reducing complexity and that it translates to thinking about collective relations.

A second alternative to ethnicity might be found in the new concept of transdifference, as developed in literature studies. The idea is that conceptual boundaries may be subdued at times and in specific social contexts, but will crop up again at other times and in other situations (cp. Antweiler 2008; Kalscheuer/Allolio-Näcke 2008). For example, religious differences might be subdued via inter-religious dialogue but crop up again if competition for a resource emerges between followers of the respective beliefs.

A third alternative would be to think more in terms of belonging instead of ethnicity (cp. Geddes/Favell 1999; Yuval-Davis 2011: 1–45, Pfaff-Czarnecka 2012: 19–46). This would place more stress on the possibility of multiple memberships (Mecheril 2003). More than with 'ethnicity', the emphasis would be on emotional familiarity and symbolic relatedness to people, places and social spaces. The last point would also be inline with the current reexamination of issues of spatial acquaintedness, nostalgia, and longing, and thus also with the problematic notion of *heimat*. A last option is to see ethnicity in modern complex societies as being of reduced importance relative to functional specialization, a specialization in work, and a differentiation of socio-cultural milieus and tendency toward pluralistic individualization. Viewed historically, these would be conceptualized as partial successors of ethnicity in large-scale societies. Sociology is the most relevant discipline here (Eickelpasch/ Rademacher 2013; Keupp et al. 2013).

The big open questions in ethnicity research do not only revolve around ethnicity as such but also pertain to the very nature of human collectives. The interconnected world of today has made flexible identities and multiple group memberships almost normal. Nowadays 'only' half of humankind lives in cities. But seen structurally, almost all humans socially and psychically exist in an urban world. They live densely packed in built environments. On a normal day they meet more people not personally known to them than a prehistoric person would meet during an entire lifetime. Strangeness itself becomes globalized, and thus an everyday cosmopolitanism becomes imperative (Calhoun 2003; Antweiler 2012a; Rumford 2013). The question is whether *spatially focused* and *ethnically* oriented collectives continue to have a place in *functionally* differentiated societies, despite the mobility of collectives and the general interconnectedness characteristic of an emerging world society. The general forms as well as the variants of human collectivity are an under-studied topic in the social sciences. There are several levels of sub-national as well as supra-national collectives. What are the principal differences between 'ethnic' collectives – such as ethnic groups, indigenous peoples, and ethnic nations – and other collectives, such as corporate cultures, subcultures, and political cultures?

It is a pity that the social sciences so often talk about collective identities without having a clear concept of collectives (cp. Hansen 2009 for a refined attempt).

I conclude:

- Ethnicity should not be conflated with endurance, stability or sustainability, and with the contents of current ways of life or traditions in human collectives.
- Ethnicity was and is used as a political resource, but the concept itself should not be reduced to this instrumental aspect.
- As a concept used strategically by members of collectives, ethnicity is a part of social reality of complex societies, and should be studied as such. Despite sympathies for ethnic groups, migrant minorities, and indigenous peoples, anthropologists and other scientists should not fall prey to the concepts used by their political leaders or representatives.

REFERENCES

Anderson, Benedict (1996 [1983]): Imagined Communities. Reflections on the Origins and Spread of Nationalism, London/New York: Verso.
Antweiler, Christoph (2012a): Inclusive Humanism. Anthropological Basics for a Realistic Cosmopolitanism, Göttingen: V+R Unipress/Taipeh: National Taiwan University Press (Reflections on (In) Humanity 4).
—— (2008): "Das Transdifferenz-Konzept auf dem Prüfstand: ethnologische Theorie und Befunde." In: Britta Kalscheuer/Lars Allolio-Näcke (eds.), Kulturelle Differenzen begreifen. Das Konzept der Transdifferenz aus interdisziplinärer Sicht, Frankfurt am Main/New York:Campus, pp. 293–315.
—— (2012b): "On Cultural Evolution. A Review of Current Research toward a Unified Theory of Societal Change." In: Anthropos 107/1, pp. 217–227.
Bailey, Frederick George (2001): Treason, Stratagems and Spoils, Boulder, Col.: Westview Press.
Banks, Marcus (1996): Ethnicity. Anthropological Constructions, London, New York: Routledge.
Banton, Michael (2014): "Updating Weber on the Racial, the Ethnic and the National." In: Journal of Classical Sociology 14/4: pp. 325–340.
Barth, Fredrik (1959): Political Leadership Among Swat Pathans., London: Athlone Press (London School of Economics Monographs 19).
—— (1966): Models of Social Organization, London: Royal Anthropological Institute (Occasional Papers 23).

—— (1983): Sohar. Culture and Society in an Omani Town, Baltimore: Johns Hopkins University Press.

—— (ed.) (1998 [1969]): Ethnic Groups and Boundaries. The Social Organization of Culture Difference, Prospect Hights, Ill.: Waveland Press.

—— (1994): "Enduring and Emerging Issues in the Analysis of Ethnicity." In: Henk Vermeulen/Chris Govers (eds.), The Anthropology of Ethnicity. Beyond Ethnic Groups and Boundaries, Amsterdam: Het. Spinhuis, pp. 11–32.

—— (2002): "Toward a richer description and analysis of cultural phenomena." In: Richard Fox/Barbara King (eds.), Anthropology Beyond Culture, Oxford: Berg, pp. 23–36.

Bateson, Gregory (1985): "Kulturberührung und Schismogenese." In: Gregory Bateson: Ökologie des Geistes: Anthropologische, psychologische, biologische und epistemologische Perspektiven, Frankfurt a. M.: Suhrkamp, pp. 99–113.

Baumann, Gerd/Gingrich, Andre (eds.) (2004): Grammars of Identity/Alterity. A Structural Approach, Oxford/New York: Berghahn.

Berreby, David (2005): Us and Them. Understanding Your Tribal Mind, New York/Boston: Little, Brown.

Breidenbach, Joana/Nyiri, Pàl (2009): Seeing Culture Everywhere. From Genocide to Consumer Habits, Seattle/London: University of Washington Press,

Bromlej, Yulian V. (1974): "The Term Ethnos and its Definition" In: Yulian Bromley (ed.): Soviet Ethnology and Anthropology Today, The Hague etc.: Mouton de Gruyter (Studies in Anthropology), pp. 5–72.

Brubaker, Rogers (2004): Ethnicity without Groups, Cambridge, Mass.: Harvard University Press.

Calhoun, Craig (2003): "Belonging in the Cosmopolitan Imaginary." In: Ethnicities 3, pp. 531–568.

Comaroff, John L./Comaroff, Jean (2009): Ethnicity, Inc., Chicago: The University of Chicago Press (Chicago Studies in Practices of Meaning).

Cornell, Stephen/Hartmann, Douglas (2006): Making Identities in a Changing World, Thousand Oaks: Pine Forge Press (Sociology for A New Century).

Eickelpasch Rolf/Rademacher, Claudia (2013): Identität, Frankfurt a.M.: transcript (Themen der Soziologie).

Erikson, Erik H. (1973). Identität und Lebenszyklus. Drei Aufsätze, Frankfurt a.M.: Suhrkamp.

Eriksen, Thomas Hylland (2010): Anthropology, Culture and Society. Ethnicity and Nationalism. Anthropological Perspectives, London: Pluto Press.

Fenton, Steve (2010): Key Concepts: Ethnicity, London/New York: Polity Press, John Wiley/Sons (Key Concepts).

Fox, Robin (2011): The Tribal Imagination. Civilization and the Savage Mind, Cambridge, Mass: Harvard University Press.
Geddes, Andrew/Favell, Adrian (eds.) (1999): The Politics of Belonging. Migrants and Minorities in Contemporary Europe, Aldershot: Ashgate (Contemporary Trends in European Social Science).
Glazer, Nathan/Moynihan, Daniel Patrick (1963): Beyond the Melting Pot. The Negroes, Puerto Ricans, Jews, Italians and Irish of New York City, Cambridge, Mass.: Harvard University Press.
Gronhaug, Reidar/Haaland, Gunnar/Henriksen, Georg (eds.) (1991): The Ecology of Choice and Symbol. Essays in Honour of Fredrik Barth, Bergen: Alma Mater Forlag AS.
Guibernau, Montserrat/Rex, John (eds.) (2010): The Ethnicity Reader. Nationalism, Multiculturalism and Migration, Cambridge/Malden, Mass.: Polity Press.
Hansen, Klaus P. (2009): Kultur, Kollektiv, Nation, Passau: Stutz (Schriften der Forschungsstelle Grundlagen Kulturwissenschaft 1).
Heinz, Marco (1993): Ethnizität und ethnische Identität. Eine Begriffsgeschichte, Bonn: Holos (Mundus Reihe Ethnologie 72).
Hutchinson, John/Smith, Anthony D. (eds.) (1996): Ethnicity, Oxford: Oxford University Press.
Jenkins, Richard (2014): Social Identity, London/New York: Routledge (Key Ideas).
Kalscheuer, Britta/Lars Allolio-Näcke (eds.) (2008): Kulturelle Differenzen begreifen. Das Konzept der Transdifferenz aus interdisziplinärer Sicht, Frankfurt a. M./New York: Campus.
Keupp, Heiner et al. (2013): Identitätskonstruktionen. Das Patchwork der Identitäten in der Spätmoderne, Reinbek bei Hamburg: Rowohlt (Rowohlts Enzyklopädie).
Krappmann, Lothar (2010): Soziologische Dimensionen von Identität. Strukturelle Bedingungen für die Teilnahme an Interaktionsprozessen, Stuttgart: Klett-Cotta.
Leach, Edmund R. (1954): Political Systems of Highland Burma. A Study of Kachin Social Structure, London: Athlone Press.
Leary, Mark R./Tangney, June Price (eds.) (2012): Handbook of Self and Identity, New York: Guilford Press.
Lewis, Bernard (1987): History. Remembered, Recovered, Invented, London: Touchstone Books.
Malešević, Siniša (2013): Nation-States and Nationalisms. Organization, Ideology and Solidarity, Cambridge/Malden, Mass.: Polity Press.
Mecheril, Paul (2003): Prekäre Verhältnisse. Über natio-ethno-kulturelle (Mehrfach-) Zugehörigkeit. Interkulturelle Bildungsforschung 13, München: Waxmann.

Meyer, Peter (2010): Menschliche Gesellschaft im Licht der Zweiten Darwinschen Revolution. Evolutionäre und kulturalistische Deutungen im Widerstreit. Soziologie. Forschung und Wissenschaft 34, Münster etc.: Lit Verlag.

Naroll, Raoul (1964): "On Ethnic Unit Classification". In: Current Anthropology 5, pp. 283–312.

Niethammer, Lutz, with collaboration of Axel Doßmann (2000): Kollektive Identität. Die heimlichen Quellen einer unheimlichen Konjunktur, Reinbek bei Hamburg: Rowohlt (Rowohlts Enzyklopädie).

Orywal, Erwin (1986): "Ethnische Identität - Konzept und Methode." In: Erwin Orywal (ed.), Die ethnischen Gruppen Afghanistans. Fallstudien zu Gruppenidentität und Intergruppenbeziehungen, Wiesbaden: Reichert (Beihefte zum Tübinger Atlas des Vorderen Orients, Reihe B 70), pp. 73–86.

Orywal, Erwin/Hackstein, Katharina (1993): "Ethnizität: Die Konstruktion ethnischer Wirklichkeiten." In: Thomas Schweizer u.a. (eds.), Handbuch der Ethnologie, Berlin: Dietrich Reimer, pp. 593–609.

Pagel, Mark (2012): Wired for Culture. Origins of the Human Social Mind, New York/London: W. W. Norton.

Pascht, Arno/Hofbauer, Christoph/Trojanow, Ilja (1999): Ethnizität. Zur Verwendung des Begriffs im wissenschaftlichen und gesellschaftlichen Diskurs. Eine Einführung, München: Akademischer Verlag.

Pfaff-Czarnecka, Joanna (2012): Zugehörigkeit in der mobilen Welt. Politiken der Verortung, Göttingen: Wallstein (Das Politische als Kommunikation 3).

Poutignat, Philippe/Jocelyne Streiff-Fenart (2008): Théories de l'ethnicité, suivi de les Groupes Ethniques et leur Frontières, par Fredrik Barth, Paris: Presses Universitaires de France (Quadrige Manuel).

Radtke,Frank-Olaf(2011):Kulturen sprechen nicht.Die Politik grenzüberschreitender Dialoge, Hamburg: Hamburger Edition.

Rumford, Chris (2013): The Globalization of Strangeness, Houndmills: Palgrave Macmillan.

Schlee, Günther/Zenker, Olaf (2009): The Formation and Mobilisation of Collective Identities in Situations of Conflict and Integration, Halle: Max Planck Institute for Social Anthropology (Working Papers 116).

Schwartz, Seth J./Luyckx, Koen/Vignoles, Vivian L. (eds.) (2012): Handbook of Identity Theory and Research, Berlin etc.: Springer.

Smith, Anthony D. (2003): Chosen Peoples. Sacred Sources of National Identity, Oxford: Oxford University Press.

Sökefeld, Martin (1999): "Debating Self, Identity, and Culture in Anthropology." In: Current Anthropology 40/4, pp. 417–31.

―― (2007): "Problematische Begriffe: ‚Ethnizität', ‚Rasse', ‚Kultur', ‚Minderheit'." In: Brigitta Schmidt-Lauber (ed.): Ethnizität und Migration. Einführung in Wissenschaft und Arbeitsfelder, Berlin: Dietrich Reimer (Reimer Kulturwissenschaften), pp. 31–50.

Taylor, Charles (1977): Sources of the Self. The Making of the Modern Identity, Cambridge, Mass.: Harvard University Press.

Tishkov, Valery A. (1992): "The Crisis in Soviet Ethnology." In: Current Anthropology 33/4: pp. 371–394.

Tomasello, Michael (2014): A Natural History of Human Thinking, Cambridge, Mass./London: Harvard University Press.

Van Den Berghe, Pierre L. (1987): The Ethnic Phenomenon, Westport, Ct.: Praeger/Elsevier.

Vermeulen, Henk/Govers, Chris (eds.) (1994): The Anthropology of Ethnicity. Beyond 'Ethnic Groups and Boundaries', Amsterdam: Het Spinhuis.

Wallman, Sandra (1986): "Ethnicity and the Boundary Process in Context." In: John Rex/David J. Mason (eds.): Theories of Race and Ethnic Relations, Cambridge: Cambridge University Press (Comparative Ethnic and Race Relations), pp. 226–245.

Wikan, Unni (2002): Generous Betrayal. Politics of Culture in the New Europe, Chicago: The University of Chicago Press.

Wimmer, Andreas (2010): "Ethnische Grenzziehungen: Ein konstruktivistischer Ansatz." In: Marion Müller/Darius Zifonun (eds.), Ethnowissen. Soziologische Beiträge zu ethnischer Differenzierung und Migration, Berlin: VS (Soziologie der Politiken), pp. 99–152.

Yuval-Davis, Nira (2011): The Politics of Belonging. Intersectional Contestations, London etc.: Sage (Sage Studies in International Sociology).

More than meets the eye

Analytical frameworks beyond race and ethnicity

FREDERIK HOLST

INTRODUCTION

"In Malaysia we have three major races which have practically nothing in common. Their physiognomy, language, culture and religion differ. [...] Nothing makes anyone forget the fact of race. So those who say 'forget race' are either naive or knaves."
(MAHATHIR 1970: 175)

Reading a quote like the one above, from former Malaysian Prime Minister Mahathir Mohamad, is likely to evoke an uneasy feeling with scholars in the area studies disciplines. The history of this nowadays very broad and transdisciplinary field has been closely tied to the colonial endeavor, often in an unholy alliance with the ancestors of today's anthropology. Today still – and not only in Malaysia – these categories are abound not only in political discourse, where violent conflicts are often traced back to contestations between ethnicized groups with seemingly homogenous interests, but also in scholarly analyses, where they remain as analytical frameworks, and often in the context of conflict.[1]

But can race and ethnicity be sound and valid analytical categories in the first place, especially in a contemporary academic context? Are they sufficiently coherent that they can be applied in every possible context, or do they rather

---

1 As an indication, the Library of Congress alone holds more than 1000 publications that deal with conflict in conjunction with race or ethnicity in their title.

only make sense when looking at the 'other'? And are there ways and means to describe the phenomena that we encounter in fundamentally different ways, rather than just replacing one shaky term with another?

In this article I want to address these questions from a trans-disciplinary area studies perspective.[2] Modern area studies, which go beyond merely studying a nation-state environment, are helpful in overcoming eurocentric approaches, which are often still very much engrained in the 'classical' disciplines. Taking inspiration from disciplines such as sociology, psychology, and discourse analysis, and adjusting and testing them outside a predominantly white, 'Western' environment may produce better results not only when looking at the area of the 'other', but also one's own area, 'at home'.

One of the outcomes of this direction is an alternative approach, in terms of concept as well as terminology, to the phenomena we often describe along the lines of race and ethnicity: the layered concept of *ethnicization as a processual framework of analysis*. In order to provide a new perspective, such an approach must go beyond classical counter-arguments with regard to race and ethnicity, with the bottom line that everything related to these is constructed. It must take into account the power that notions of race and ethnicity have in real life, but at the same time avoid reinforcing notions of homogeneity, and instead underline the processual aspect of group and identity formation. This may not be an easy task, and might challenge accustomed and convenient categories often used when analyzing group dynamics and relations. But in the end it is a worthwhile endeavor that opens up more differentiated views of the underlying issues at stake, which are all too easily overlooked when focusing on the rather static categories of race and ethnicity.

AMBIGUITIES OF RACE AND ETHNICITY

> "The concept of a single, exclusive, and unchanging ethnic or cultural or other identity is a dangerous piece of brainwashing."
> (HOBSBAWM 1996: 1067, emphasis in original)

When talking about aspects of identity, one can often make an interesting observation: Hardly anyone would regard one's own identity or personality as

---

2   This chapter is a condensed version of the theoretical framework of manifestations and implementations of ethnicization which I have developed in greater detail, and with specific regard to the Malaysian scenario, elsewhere (Holst 2012).

static, or even interchangeable with someone else's. Yet there often seems to be no problem in assuming the existence of large-scale, homogenous ethnicized groups and assigning individuals membership of one of these, or other, identity groups. This obvious contradiction is often not realized – which may have to do with the different meanings and ways in which terms like 'race' and 'ethnicity' have developed. A cursory overview of the genesis of these terms is therefore a good point of departure for this analysis.

Although modes of differentiation and discrimination have existed in most societies across the world for centuries and more – where those living in the periphery have often been termed 'barbarians' or similar by those in the center – race as a concept became manifest at a time when Europeans encountered people whose physical appearance was outright different.

Banton states that these "contacts were important to the development by Europeans of racial categories" (1977: 13), and Barot and Bird add that "issues of corporeality were central to developing racial discourses and were seen as signs of something else, that is, signs of superiority and inferiority" (2001: 607). Race and perceived racial differences were readily incorporated into justifications of colonialism which were at best based upon the twisted notion of "bringing development to the inferior" (2001: 607).

With the advent of the Enlightenment and its stress on rationalism, racist ideologies needed adequate fundamentals. Darwin's *On the Origin of Species* (1859) provided a scientific foundation for a biological perspective on human development. It is this natural science approach to race that has dominated the discourse until today. Van den Berghe (1995), for example, argues that "social organisms" could only evolve because of nepotistic behavior, as altruistic investments into non-related organisms would be biologically "wasted". As a consequence, social concern is based on common biological descent and biologically rooted nepotism, even when the markers that determine on a larger scale who shares a common descent with someone else are primarily cultural.

However, most scholars in the social sciences and humanities have abandoned the concept of race as a category of distinction because biological and genetic markers have been proven to be far too broad and unspecific to explain meaningful differences between large groups of populations in general terms (Tonkin et al. 1989; Rustin 1991; Banton 1998). To some degree this has also happened in the medical sciences (Goodman 2000), with the most striking point being the lack of a clear definition and differentiation of race as a scientific category (Schwartz 2001; Cooper 2003; Bamshad et al. 2004).

The term and concept of 'race' have thus undergone changes in their meaning and use. Whereas in a German context, it would be inappropriate to use *rasse* as an academically sound category, the term has been transformed in Anglo-American academia. One example is its use as a category to justify affirmative action policies, e.g. in the USA. One argument in favor of maintaining the concept of race is that it is a result of a social and political process, and that it is necessary in order to highlight the position of those who have been oppressed by racial policies in the past. Regarding affirmative action policies in the USA, Mosley argues that "we need not expect the elimination of racial categories to eliminate the problems introduced by racism. At best our problems would no longer be 'racial problems'" (1997: 102). While it is true that a mere change of terminology does not change the underlying problems – as the next paragraphs will show – it is important to note that race here is not an analytical category in the sense of describing a certain group, but an attribute describing the outcome of a process of discrimination. What remains problematic is that relying on the term 'race' contributes – at least discursively – to the persistence of the idea that distinctive racial groups exist, for example, through the frequent ticking of the 'race box' in various forms. Such forms of self-categorization as 'black', 'white', etc. further reinforce racial group identities, thus running at least partly counter to the intentions of affirmative-action policymakers.

In contrast to 'race', the term 'ethnicity' seems to be a rather "new" (1975: 1) concept, as Glazer and Moynihan state in one of the first compilations discussing the term. The question remains as to whether it provides a more open approach towards categorization that takes into account more than just biological or genetical factors. The difficulty again lies in the definition, as the general meaning of ethnicity still remains fuzzy today, ranging from the essence of an ethnic group, to the feeling of belonging to such a group, to the marker of difference from other ethnic groups (Tonkin et al. 1989). Most recent theoretical literature follows an "umbrella classification" (cp. Chandra 2006: 397 for a more comprehensive list), in which a shared culture, a common ancestry/kinship (real or imagined) and some form of group membership are central aspects of defining an ethnic group.

Barth (1969) raises a fundamental critique against defining an ethnic group in this 'traditional' manner, especially because "while purporting to give an ideal type model of a recurring empirical form, it implies a preconceived view of what are the significant factors in the genesis, structure, and function of such groups" (Barth 1969: 11). The result is "a world of separate peoples, each with their culture and each organized in a society which can legitimately be isolated for description as an island to itself" (ibid: 11).

However, not everybody seems to see themselves as part of such an island: Hutchinson and Smith highlight that the usages of the term 'ethnicity' "refer to other peoples who, like animals, belong to some group unlike one's own" (1996: 4). The implication that it is the 'others' who are characterized by ethnicity is a notable difference to the concept of race. As Tonkin et al. put it: "Within the discourse of race, everybody had one, everybody belonged to one. In actual use, however, not everybody belongs to an 'ethnic group', or has an 'ethnicity'. In their common employment, the terms have a strong and familiar bias towards 'difference' and 'otherness'" (1989: 15). Elwert points out that in many cases it was scholars from within the colonial system that attached an ethnic group definition to a certain set of people. Geographical identifiers were frequently used to define a group with perceived similar cultural traits, but more often than not these definitions were far from being specific or clear (Elwert 1989: 443-446). In a similar way, the term 'ethnic group' has also become synonymous with (mostly non-white) minorities in certain contexts: Guibernau and Rex (1997: 4) note that it is used in Britain for non-white immigrants, in Australia for the Aborigines, in Scandinavia for the Sami, and in Southeastern Europe for the Roma. The example of the Sami points to the fact that an element of 'backwardness' is implied here as well: They are a 'white' minority that is associated with the ethnic minority attribute, whereas it is not common to refer to the Welsh or Scots in Britain as an ethnic group, for example.

Is an ethnic group now any different from a racial group? Eriksen points out that the "boundaries between race and ethnicity tend to be blurred, since ethnic groups have a common myth of origin, which relates ethnicity to descent, which again makes it a kindred concept to race" (2002: 6). Smelser et al. summarize the problem that lies in the ambiguity of the identifying characteristics of race and ethnicity: They point out that both terms comprise complex social phenomena that are hardly possible to describe or measure accurately, especially when it comes to identifying the principal characteristic, of which there are many to choose from: attributed physical markers, common descent, legal definitions, or the attribution of others or one's own self-identification (2001: 4).

ETHNIC VS. SOCIO-CULTURAL IDENTITIES

If ethnic identity is constructed yet at the same time is used to explain social realities, the scholarly task is to provide a model that does not depend on essentialization, yet which can still explain those social realities often seen to be based on race and ethnicity.

Ethnicity is often conflated with identity. However, ethnicity is more static, in cases where biological traits are included, or more fluid, if it is based upon an (imagined) community (Anderson 1983). In contrast, theories of identity acknowledge its possibility of change and adaption. The result of this conflation – the notion of an ethnic identity – is therefore not going to provide substantial explanations of group relations (cp. Chandra 2006).

Regarding the linkages between ethnic identity and culture, Eriksen shows the incongruences between the two:

"Cultural differences cut across ethnic boundaries; and [...] ethnic identity is based on socially sanctioned notions of cultural differences, not 'real' ones. While ethnic identity should be taken to refer to a notion of shared ancestry (a kind of fictive kinship), culture refers to shared representations, norms and practices. One can have deep ethnic differences without correspondingly important cultural differences [...]; and one can have cultural variation without ethnic boundaries" (Eriksen 2001:43, emphasis in original).

However, this would render it difficult to make any kind of statement about any group, because one would never have an accurate definition of what is being examined in the first place. For this reason Tonkin and colleagues present two contrasting notions of the term 'identity':

"[O]ne more-or-less essentialist notion, with identity as something (an attribute, entity, thing, whatever) which an individual or a group has in and of itself [...]; and another much like that of ethnicity as already discussed – a notion only existing in a context of oppositions and relativities" (Tonkin et al. 1989: 17).

For the current analysis, I propose to take the basic notion of this duality of identity that Tonkin and colleagues have described here and specify it with the adjective 'socio-cultural'. Rather than an excessively broad and static notion of ethnic identity, it is the conglomerate of social and cultural identity components and interactions that will provide significant insights into group and community relations, because it is in this sphere where the most significant interaction between groups takes place. Lasting group affiliations will therefore have to have ties on a social as well as a cultural level in order not to fizzle out after a while.

If we extend this two-dimensional model to a three-dimensional one by adding some 'depth' to it, the model also helps to explain why certain socio-cultural identities are more prevalent than others: On a very small scale, between two individuals for example, the socio-cultural identities that might provide a basis for the individuals to 'connect' to each other could be quite sophisticated. For example, an individual in Malaysia who is a left-leaning social activist, plays piano, likes punk music, speaks Malay, and is of Muslim faith may be lucky enough to find another person with similar socio-cultural identities (for example, if they both live in a large enough city). However, to find more than a few people like this might be a difficult task. Furthermore, at work or on other occasions where group membership is not fully voluntary, a number of these socio-cultural identities will not be entertained.

Still, this person is required to 'connect' to others if he or she does not want to become an outsider. Thus, the larger the reference group becomes, the more abstract become the socio-cultural identities that provide for ties that bind. This left-leaning social activist might therefore focus on being an activist in a larger reference group, because he or she might think that being left-leaning is one aspect of being an activist. Alternatively this person could focus on the socio-cultural identity of being a religious person, and see his or her political affiliation as part of this socio-cultural identity. In an even larger reference group, for example when it comes to political party affiliation, this person might just refer to him- or herself as 'left-leaning', if this is what this person sees as the most encompassing socio-cultural identity in that context.

Now, what are the socio-cultural identities that become most prevalent in societies, and which can be used to form national or ethnic identities? As I have argued elsewhere (Holst 2012) it seems that socio-cultural identities based on language and on (moral) value systems such as religion can easily become salient points of reference in a society. When we now regard ethnic group membership rather as a socio-cultural identity that is defined, for example, by the criteria of speaking a certain language and practicing – or at least being influenced by – a specific religion, two things become evident: First, for most people in a given society, language as well as (moral) value systems such as religion are among the few elements that define them from childhood onwards. Second, these aspects constitute probably the largest reference groups that people can somehow relate to – at least on an abstract (or in Anderson's terms, "imagined" (1983)) level – because the former enables people to communicate about the values derived (or seen to be derived) from the latter. Thus, coming back to our multi-faceted left-leaning social activist, he or she would somehow still be able to relate to a socio-cultural identity defined as 'Malay' – although most likely inadequately and uncomfortably.

This model shares some similarities with Barth's (Barth 1969) analysis of the construction of ethnic groups and their boundaries regarding the permeability of borders between groups, for example, or the possible changes of identity.

Eriksen's (2001) criticisms of ethnic identities are acknowledged here, as is Nagata's proposition that "certain cultural items and behaviors, far from being uniquely or inalienably attached to particular ethnic groups, are in fact amenable to manipulation according to the current choice of reference group" (Nagata 1974: 333). However, in my opinion, apart from principally maintaining the shaky concept of *ethnie*, these approaches do not adequately acknowledge the influence of social-cultural identities that help to view the individual as being defined in more than just one (i.e. ethnic) way. In this regard, the model I propose has two advantages:

On one hand it provides a basis for explaining what other models have termed 'ethnic identity', as I have shown in the previous paragraph: A person labeled as 'Malay', 'Chinese', or 'German' might to a certain extent live, think, and act outside the mainstream of what is generally or normatively associated with that group or community. However, the power of these group identifiers will nevertheless force him or her to act (or be seen as acting) accordingly, at least in certain situations.

His or her socio-cultural identity is formed through interaction with others, and at least to a certain degree it will have to harmonize with the corresponding surroundings. Some systems might pressurize individuals to emphasize a particular socio-cultural identity while marginalizing another, thereby increasing the pressures associated with homogenization, possibly resulting in conflict. Again, these socio-cultural identities need not be similar to what is otherwise understood as ethnic identity. It can be a focus on descent or kinship, but it can also incorporate gender, religion, social class, or other factors. Herein, this model connects to what Elwert (1989) has described as 'We-group processes' in which he points out different motivations for group affiliations, and argues that nationalism and ethnicity are not the only manifestations of these social processes.

On the other hand, this model opens up the space for acknowledging the fluidity and transformability of identities in general. Thus, an individual has the option of choosing certain affiliations or identities that are more meaningful to him or her and reduce others to a necessary minimum. Some of these identities will be stronger than others and thus more unlikely to change, but hardly any are cast in stone.

This helps to explain the power that ethnic group identifiers may have on people, such as being labeled 'Malay' or 'Chinese' or 'German' for example, because these identifiers have a real impact on people's lives, and it would be wrong to ignore them. These ascriptions are also instrumental in creating and stabilizing discursively dominant ethnicized groups. However, it is important for the analytical perspective to keep in mind that members of these (rather large) socio-cultural groups also possess a number of additional socio-cultural identities which may be more meaningful and decisive for their lives, and thus it would be wrong to assume a homogeneity of what is commonly referred to as 'Malays' and so on.

For the course of this work, this approach has two consequences: One is the understanding of group identities such as Malay etc. not as one homogeneous set of attributes but rather as one aspect of identity out of many others: The analytical focus shifts from conflicts apparently inherent in these groups' relations to facets of identity that actually provide a common basis for mutual cooperation. The other consequence is derived from this understanding: If these groups are characterized by individuals associating with a certain set of socio-cultural identities, they cannot be 'ethnic' *per se* in the sense that they carry a primordial notion of ethnicity within themselves. Group labels that build upon ethnic markers are thus external constructs, becoming salient through processes of manifestation and implementation of ethnicization, which shall be explored further below in this article. These group labels are nevertheless powerful and have an impact on people's everyday lives, and thus cannot simply be ignored. At the same time, the processual aspect of identity ascription should remain evident, at least in scholarly terminology. As a consequence, I refer to these groups as ethnicized rather than ethnic. This acknowledges the fact that group identity formation does take place, but underlines the processual aspect rather than reinforcing notions of staticity. With this precursory disquisition, a conceptual terminology has been established with the aim of reducing ambiguity, in order to deal with the various contexts where ethnicization takes place.

RATIONAL CHOICE OR SITUATED AGENCY?

Despite ethnicity remaining a rather ambiguous concept, it is nevertheless still a common explanation and foundation for identity-group formations. On the one hand this section takes a closer look at the arguments supporting ethnicity as a resource in advancing one's own causes, where a vertical category, based on group-inherent traits such as ethnicity, seems to override horizontal ones, based on socio-economic conditions, such as class. On the other hand it also describes an alternative model that takes into account not only individual benefits but also the many (and often complex) situations in which individuals cannot make strategic decisions solely on the basis of personal gain.

Rational choice theory is one of the more prominent explanations for the prevalence of group and identity formation based on ethnicity (Banton 1995;

Banton 2004). In short, the theory states that individual actors make a choice of action guided by constraints and opportunities that form the basis of rational responses. Collective identity can become a resource that can be controlled and used strategically by single actors (Eder et al. 2002: 78). The concept, quite closely connected to game theory in economics, has drawn significant criticism (Macy and Flache 1995; Boudon 1998; Christiano 2004; White 2004).

Some of the critical points raised by Eder et al. (Eder and Schmidtke 1998; Eder et al. 2002) will be looked at in more detail here, as they take these as points of departure to develop their own model of *situated agency*. They acknowledge the capacity of individuals to act rationally in line with their interests and preferences, which are deemed important on a subjective level. However, they dispute the stability of collective identities that would be a prerequisite for making a substantial choice for three reasons(Eder et al.2002:78).

Firstly, identity construction is a continuous struggle that prevents ethnic identities from becoming stable. Collective identities are in a constant process of symbolic dispute over their meaning, thus calculating the cost and benefit of ethnic action can only take place in an ongoing process of negotiation and interaction. Recognition of the collective identity, rather than scarce resources and privileges, becomes a good in itself and thus a key objective of ethnic action.

Furthermore, individuals are limited in making choices because their knowledge and competence with regard to weighing the costs and benefits of sharing a collective identity is limited. Especially regarding ethnically framed identities, the individual is often drawn into them against his or her rational interest. Identity formation is not characterized by an 'open market situation' where individuals can choose between a number of offers equally, but is rather an "incalculable object matter which undermines any attempt of rational action" (Eder et al. 2002: 78). Especially in terms of ethnic mobilization and conflict, individual approaches to collective action are limited, because "[w]ithout a collective identity as the basis for defining oneself as a rational actor the rationalist framework becomes spurious" (ibid: 78).

Finally, the values that should help in gauging the effect of an action cannot be assumed as certain. Individual actors are in continual interaction while negotiating and figuring out what they share with each other and what creates differences. It is the situation in which they interact that has a strong influence on their negotiating of social order in terms of identity and difference: "Their 'rational choice' is made neither before nor after the interaction with others. Preferences and interests are formed in the process of interacting with others" (ibid: 79).

Eder et al. proceed to offer a model that is able to explain rational choice as one factor among others, using the approach of situated action. In this model, they do not assume the existence of strategic actors using collective identities to maximize their individual benefit; collective identities are rather created by pluralities of individuals in concrete social actions. The motivations that drive these individuals can be manifold: "from such greed to a sense of shame or shyness, to a sensitivity to the feelings of others and fear and avoidance of conflict with those present" (ibid: 81). These motivations, combined with other constraints and rational intentions (the existence of which of course Eder et al. do not deny), guide individuals' actions and choices. However, processes of identity construction, maintenance and conflict do not come about solely as the results of individual and deliberate choices. The key aspect for Eder et al. is that these processes are "processes of communicating signs [...] [which] consist in myriad acts of interaction between individual actors as they make conscious and unconscious claims to belonging which are – or are not – recognized by others" (ibid: 81, emphasis in original).

The 'currency' in these processes is made up of "symbolic codes of distinction and classification which are communicated in social situations" (ibid.). It is in these situations that codes and processes are linked, as "[c]odes are embodied in processes of communication" (ibid: 84). Within these processes of communication, Eder et al. locate three structural positions, each of which can make use of codes depending on the circumstances: *Ego*, the actor; *Alter*, who – as *Ego* knows – is the reacting and responding party; and Other – who in principle could participate, but is not addressed directly – such as bystanders, other groups or society as a whole. The possible configurations in which the three relate to each other constitute various social situations.

This Other is the main difference in this model compared to theories dealing with rational choice. Those theories "depend on extremely restricted assumptions about social action in situations" (ibid: 91), in which *Ego* and *Alter* are actors that can negotiate with minimal external pressure over what can be gained and what might be lost. Such models therefore lack "a constitutive element of social situations: the third party in an interaction situation, the Other who is to be taken into account by actors in a situation and who shapes the logic of agency" (ibid: 91). It is this third observer who "opens the analytical perspective to collectively shared ideas, cultural definitions, and communication processes which structure the environment in which single actors make their claims", and it is *Ego's* and *Alter's* actions which are dependent upon the attention and recognition of an observing Other (ibid: 90).

Eder et al. focus on those situations that generate a cleavage between *Ego* and either *Alter* or the Other, especially in identicization processes, because the aforementioned neglect of the Other in rational choice approaches and game theory becomes most evident here: In situations of ethnic conflict, "boundary construction is not only directed against an *Alter*, but also involves the invocation of a third Other as proof, 'recognition' of the construction" (ibid: 91).

Thus, their conclusion is that rational choice exists, but not in the sense of independent choice, motivated by a clear evaluation of personal gains and losses; it is rather a choice that is embedded in situations and public perspective: In real life, when defining his collective identity no actor acts without taking into account the public, which serves as a reference context for staging and negotiating an identity. Impression management not only refers to *Alter* but also to the third party, Other. Claiming an ethnic identity is first of all a form of impression management, and then a struggle for recognition within a society. There is rational action, but it is embedded in situations which transcend the meanings that rational actors attribute to their action (ibid: 92).

It should be stressed again that this approach does not eliminate individual choice. The individual is not acting in an environment that is entirely determined by the Other, thus making it exploitable by an elite. As Eder et al. state: "Leaders often get an intuitive sense of the value of collective identity constructions and can have a steering effect on identity construction, but the process is structured by macro-factors and micro-situations in which actors communicate their identities" (ibid: 84).[3]

ETHNICIZATION: A PROCESSUAL AND LAYERED APPROACH

With this perspective in mind, the focus expands from the individual benefits that a person might have, to the inclusion of the processes in which these "macro-factors and micro-situations" (Eder et al. 2002: 17) advance the creation of collective identities. Eder et al. refer to this process as ethnicization, "the chain of events through which objective conditions of economic or political grievances become the basis of political claims justified by reference to a

---

3   For a more concrete example of their concept of *Ego*, *Alter* and Other cp. Eder et al. (2002) in which their theoretical model is intertwined with a well-written fictional "storyline of ethnicization" where the development between "Landlandians" and "Alternians" greatly helps to elucidate their argument.

collective identity" (ibid: 17). This chain of events is, however, often examined mainly from a top-down perspective, where a powerful elite is the center of academic (as well as activists') attention. This might lead to the impression that the elites are able to actively control the processes of ethnicization while ordinary people are unaware of their manipulation. I argue that some aspects of ethnicization have become so engrained in society's everyday life that they are difficult to identify as such, even for elite actors. Other aspects may have been initiated by actors in the center of power, but may not develop along the lines of a typical instrumentalist perspective. They might even backfire and harm the interests of the initiator or be taken up and reinforced by actors outside the typical realms of power, and thus develop their own, uncontrolled dynamics.

To account for these dynamics, I have developed a layered model of manifestations and implementations of ethnicization to distinguish between those aspects where dominant reference points of ethnicization have become developed largely independently from external influence, and those processes where actors intentionally engage in and react to ethnicized politics or policies. Nevertheless, there is not always a clear-cut line between the two, and in many cases there is a strong interdependence where one provides the foundation for or reinforces the other and implementations can themselves result in further manifestations over time. However, differences and even contradictions may occur if, for example, long-term developments of ethnicization and their manifestations run counter to implementations of short-term ethnicized political agendas.

Manifestations of ethnicization shall be defined as occurrences of ethnicization that have shaped a certain societal sub-system to such an extent that ethnicity has become a dominant reference point, and associated policies no longer need to be pushed through in order to achieve their implementation. Often policies of ethnicization develop independently from a larger political framework once they become common practice. They therefore also become difficult to change or adjust, even if that were the aim of those actors who put them into practice in the first place. These manifestations have become deeply entrenched in various areas of society in which ethnicity has become a core pillar of a societal sub-system. In the political and economic field, for example, ethnicized manifestations may be characterized by a certain routineness. They have shaped and influenced these areas in such a way that referencing to ethnicity has become a matter of course, or even unavoidable. Some segments of society may contest these aspects, but still they remain the (or among the) main points of reference – even for those who challenge this – because they have gained such a dominant position in politics, policies, and related discourses. Typical examples of manifestations of ethnicization would be an ethnicized party system where ethnicized groups supersede class-based interests, or an ethnicized economic system where ethnicized group membership determines – either *de facto* or *de jure* – access to resources in the (political) economy. The origins of these manifestations may lie in a colonial system, but other sources of reinforcement must also be involved to explain their persistence.

This is why the manifestations of ethnicization provide a fertile ground for ongoing ethnicized policies, but the circumstances in which these policies are initiated and put into practice – their implementation – are equally important to examine. Analyzing ethnicized policy-making that focuses on top-down structures or similar cause-and-effect chains risks being limited to examining only aspects of instrumentalization. As the term implies, a certain issue or conflict becomes the instrument of another group in order to gain political leverage. In the context of ethnicization, instrumentalization would describe the process of exploitation of ethnicized fault-lines in order to create antagonisms between ethnicized groups with the aim of strengthening one group's position at the expense of others. However, this perspective has its weaknesses: Sticking to the root of the word, an instrument is a tool that is usually used by a person who has a clear idea of the achievable results if the instrument is used properly. Thus, the perspective of instrumentalization is often one that creates a focus on a central or dominant power that not only has a clear-cut goal, but also more or less knows a way that leads to it. As a consequence, this runs the risk of conjuring the image of a 'core of all evil' that is pulling the strings, and which just needs to be removed in order to get rid of the system and affected policies. However, manifestations of ethnicization may have become so prevalent that it is impossible to remove notions of ethnicization by simply identifying and removing a central power that controls the various instruments of ethnicization. It is instead a multitude of actors that incorporate ethnicized policies into their agendas, although their aims and goals may not be primarily based on ethnicized notions. They rather realize that ethnicity is a major reference point on the way to achieving or remaining in their position of power – and power, again, not in terms of any kind of central power, but rather in more widespread terms, across the societal sub-systems. These actors therefore implement policies based upon ethnicization, knowing that there are solid manifestations to build upon. However, with a multitude of actors and various levels of ideological fervor, the impact and direction of these policies in the process of achieving their goals is often unclear. Despite all target-orientation, implementations of ethnicization can only be influenced to a certain degree, and might develop a life on their own, eventually even becoming challenges for those political actors who implemented them in the first place. Sometimes this may lead either to excesses in ethnicized policymaking, or to contradicting approaches that result in flip-flop policies that need to be topped with layer after layer of policy reactions to conceal their inherent inconsistencies. These two aspects – beneficial and obstructive – that implementations of ethnicization can have for political actors must be addressed, in order to underline the claim that ethnicization in the political system is not merely a top-down approach that can be safely managed and controlled. Examples of implementations of ethnicization would be ethnicized policies governing language or religion, where these are advanced or restricted in their practices in multi-lingual or multi-religious societies. An especially extreme example of ethnicized flip-flop policies would be Malaysia's ethnicized labor migration policies, where at times several hundreds of thousands of undocumented workers were deported from the country, only to be brought back weeks later after the construction sector came to a virtual standstill (Holst 2007).

WHERE DO WE GO FROM HERE?

The question remains whether a critical take on ethnicity and a shift in the conceptualization of the underlying factors can result in a meaningful new approach to the issues at stake, or whether it remains an academic exercise for the sake of securing one's position. And in fact many scholars go into lengthy deconstructions of the use and accuracy of concepts such as race and ethnicity, but nevertheless fall back on using these same terms to explain the societal systems they are dealing with. However, when categories are being used that lump together large parts of a population, it is almost inevitable that complex cultural and social dimensions are lost to the observer. Especially since race and ethnicity have such a vast scope and are discursively so prevalent, it is often very tempting to just follow the well-trodden paths and refer to the same groups that have been examined for decades and even centuries along the same lines. Authors of well-meaning analyses of 'the Karen', 'the Malay', or 'the Sami' in regard of their respective cultures/societies/plights may certainly have good intentions, but from a scholarly perspective the question remains as to whether such approaches could actually produce meaningful results; presumably, no more than any broad analysis of 'the French', 'the Germans' or 'the Americans' would be able to. Still, it would not be a solution to just leave concepts of race and ethnicity out of the equation altogether. These notions have very real impacts on concrete lives, and simply stating the constructedness would be stopping halfway down the road.

I would therefore propose a two-step approach: Firstly, to identify whether the issue at stake must necessarily be framed along the lines of identity-group categories, especially when a certain degree of conflict is involved. Conflicts 'at home' would first and foremost be examined along the lines of more complex categories, such as class, gender, state power, or center-periphery relations. Certainly, this requires a much deeper understanding of the specific society, but in regard to the resulting findings, this is certainly a much more worthwhile endeavor than oversimplifying one's perspective by using excessively broad categories. Secondly, if the subject of analysis is a conflict in which specific reference to identity groups is obvious and also works as a (key) mobilizing factor, then I would argue that a processual approach provides more accurate results than just taking the group formations as a given. The concept of ethnicization, including the layers of manifestations and implementations, provides a framework which does not reinforce static notions of group identity and belonging, but rather helps to disentangle the manifold ways in which race and ethnicity have become rooted in various societies, and can (and should) even be applied 'at home'.

As a consequence, speaking of 'ethnicized' rather than 'ethnic' groups is more than just another supposedly 'politically correct' term, as it underlines a fundamentally different approach when describing identity-group formation processes: whereas the ascriptive 'ethnic' stands for mostly homogeneous groups, the adjective 'ethnicized' represents not only the constructedness of such concepts but also the powerful processes that lead – at least discursively – to identity-group formation.

When we take up the introductory quote from Mahathir, in which he labeled those who say "forget race" (Mahathir 1970: 175) as either naive or knaves, he is correct if we take him literally: race and ethnicity cannot simply be forgotten. However, he is incorrect if he assumes that not forgetting race and ethnicity means simply accepting them, which would mean, in the end, actually reinforcing them. It remains a not always easy task, both scholarly and in everyday lives, to find a suitable approach to address the issues at stake in different contexts in a meaningful way. The framework of manifestations and implementations of ethnicization can be one of them.

REFERENCES

Anderson, Benedict (1983): Imagined Communities – Reflections on the Origin and Spread of Nationalism, New York: Verso.

Bamshad, Michael, et al. (2004): "Deconstructing the relationship between genetics and race." In: Nature Reviews Genetics 5/8, pp.: 598–609.
Banton, Michael (1977): The Idea of Race, London: Tavistock Publications.
—— (1998): Racial Theories, Cambridge: Cambridge University Press.
—— (1995): "Rational choice theories." In: American Behavioral Scientist 38/3, pp. 478–497.
—— (2004): "Are Ethnicity and Nationality Twin Concepts?" In: Journal of Ethnic and Migration Studies 30/4, pp. 807–814.
Barot, Rohit/Bird, John (2001): "Racialization: The Genealogy and Critique of a Concept." In: Ethnic and Racial Studies 24/4, pp. 601–618.
Barth, Fredrik (1969): "Introduction." In: Fredrik Barth (ed.), Ethnic Groups and boundaries – The social organization of culture difference, London: Allen & Unwin, pp. 9–38.
Boudon, Raymond (1998): "Limitations of rational choice theory." In: American Journal of Sociology 104/3, pp. 817–828.
Chandra, Kanchan (2006): "What is Ethnic Identity and Does It Matter?" In: Annual Review of Political Science 9, pp. 397–424.
Christiano, Thomas (2004): "Is Normative Rational Choice Theory Self-Defeating?" In: Ethics 115/1, pp.: 122-141.
Cooper, Richard S. (2003): "Race, genes, and health – New wine in old bottles?" In: International Journal of Epidemiology 32/1, pp. 23–25.
Darwin, Charles (1859): The origin of species by means of natural selection or the preservation of favoured races in the struggle for life, London: John Murray.
Eder, Klaus, et al. (2002): Collective Identities in Action – A Sociological Approach, Aldershot: Ashgate.
Eder, Klaus/Schmidtke, Oliver (1998): "Ethnische Mobilisierung und die Logik von Identitätskämpfen. Eine situationstheoretische Perspektive jenseits von 'Rational Choice'." In: Zeitschrift für Soziologie 27/6, pp. 418–437.
Elwert, Georg (1989): "Nationalismus und Ethnizität – Über die Bildung von Wir-Gruppen." In: Kölner Zeitschrift für Soziologie und Sozialpsychologie 41, pp. 440–464.
Eriksen, Thomas Hylland (2001): "Ethnic Identity, National Identity, and Intergroup Conflict – The Significance of Personal Experiences." In: Richard Ashmore et al., Social Identity, Intergroup Conflict, and Conflict Reduction, Oxford: Oxford University Press, pp. 42–70.
—— (2002): Ethnicity and Nationalism, London: Pluto Press.
Glazer, Nathan/Moynihan, Daniel P. (1975): "Introduction." In: Nathan Glazer/Daniel Moynihan (eds.), Ethnicity – Theory and Experience, Cambridge Harvard University Press, pp.1–26.

Goodman, Alan H. (2000): "Why Genes Don't Count (for Racial Differences in Health)." In: American Journal of Public Health 90/11, pp. 1699–1702.

Guibernau, Montserrat; Rex, John (1997): "Introduction." In: Montserrat Guibernau/John Rex (eds.), The Ethnicity Reader - Nationalism, Multiculturalism, and Migration, Malden: Blackwell Publishers, pp. 1–9.

Hobsbawm, Eric (1996): "Language, Culture and National Identity." In: Social Research 63/4, pp. 1065–1080.

Holst, Frederik (2012): Ethnicization and Identity Construction in Malaysia, London: Routledge.

——(2007): "(Dis-)Connected History – The Indonesia-Malaysia Relationship." In: Eva Streifeneder/Antje Missbach (eds.), Indonesia – The Presence of the Past – A festschrift in honour of Ingrid Wessel, Berlin: RegioSpectran, pp. 327–340.

Hutchinson, John/Smith, Anthony D. (1996): "Introduction." In: John Hutchinson/Anthony D. Smith (eds.), Ethnicity, Oxford: Oxford University Press, pp. 3–14.

Macy, Michael W./Flache, Andreas (1995): "Beyond rationality in models of choice." In: Annual Review of Sociology 21/1, pp. 73–91.

Mahathir, Mohamad (1970): The Malay Dilemma, Singapore: D. Moore for Asia Pacific Press.

Mosley, Albert (1997): "Are Racial Categories Racist?" In: Research in African Literatures 28/4, pp. 101–111.

Nagata, Judith A. (1974): "What is a Malay? Situational Selection of Ethnic Identity in a Plural Society." In: American Sociologist 1/2, pp. 331–350.

Rustin, Michael (1991): "Psychoanalysis, Racism and Anti-Racism." In: Michael Rustin (ed.), The Good Society and the Inner World – Psychoanalysis, Politics, and Culture, London: Verso, pp. 57–84.

Schwartz, Robert S. (2001): "Racial Profiling in Medical Research." In: New England Journal of Medicine 344/18, pp. 1392–1393.

Smelser, Neil J., et al. (2001): "Introduction." In: National Research Council (ed.), America becoming – Racial Trends and their Consequences, Washington D.C.: National Academy Press, pp. 1–20.

Tonkin, Elizabeth, et al. (1989): "Introduction – History and Social Anthropology." In: Elizabeth Tonkin/et al (eds.), History and Ethnicity, London: Routledge, pp. 14–15.

van den Berghe, Pierre (1995): "Does Race Matter?" In: Nations and Nationalism 1/3, pp. 357–368.

White, Mark D. (2004): "Can homo economicus follow categorical imperative?" In: Journal of Socio-Economics 33/1, pp. 89–106.

The universal and the particular
Contrasting nomothetic and idiographic comparisons

TOBIAS SCHWARZ

Studying the political uses of ethnicity profits greatly from cross-cultural comparative research, because only comparisons can show the specificity of any case under scrutiny. This essay sketches out the basic characteristics of an anthropological approach to comparison by drawing on existing research on naturalizations with a cross-cultural perspective. Comparative methods are often associated with deductive-generalizing designs on the basis of a large number of cases (large-N) but the link between comparison and deduction is not a necessary one. Research in social and cultural anthropology[1] is always comparative, as it begins with the assumption of both a contrast between one's own and other societies on the one hand, and certain basic similarities common to social life everywhere on the other, thus assuming the possibility of comparison. Yet for the most part this implicit comparative perspective is not made explicit. While in anthropological work the quality of methodological deliberations is generally very high – for instance concerning the role of the researcher in the field – the methodology of comparison is often not elaborated upon when reporting on ethnographic fieldwork or *micro*-analytical case studies. In stark contrast to empirical work in sociology and political science, where the use of a comparative approach is often justified with methodological scrutiny, anthropology scholars can legitimately make do without such rigor. Nevertheless, the small-scale comparisons anthropologists make do rely on certain methods, only they are often left implicit or are not reflected upon.

---

1 When I mention anthropology in what follows, I am concerned with both the 'cultural' and the 'social' traditions, and do not touch upon archaeology, linguistics, or physical anthropology.

In what follows, I will use the term *idiographic comparison* to refer to the typical anthropological approach. This will be contrasted with a typical sociological/political science approach, that of *nomothetic comparison*.[2] I will argue that the idiographic approach aims at opening up the perspective, allows for alternative interpretations, and helps to find new insights, which in turn can lead to a more detailed understanding of each of the cases compared. It does not aim at creating models or (universal) theories that reach beyond the empirically analyzed cases, as is typical of the deductive-generalizing comparison prevailing in social science research. Small-scale idiographic comparisons are useful for better understanding each case at hand (by contrasting it with at least one other case) or for discovering new aspects of each case, and also for discovering connections between cases.

My own research is dedicated to naturalization ceremonies worldwide, and employs a cross-regional comparative framework. This text will therefore draw on research on naturalizations from both political and anthropological scientists, to illustrate the juxtaposition of idiographic and nomothetic comparisons. The following section explains the connection between ethnicity and naturalizations.

ETHNICITY, NATIONALITY, NATURALIZATION

How is naturalization related to ethnicity? Following Gabbert, I understand ethnicity as a process of differentiation between groups on the basis of (perceived) cultural or phenotypic characteristics, and primarily with reference to an (imagined) common origin (Gabbert 2006: 90). Among other things, ethnicity is about who can be or should become member of the We-group, and how this quality is transmitted trans-generationally. In a nation state, membership of the We-group is organized by nationality law.

Nationality in all nation states derives automatically from birth (to parents who are already members, or inside the national territory), and individuals can

---

2   This is not to assume that only anthropologists would adhere to idiographic research designs, because there is of course a longstanding tradition of interpretative social science research (cp. e.g. Deegan 2001 on the Chicago School of ethnography). Neither is it possible to neglect the systematic comparative tradition within anthropology, which strove to find explanations of the variations of human culture, often by comparing isolated elements (variables), and pursued the objective of producing universally applicable explanations (cp., e.g. on the "Human Relations Area Files", Ember 1997).

neither influence this nor escape this ascription. Born into a nation state, all individuals acquire their status as members by chance. To Joppke, therefore, the formal legal attribution of membership in a nation state is intrinsically an "ethnic" ascription (2003: 436). The automatic categorization of individuals as nationals or foreigners purely with reference to their origins results in the perpetuation of a collective by assumed kinship relations (in terms of Weber's *Abstammungsgemeinsamkeit*, regardless of "whether or not a similarity of blood objectively exists" (1990: 237, my translation). To this effect, the national paradigm produces an assumed similarity beyond the active will of the individuals, and national membership is ethnic in the sense that it is passed on down the generations.

There is also another reason why the current relevance of ethnicity as a political resource is first and foremost related to the rise of the modern nation state: The imagined ethnic similarity of all members of the nation became crucial to legitimizing dominance only when nation states started to define their domain by the assumed common bond among all their respective members. While prenational imperial rule never relied on ethnic classifications to maintain political boundaries, the nation state needed to define its institutional boundaries in ethnic terms: the rulers and the ruled should be of the same people (Wimmer 2008: 991).

The ethnic legitimation of the nation, i.e. by primary reference to common descent, is sometime juxtaposed with civic legitimation.[3] According to the latter concept, membership in the nation can derive from personal will alone, through the decision on the part of the potential member to become associated. The theoretical ideal types, *ethnic* and *civic*, have been taken up as part of an influential typology of nationalism by Hans Kohn (Kohn 1944). He applied the distinction between ethnic and civic nationalism in different European nation states, and contrasted what he saw as the 'civic' Western type with his depiction of the 'ethnic' Eastern nationalism.

These two opposing understandings of nationhood are often correlated with different approaches to nationality law. The transfer of membership to biological descendants – *jus sanguinis* – is understood as ethnic, while the attribution of membership through birth on national territory – *jus soli* – is deemed more civic. This juxtaposition of an 'ethnic' law of filiation and a 'civic' territorial law has been used in historical and political science literature. Early comparative studies

---

3   The ethnic vs civic rationale for peoplehood relics on the theoretically assumed difference between unifying criteria that are on the one hand a priori given and inalterable, and on the other hand politically shaped and influenced by the will of individuals. These contrasting attributions have been termed "Ethnos" and "Demos" by Francis (1965).

contrasted Germany with France, the United Kingdom, or the United States, and distinguished primordial from revolutionary understandings of the nation (Brubaker 1992; Gosewinkel 1998; Baumann 1999; Bös 2000). Since then, research has shown several times that it is not possible to assign the theoretical contrast between ethnic and civic to the empirical occurrence of *jus sanguinis/soli* (Weil 1996; Giesen/Junge 1998; Fahrmeir 2000; Hansen 2004: 6). In reality, the two presumed ideal types overlap much more than the model suggests. Though some scholars criticize the ethnic-civic-opposition as empirically wrong (cp. Giesen/Junge 1998 on Brubaker, and Kuzio 2002 on Kohn) or theoretically not useful at all (Sciortino 2012: 378), others suggest placing them on a continuum rather than seeing them as mutually exclusive antipodes (Smith 1991: 13). Others still have upheld Kohn's typology for the purpose of comparative arguments (Koning 2011). From a social-theoretical angle, however, it is not the supposed contrast between *ethnos* and *demos* that seems to offer an appropriate perspective, but rather it is the overlapping or consecutive "de- and re-ethnicizations" (Joppke 2003: 429) of national membership rules that becomes the research topic.

I think the issue is not about finding the right label. The main reason why a comparison of such ideal types can still be worthwhile is not because of what the respective norms are based on, but that the legal membership regimes have different consequences (cp. Schwarz 2013: 24–27). The consequences are most visibly different concerning the nationality of future generations of immigrants. In a pure *jus soli* regime, all children born inside the national territory will be considered members. Hence, incentives for families to naturalize are considerably smaller than in countries without any *jus soli* provision, because there the offspring of immigrants would remain foreign over generations, unless naturalization were possible (like the descendants of labor migrants in Germany before 2000, or Koreans in Japan today; cp. Bade 2001; Refsing 2003).

Finally, what I think is especially noteworthy in this discussion is that both in ethnic and civic contexts there can be a tendency to demand assimilation to a hegemonic culture from those naturalizing into the national collective later in life. And sometimes the civic understanding of the nation can give way to an even more forceful demand for assimilation than the ethnic. "Civic nationalism may in practice prove more 'homogenizing' than ethnic variants. While the belief that members of the nation naturally belong together may give rise to some quite relaxed views regarding allegiance, civic nationalists will be anxious to educate citizens into respect for the constitution and to instill loyalty and respect for the key values and principles enshrined in the constitution" (Baumeister 2003: 411). A similar result draw Ceuppens and Geschiere while discussion policies of belonging in Belgium, as "both ethnic and civic citizenship can imply a process of complete assimilation, either to a specific ethnic culture or to a public, political culture that is represented as universal and, as such, is oblivious of its own culturalness" (2005: 399).

In what follows I will give examples of why it does not matter so much whether naturalization policies can be categorized as more or less ethnic, but rather how differently the understanding of a shared national culture can be played out.

THE THEORETICAL DIFFERENCE BETWEEN IDIOGRAPHIC AND NOMOTHETIC COMPARISONS

The terms 'nomothetic' and 'idiographic' (or 'generalizing' and 'individualizing') grew out of attempts to classify natural sciences and humanities in the German philosophical tradition around 1900 (cp. Windelband 1894 and Rickert 1899). Since then, they have often been criticized for too rigidly juxtaposing the two tendencies, but I take them as pointing to exactly that: tendencies, rather than strict demarcations.[4]

The objective of *nomothetic approaches* is the production of general theories ('universal laws') or models applicable to all possible cases (generalizations). The comparison is put at center stage, i.e. the results of such comparisons aim to prove (or falsify) a hypothesis that derives from previously detected principles. Hence the process of comparison is theory-driven (deductive; i.e. the truth of its conclusion relies on the truth of its premises). This is done by categorization of cases along some (usually many) selected elements and by scrutinizing the relation between these elements (looking for patterns of co-occurrence, for instance).

Idiographic approaches start from single cases, which they aim to understand by in-depth description and interpretation. The end of any comparison within an idiographic approach is to find specific qualities of a few

---

4   Even if this contrast seems too rigid in light of possible nuances and combinations between the two camps I will comment on below, it is still a useful and almost classic typology that has been employed before (cp. for instance Rohner 1977 on anthropology, Seipel/Rippl 2013 on sociology, and Kaelble 1999: 26–27 on historiography). Contrasting nomothetic and idiographic approaches informed for instance Charles Tilly's famous classification of different modes of historical comparison, two of which he called "individualizing" and "universalizing" (1984: 59).

cases through an inductive (evidence-based) search for similarities and differences among them. To achieve this, cases are sampled in terms of criteria suggested by theoretical assumptions ('universal characteristics') and can be further selected theoretically to produce contrasts and parallels, but the thereby resulting comparison is not an end in itself. What is to be accomplished primarily is the more detailed understanding of specific cases – hence this approach can be considered individualizing.

More than other disciplines, anthropology allows the combining (or blending) of methods, according to the basic principle that methods have to "do justice to the complexity of the objects under study" (Flick 2002: 5). Consequentially, the methodology used should not be determined *ex ante* by the academic discipline the researcher locates him or herself in. Personally, I freely take from ethnographic fieldwork, interpretative sociology, discourse analysis, and statistics whatever tools I consider most promising to help me to understand the subject under scrutiny. Nevertheless, I see the mayor strength of anthropology as being its endeavor to generate in-depth accounts of particular social situations (usually done through prolonged fieldwork in one particular location), and believe that most anthropologists would agree with me on that. The term 'idiographic approach' is a shorthand for this.

A glance at the following examples of (comparative) studies on naturalizations will help to better illustrate the advantages and shortcomings of both types of comparison – and also make clear that I am not arguing that there would be only one 'right' way to make comparisons: both are useful, they just follow different agendas.

CHARACTERISTICS AND DIFFICULTIES OF NOMOTHETIC COMPARATIVE STUDIES ON (WESTERN) EUROPEAN NATIONALITY POLICIES

During the last decade, a number of comparative studies were conducted on the (Western) European situation regarding nationality, naturalization, and access to citizenship rights (Koopmans et al. 2005; Bauböck et al. 2006; Howard 2009; Huddleston/Niessen 2011). Such studies covered a large number of cases, from medium-N analysis of selected cases (Goodman 2014) to a number of studies covering the 15 'old' member states of the EU, to 38 countries throughout Europe in a study on ethnic preferences for the acquisition of nationality (Dumbrava 2014), some of them explicitly comparing naturalization policies (cp. for instance Huddleston 2013 who measured naturalization procedures in 35

European countries). Other works have focused on the Americas (Vonk 2015) or the Middle East and North Africa (van Waas 2014), among other regions. This type of comparative study is mostly done by political/social scientists and legal scholars.

Comparative works of this kind produce broad comparative overviews, which are very useful for the purposes of informing interested scholars about the current situation. They collect descriptions of the state of nationality law; i.e. how nationality is attributed by birth, when and how foreigners can be naturalized, and so on. They also show contrasts between different national settings and allow the clustering of different cases according to similarities, or even allow with the formulation of typologies (for instance, more inclusive versus more restrictive (Goodman/Howard 2013), or de-ethnicized versus re-ethnicized (Joppke 2003) national legislations on nationality). According to the nomothetic logic of large-N comparisons outlined above, they aim to *explain* the nature of these configurations or shifts from one type to the other. This perspective can be exemplified with the goals of Marc Howard's study, which compared the citizenship policies of the EU-15 member states. His approach stands out for its use of a rather simple and straightforward set of indicators, because he combines only three components to produce what he calls the "Citizenship Policy Index" (CPI) (2009: 19). These components are:

- How newborns acquire their nationality (numerically ranging from 0 points if there are no ius soli provisions, to 2 points in the case of the least restricted version of ius soli);
- How easy or difficult it is for immigrants to naturalize (measured in years of residence required, again resulting in scores from 0 in cases of ten years or more required, to 2 in cases of 3 years or less, reduced by either .25 or .5 points if 'civic integration' is required, depending on how difficult the tests that must be passed are);
- Whether dual citizenship is allow or not (points between 0 for policies that explicitly forbid it, to 2 points where there are no restrictions at all; ibid: 19–26). The combined scores from all three components give a CPI score for each country, ranging from 0.00 for Austria and Denmark to 5.22 for Sweden and 5.50 for Belgium in 2008, according to which they are then grouped into one of three categories: "restrictive", "medium", or "liberal" (ibid: 28). With this approach to measuring the nature of 15 different national citizenship policies, Howard outlines the theoretical arguments of his book, with the aim to "explain why four of the countries developed what can be considered 'historically liberal' policies" and "why, of the eleven historically restrictive countries, six have liberalized their

citizenship policies since the 1990s, whereas the other five remain restrictive" (ibid: 2). He addresses these questions by taking into account the impact of colonialist histories, the evolution of democracy, and the impact of public mobilizations in the 15 cases under scrutiny.

To be able to manage large datasets, the nomothetic approach basically relies on counting and sorting. What it does well is to classify objects according to selected characteristics, and then either sort them into groups defined by one or more classifying markers or use these markers to relate the cases to each other on a numeric scale. These markers represent certain objective characteristics of the case at hand, and by taking them out of their context they are made comparable in the strictest sense, i.e. they are understood as representing the same kinds of characteristics in all cases. This method isolates the items from their context. Instead of analyzing the complex legal/administrative constellation within its societal context, this approach dissects isolated elements that in some way represent the subject under scrutiny (hence the proliferated term 'indicator'). Each indicator can be measured individually, and their combination ostensibly allows the assumed totality of the specific issue at hand to be measured. Consequently, to answer its theoretical questions the nomothetic approach is primarily concerned with the question of the criteria according to which the cases should be sorted. The peril of reductionism is countered by defining increasing numbers of categories, resulting in ever-growing number of separately coded indicators (the *Migrant Integration Policy Index*, for instance, combines 148 indicators; cp. Huddleston/Niessen 2011: 212–213).

But every single category/indicator has its own associated problems. As an example, one can count the amount of persons naturalized. Such total number has the advantage of being objectively comparable – e.g. higher figures represent more naturalizations – and can seemingly be formally interpreted in a precise way. In this example, more naturalizations ostensibly indicate a more liberal or more inclusive immigration regime. But obviously such interpretation must be contextualized; that is, the figures should be given as relative amounts: as a percentage either of the total population, or of the foreign population, or of the foreign population eligible for naturalization. Which would be the most appropriate relation (a dissent elaborated upon by Bauböck/Helbling 2011)? This first short example shows how difficult it is even to identify the precise unit of comparison.

As a second example, in order to analyze the naturalization procedure one could also compare the legal requirements – for instance, the minimum time of residency required for naturalization. This seems like a conveniently isolated, numeric item, because every country inside the EU defines a threshold, based on the number of years immigrants must have been living within is territory before they can become citizens (between 3 and 12 years). Even while EU member states' policies are relatively similar, in contrast to those in other regions of the world, a closer look shows that it is not an easy task to compare even this item, because 'residency' might mean different things in different legislations (i.e. permanent or temporary; lawful or *de facto*; uninterrupted or considered as total amount; directly prior to application or within a certain time range; or not specified at all; cp. table 2 in Goodman 2010: 41). On top of that, to be able to evaluate how easy or difficult it is for immigrants to naturalize in the countries compared, it is crucial to take into account how difficult it is to become a lawful resident – and the category 'residency requirement in years' does not account for that at all. Last but not least, the only statement possible in this context is about 'ordinary' naturalization, while some countries (like Germany) allow for an additional discretionary naturalization, for which fewer years of residency are required.

Even if the former problematic of how to define the unit of comparison could be solved by cooperative work by country experts who, in the manner of idiographic case studies, really get "the characteristics of the case at hand right" (Tilly 1984: 59), the second group of examples points to an enduring problem. This is the danger of falling prey to *faux amis*: some indicators seem to be similar enough to be compared numerically or by exact sorting techniques, but in fact they are not. Translators know of this pitfall in the potential for hastily assuming similar meanings when a similar-seeming term appears in several languages. Every German speaker knows the joke 'Can I become a beefsteak?', which picks on the similarity between the German *bekommen* ('to get') and the English 'to become'. The trap in translating such *faux amis* is obvious and well known, and nomothetic comparisons are not exempt from it. There, however, the problematic arises not during the interpretation of data, but in the process of sorting, as I have just illustrated. To generate universal terminology out of specific emic vocabulary is an inevitable difficulty for large-scale, multivariant, generalizing, comparative designs.

In summary, the nomothetic comparison dissects the subject matter into isolated units. Thereby, it can at best detect the essential details. At worst, however, the fragmentation makes any reference to the actual subject matter disappear (almost) completely, and the result might even be a mere artefact of the respective question.

DIFFICULTIES AND BENEFITS OF IDIOGRAPHIC CASE STUDIES OF NATURALIZATION PROCEDURES OR CEREMONIES

Parallel to the above-mentioned large-N comparisons of nationality policies has emerged a growing number of detailed case studies on how the policies of naturalization are carried out, from the legal basics (like the introduction and the content of citizenship tests, e.g. van Oers 2014) to administrative practices (such as how naturalization interviews are carried out; Fassin/Mazouz 2009). Some of these studies take complex social situations as their point of departure and either view them from a historical angle or follow an ethnographic approach, or use a combination of both, which places empirical and observable interactions in a context in which broader power relations play out. Especially regarding naturalization ceremonies, there are a few detailed cases studies from Western countries (Damsholt 2009; Aptekar 2012; Byrne 2012).

The problems facing any inductive-individualizing approach that attempts to engage in comparisons are obvious. If more than one case is to be studied thoroughly, the workload and the demands on the researchers increase linearly. While in large-N deductive-generalizing designs, one national dataset may be more or less like another in terms of study design or data-processing power (admittedly, getting access to the data often requires tedious work), in ethnographic fieldwork, gaining access to more than one site and data-gathering there requires time funds to be spent many times over. The more distant the locations are from one another, the more demanding movement between them becomes. And, most importantly, if different cases are to be analyzed in depth, a high level of specific competency is needed, including knowledge of various languages.

Not surprisingly, there are only few explicitly comparative studies so far; for instance the recent interpretative comparisons of naturalization ceremonies in the US, Canada, Australia, and Great Britain (Byrne 2014), all English speaking countries. Another explicit comparative project was designed with considerable historical depth and takes into account 18th and 19th century political culture to unravel the roots of current naturalization ceremonies in West European countries (Damsholt 2008a). Apart from this historical perspective, the work of Tine Damsholt placed a lot of emphasis on the participant observation of current ceremonies in Denmark, Sweden, Norway, and Great Britain. Her ethnography shed light on the material practices: how citizenship is 'ritualized' at the ceremonies, and how it is 'materialized' in (for instance) the form of certificates, medals, gifts, etc. (2009). During her participant observations at the ceremonies, Damsholt systematically looked into – or rather, listened into – various 'soundscapes' created by the social and special arrangements of the rituals. Among them was the collective recitation of oaths, the performance of folk music, the collective singing of national anthems, the noise of children playing in the background, and of course silence (to produce a 'sacred' atmosphere, ibid 2008b).

Damsholt's approach seems to me to be a very important contribution to the study of naturalizations, because with her focus on the emotions, sounds, and activities of those involved in the ceremonies she stresses the importance of experienced or even embodied communities in the everyday functioning of the 'imagined community' of the nation state. If it was still necessary to underline the value of participant observation, the focus on subjective participation in such ceremonies and on the perspective of the attendees makes the point. Observational data of that kind can hardly be standardized, because the ethnographers' impressions are also highly subjective, hence no objective reproduction of what happened at the ceremonies is possible. How "national soundscapes" (2008b: 61) are to be compared across cases is a question that cannot be answered with a nomothetic approach.

Oskar Verkaaik, a Dutch anthropologist, looked at the way in which local civil servants organized and performed naturalization ceremonies in the Netherlands, and detected some unintended consequences that their interpretation of the national imagery had. The political decision-makers, he wrote, intended the ceremonies to be "a kind of disciplinary initiation ritual" (Verkaaik 2010: 69): they were meant to remind the new members of the nation of seemingly typical Dutch "norms and values" (ibid: 69), and were meant to stress their "duties" (ibid: 69) as good citizens. In doing so, the ceremony, which was actually meant to be a "welcoming gesture" (ibid: 73), depicts the nation as something already there, constituted to large extent by a national "culture" (ibid: 77) that immigrant others can be initiated to.

Verkaaik's interpretation of what was actually happening at the ceremonies is quite different. Many of the civil servants (those determining how these ceremonies are actually conducted) felt embarrassed by the government's ideal of depicting Dutchness at the ceremonies. Hence, they ridiculed the way in which Dutch folklore was presented, or they presented it in an ironic way, and thereby distanced themselves from any assumed duty to assimilate to it. Or, if they had the power to organize the ceremonies the way they wanted to, they sometimes made them resemble other ceremonies they used to run in their town halls, such as weddings, without any reference to the Dutch nation and without featuring any key symbols (ibid: 76).

Though only implicitly, Verkaaik also used a comparative method when he chose to look both at political speeches and mediated debates on the one hand,

and at local bureaucrats and their practices on the other; in this way he discovered a stark contrast between strategically intended and actively practiced self-representations of the Dutch nation. In addition, he chose various different locales for his observations, including smaller and larger municipalities, and more rural and more suburban settings. In investigating different locations, he observed very similar things going on, and he assembled them to form a pattern: the national was spelled out in terms of *local* food, crafts, or celebrities. "Whereas Dutch intellectuals were busy defining Dutch culture in terms of European civilization, the naturalization ceremony linked it to nationalist history and local folklore" (ibid: 74). But he also made out differences among the local ceremonies, which led him to interpret the ceremonies as a form of disciplinary initiation ritual, as mentioned above. This conclusion he draws, at least partly, from insights gained from a comparative perspective. Only by observations in more than one location did he notice that in some municipalities some of the local civil servants actively opposed the exhibition of Dutchness as defined by the state. They thereby made visible what would otherwise have largely remained (and in other places continued to be) implicit.

This contribution is of great value, because it shows how much more insight scholars can gain from looking at how things are actually done than they might from focusing only on how things are intended to be, or on how people talk about them. Because a lot of knowledge is tacit or embodied, it remains largely non-verbal, and must be observed in what people do. In other words: though time-consuming, participant observation can be worth every moment spent.

IDIOGRAPHIC COMPARISONS AS TRANSLATIONS

The analogy to the practice of translation, which I have already used above, holds true for the inductive-individualizing comparison. Its core element is the relation of certain social configurations in one context (i.e. specifically combined characteristics) to comparable configurations in other contexts – not merely to relate collections of artificially isolated characteristics to one another. Hence I suggest viewing this approach as a form of translation. The direct, unambiguous transfer of the meaning of a text written from one language into another language is just as impossible as the objective, universally valid comparison of two cultural configurations. A good translation is never based on mere literal equivalence, but rather creates a consistent image, a text that 'works' in the target language. Comparisons in the idiographic approach can be seen as an ongoing process of translation back and forth that never exactly reproduces the meaning, but rather connects and mediates between cases. This mode of comparison seems to me to involve a change of perspectives on the subject, which cannot lead to an 'objective' or definite description, but which should account for the differences between the distinct perspectives (cp. Kaschuba 2003: 347). Hence, the idiographic approach can help uncover unexpected dimensions of the cases, even if the scientific attention was not directed at them in the beginning. What is more, alongside comparable elements, the inductive idiographic design can integrate formerly unknown transfers and entanglements between the cases more easily than the deductive design can. And after all, a possible finding of an idiographic comparison may well be that the cases are not comparable at all – in terms of an inductive research design, this is a legitimate and useful result.

As has been mentioned above, an idiographic approach always requires a small-N design. The interest in the context of social interactions usually necessitates prolonged fieldwork as the preferred method, instead of the short-term contact involved in, say, gathering survey data with a questionnaire. This may give results that seemingly lack significance when compared with those of large-N studies, because the degree to which the results can be generalized is limited. Therein lies another difference from nomothetic designs: the applicability of the results does not extend further than the cases under scrutiny. The deeper understanding of single (few) empiric cases is the final goal, not the discovery of 'general laws'. Nevertheless, even in the absence of generalizations, it is perfectly possible to build a typology of the few cases under scrutiny.

THE TWO MODES OF COMPARISON COMPARED

This text explained the special features of the anthropological approach to comparison, which I have called an *ideographic* comparison. Its main specificity is to focus on only a few cases, to consider them as complex constellations, and to compare them to each other with the main aim of better understanding both the specificity of each case at hand and the parallels, or connections, between them. I contrasted this approach with a *nomothetic* approach, whose aim is to formulate universal laws or establish universal models that can help to explain all possible cases.

The juxtaposition of the idiographic and the nomothetic approach is somehow artificial, insofar as few disciplines in the humanities and social sciences are 'purely' idiographic or nomothetic. Furthermore, many actual studies might in fact integrate both perspectives, or might draw on methodology from both camps. In this article, the contrast between the two serves the purpose of stressing conceptual particularities. Among the differences between the two approaches, one stands out: the nomothetic perspective engages with its cases via isolated, decontextualized features (variables), while the idiographic approach understands each case as a complex configuration of social relations within their societal context. This results in very different problems associated with the respective approaches, some of which I commented above.

While it certainly cannot have gone unnoticed that I support the idiographic approach, let's not forget that the nomothetic comparison also has much to offer. Only macro-comparative approaches allow for theory-building around encompassing models; for instance that of a 'restrictive turn', or of 'converging policies' among member states of the EU (Hansen/Weil 2001; Goodman/ Howard 2013). To produce a broad overview is legitimate for some purposes, but to my understanding should not be the end of comparisons. Without in-depth cases studies the question of what is really happening on the ground would not be addressed. A comparison between two (or more) cases should aim to *open up* the perspective, to allow for alternative interpretations by contrasting one case with others, and, at best, to help to find *new* insights. It can help to draw attention to possible parallels and differences between the cases compared, which in turn could lead to more detailed understanding of each of them.

The examples of idiographic studies of naturalization policies I mentioned above hint at what idiographic comparisons can accomplish: Not only discerning *whether* those policies stem from an ethnic concept of the nation, and *whether* they are prone to push immigrants more or less to assimilate, but also finding out *what* they are asked to assimilate to, and *how* this is forced upon them – and even how the participants navigate and partly undermine these assimilatory attempts.

REFERENCES

Aptekar, Sofya (2012): "Naturalization ceremonies and the role of immigrants in the American nation." In: Citizenship Studies 16/7, pp. 937–952.
Bade, Klaus J. (2001): "Immigration, Naturalization, and Ethno-national Traditions in Germany: From the Citizenship Law of 1913 to the Law of 1999." In: Larry Eugene Jones (ed.), Crossing boundaries. The exclusion and inclusion of minorities in Germany and the United States, New York: Berghahn, pp. 29–49.

Bauböck, Rainer et al. (2006): Acquisition and loss of nationality. Policies and trends in 15 European states, Amsterdam: Amsterdam Univ. Press.

Bauböck, Rainer/Helbling, Marc (2011): "Which indicators are most useful for comparing citizenship policies?" EUDO Citizenship Observatory, EUI Working Papers 54, (http://hdl.handle.net/1814/19015).

Baumann, Jochen (1999): "Staatsangehörigkeit und Citizenship. Das deutsche Staatsbürgerrecht im europäischen Vergleich." In: Jochen Baumann/Andreas Dietl/Wolfgang Wippermann (eds.), Blut oder Boden. Doppelpaß, Staatsbürgerrecht und Nationalverständnis, Berlin: Elefanten-Press, pp. 49–106.

Baumeister, Andrea (2003): "Ways of Belonging: Ethnonational Minorities and Models of 'Differentiated Citizenship'." In: Ethnicities 3/3, pp. 393–416.

Bös, Mathias (2000): "Die rechtliche Konstruktion von Zugehörigkeit. Staatsangehörigkeit in Deutschland und den USA." In: Klaus Holz (ed.), Staatsbürgerschaft. Soziale Differenzierung und politische Inklusion, Wiesbaden: Westdt. Verl., pp. 95–120.

Brubaker, Rogers (1992): Citizenship and Nationhood in France and Germany, Cambridge/MA: Hervard University Press.

Byrne, Bridget (2014): Making citizens. Public rituals and personal journeys to citizenship, Basingstoke: Palgrave Macmillan.

―― (2012): "A local welcome? Narrations of citizenship and nation in UK citizenship ceremonies." In: Citizenship Studies 16/3-4, pp. 531–544.

Ceupens, Bambi/Geschiere, Peter (2005): "Autochthony: Local or Global? – New Modes in the Struggle over Citizenship and Belonging in Africa and Europe." In: Annual Review of Anthropology 34, pp. 385–409.

Damsholt, Tine (2008a): "Making Citizens. On the Genealogy of Citizenship Ceremonies." In: Per Mouritsen (ed.), Constituting communities. Political solutions to cultural conflict, Basingstoke: Palgrave Macmillan, pp. 53–72.

―― (2008b): "The sound of citizenship." In: Ethnologia Europaea 38/1, pp. 56–65.

―― (2009): "Ritualizing and Materializing Citizenship." In: Journal of Ritual Studies 23/2, pp. 17–29.

Deegan, Mary Jo (2001): "The Chicago School of Ethnography." In: Paul Atkinson/Amanda Coffey/Sarah Delamont/John Lofland/Lyn Lofland (eds.), Handbook of ethnography, London, Thousand Oaks, Calif.: Sage Publications, pp. 11–25.

Dumbrava, Costica (2014): Nationality, citizenship and ethno-cultural belonging. Preferential membership policies in Europe, Basingstoke: Palgrave Macmillan.

Ember, Melvin (1997): "Evolution of the Human Relations Area Files." In: Cross-Cultural Research 31/1, pp. 3–15.

Fahrmeir, Andreas (2000): Citizens and aliens, New York: Berghahn.

Fassin, Didier/Mazouz, Sarah (2009): "What Is It to Become French? Naturalization as a Republican Rite of Institution." In: Revue française de sociologie 50/5 pp. 37–64.

Flick, Uwe (2002): An introduction to qualitative research, London, Thousand Oaks, Calif.: Sage Publications.

Francis, Emerich K. (1965): Ethnos und Demos. Soziologische Beiträge zur Volkstheorie, Berlin: Duncker & Humblot.

Gabbert, Wolfgang (2006): "Concepts of Ethnicity." In: Latin American and Caribbean Ethnic Studies 1/1, pp. 85–103.

Giesen, Bernhard/Junge, Kai (1998): "Nationale Identität und Staatsbürgerschaft in Deutschland und Frankreich." In: Berliner Journal für Soziologie 4, pp. 523–537.

Goodman, Sara Wallace (2014): Civic integration and membership politics in Western Europe, Cambridge: Cambridge University Press.

⸺ (2010): "Naturalisation Policies in Europe: Exploring Patterns of Inclusion and Exclusion." Edited by EUDO Citizenship Observatory. (http://cadmus.eui.eu/handle/1814/19577).

Goodman, Sara Wallace/Howard, Marc Morjé (2013): "Evaluating and Explaining the Restrictive Backlash in Citizenship Policy in Europe." In: Studies in Law, Politics & Society 60, pp. 111–139.

Gosewinkel, Dieter (1998): "Untertanschaft, Staatsbürgerschaft, Nationalität. Konzepte der Zugehörigkeit im Zeitalter des Nationalstaats. Anmerkungen zur Begriffsgeschichte in Deutschland, Frankreich, England und den USA." In: Berliner Journal für Soziologie 4, pp. 507–522.

Hansen, Georg (2004): "Die Ethnisierung des deutschen Staatsbürgerrechts und seine Tauglichkeit in der EU." In: Fakultät für Kultur- und Sozialwissenschaften (ed.), Zweites Forschungskolloqium des Fachbereichs Kultur- und Sozialwissenschaften "Gesellschaftliche, kulturelle und politische Formierung Europas", Fern Universität Hagen.

Hansen, Randall/Weil, Patrick (2001): "Citizenship, Immigration and Nationality: Towards a Convergence in Europe?" In: Randall Hansen/Patrick Weil (eds.), Towards a European nationality. Citizenship, immigration and nationality law in the EU, Basingstoke, Hampshire: Palgrave, pp. 1–23.

Howard, Marc Morjé (2009): The politics of citizenship in Europe, Cambridge, New York: Cambridge University Press.

Huddleston, Thomas (2013): "The naturalisation procedure: measuring the ordinary obstacles and opportunities for immigrants to become citizens." EUDO Citizenship Observatory, EUI RSCAS Policy Paper, 16 (http://hdl.handle.net/1814/28122).

Huddleston, Thomas/Niessen, Jan (2011): "Migrant Integration Policy Index (MIPEX) III." British Council; Migration Policy Group, Brussels. (http://www.mipex.eu/sites/default/files/downloads/migrant_integration_policy_index_mipexiii_2011.pdf).
Joppke, Christian (2003): "Citizenship between De- and Re-Ethnicization." In: European Journal of Sociology/Archives Européennes de Sociologie 44/3, pp. 429–458.
Kaelble, Hartmut (1999): Der historische Vergleich. Eine Einführung zum 19. und 20. Jahrhundert, Frankfurt/Main: Campus Verlag.
Kaschuba, Wolfgang (2003): "Anmerkungen zum Gesellschaftsvergleich aus ethnologischer Perspektive." In: Hartmut Kaelble/Jürgen Schriewer (eds.), Vergleich und Transfer. Komparatistik in den Sozial-, Geschichts- und Kulturwissenschaften, Frankfurt/Main: Campus-Verl., pp. 341–350.
Kohn, Hans (1944): The idea of nationalism. A study in its origins and background, New York: MacMillan.
Koning, Edward A. (2011): "Ethnic and civic dealings with newcomers: naturalization policies and practices in twenty-six immigration countries". In: Ethnic and Racial Studies 34/11, pp. 1974–1994.
Koopmans, Ruud et al. (2005): Contested citizenship. Immigration and cultural diversity in Europe, Minneapolis: University of Minnesota Press.
Kuzio, Taras (2002): "The myth of the civic state: a critical survey of Hans Kohn's framework for understanding nationalism." In: Ethnic and Racial Studies 25/1, pp. 20–39.
Refsing, Kirsten (2003): "*In* Japan, but not *of* Japan." In: Colin Mackerras (ed.), Ethnicity in Asia, London, New York: RoutledgeCurzon (Asia's transformations), pp. 48–63.
Rickert, Heinrich (1899): Kulturwissenschaft und Naturwissenschaft. Ein Vortrag, Tübingen: Mohr.
Rohner, Ronald P. (1977): "Advantages of the Comparative Method of Anthropology." In: Cross-Cultural Research 12/2, pp. 117–144.
Schwarz, Tobias (2013): "Policies of Belonging: Nationale Mitgliedschaft und Zugehörigkeit in Lateinamerika." Kompetenznetz Lateinamerika – Ethnicity, Citizenship Belonging (KLA Working Paper Series 2) (http://www.kompetenzla.uni-koeln.de/fileadmin/WP_Schwarz.pdf).
Sciortino, Giuseppe (2012): "Ethnicity, Race, Nationhood, Foreignness, and many other things: Prolegomena to a Cultural Sociology of difference-based interactions." In: Jeffrey C. Alexander/Ronald N. Jacobs/Philip Smith (eds.), The Oxford handbook of cultural sociology, Oxford: Oxford Univ. Press, pp. 365–389.

Seipel, Christian/Rippl, Susanne (2013): "Grundlegende Probleme des empirischen Kulturvergleichs. Ein problemorientierter Überblick über aktuelle Diskussionen." In: Berliner Journal für Soziologie 23/2, pp. 257–286.

Smith, Anthony D. (1991): National identity, London: Penguin.

Tilly, Charles (1984): Big structures, large processes, huge comparisons, New York: Russell Sage Foundation.

van Oers, Ricky (2014): Deserving citizenship. Citizenship tests in Germany, the Netherlands and the United Kingdom: Brill; Nijhoff.

van Waas, Laura (2014): "A Comparative Analysis of Nationality Laws in the MENA Region." In: SSRN Journal (http://ssrn.com/abstract=2493718).

Verkaaik, Oskar (2010): "The cachet dilemma: Ritual and agency in new Dutch nationalism." In: American Ethnologist 37/1, pp. 69–82.

Vonk, Olivier W. (2015): Nationality law in the western hemisphere. A study on grounds for acquisition and loss of citizenship in the Americas and the Caribbean, Leiden, Boston: Brill.

Weber, Max (1990): Wirtschaft und Gesellschaft. Grundriss der verstehenden Soziologie. 5th ed., Tübingen: Mohr.

Weil, Patrick (1996): "Nationality and Citizenships: The Lessons of the French Experience for Germany and Europe." In: David Cesarani/Mary Fulbrook (eds.), Citizenship, nationality and migration in Europe, London [u. a.]: Routledge, pp. 74–87.

Wimmer, Andreas (2008): "The Making and Unmaking of Ethnic Boundaries: A Multilevel Process Theory." In: The American Journal of Sociology 113(4), pp. 970–1022.

Windelband, Wilhelm (1894): Geschichte und Naturwissenschaft, Straßburg: Heitz & Mündel.

Rethinking 'race' from Asian perspectives

YASUKO TAKEZAWA

INTRODUCTION

In continental Europe, there has been a tendency to avoid using the term 'race' in favor of 'ethnicity'. In the United States, on the other hand, there is abundant literature on race – far more than that on ethnicity – and in Latin America, racism and skin pigmentation are attracting increasing attention since the strong correlation between pigmentation and socioeconomic hierarchy has been revealed (cp. for example, Telles and PERLA 2014). The usage of the terms thus varies depending on the region and its historical/social context.

Race in general is defined as a group identified by what are perceived to be physical differences. In Encyclopaedia Britannica, Peter Wade writes, "What most definitions have in common is an attempt to categorize peoples primarily by their physical differences." The third edition of Oxford Dictionary of English, for example, defines race as "each of the major divisions of human kind, having distinct physical characteristics" (Stevenson 2010).

Such understandings of race have been developed mostly in the U.S. and Europe based on Euro-American experiences. However, as long as visible physical features are considered the primary criteria for identifying race, only minorities discriminated against on the basis of the European and American idea of race are likely to have social recognition as the victims of 'racial discrimination'.

I consider the following characteristics as inherent in the idea of race. First, racial characteristics are believed to be 'inherited' from generation to generation, mediated by bodies, and thus cannot be (easily) changed. Second, there is a strong tendency for those who draw the boundary between the self and other to exclude the latter, and often to assume a hierarchy between groups. Third, since exclusion and hierarchy manifest themselves in collusion with political, economic, and social institutions and resources, they are not limited to a consciousness of differences based on simple prejudice and ethnocentrism. That is to say, they are related to interests through institutional differentiation.

If race then includes physically invisible groups, how is it different from ethnicity? An ethnic group basically continues to construct and confirm its unity and solidarity through the awareness and imagination of sharing 'something special' in past historical experience, 'culture', or values, even though its label and category may have been mobilized in the process of modern state formation. However, though the ideas of race and ethnicity are not mutually exclusive, and may refer to the same groups, they should be distinguished as analytical concepts.

I argue that the idea of race is neither a modern Western product, nor a universal phenomenon. My thesis claims that when we abstract the highest common factors from the various phenomena constituting the idea of race, we can identify three dimensions, which I call *race*, *Race*, and *RR* (Race as Resistance) respectively. In the following, I will discuss these three dimensions of the idea of race based on Asian perspectives. I can provide only a small number of examples due to limited space. However, the model may be applied to rethinking race on a global level (Takezawa 2011).

RACE IN THE LOWER CASE SENSE

What I refer to as *race* (with a lower-case 'r') indicates cases where differences observed in a particular society between socially differentiated groups are understood to be inherited over generations and cannot be changed (or easily changed) by the environment. These differences are represented in political, economic and social institutions accompanied by a clear hierarchy, and manifest an exclusive nature. *race* in the lower-case sense does not exist in human society across all time and space, and can only occur in contexts where social stratification has developed to a certain extent.

Examples of *race* in this sense include the Pakejong in Korea (Kim 2013); the slavery system of the Toba Batak of Southeast Asia (Reid 1983); the Micronesian low caste, whose members engage in 'polluted' work and cannot own land (Chappell 1998); the socially low-status Milingai of Yap island, who are 'impure' and also cannot own land (Ushijima 1987); the Irish from the viewpoint of the English; and the Jews and the Roma in various parts in Europe.

Let us take the example of the Burakumin in Japan. It has long been a taboo to consider the Burakumin in terms of race, but at the 2001 Durban conference, the Buraku Liberation League and a Dalit group in unison formed a session to appeal for their rights, claiming that they have been suffering racism based on work and descent. The history of the Burakumin – a heterogeneous group – is complicated, but in brief, the group was designated as outcaste during the early modern period, and were formerly often referred to as *eta* (literally, 'defilement-abundant'). Many of them were engaged in slaughtering animals and producing leather, or other work considered undesirable by the majority, while in reality their products and labor were indispensable in their society, especially for the rulers (for Buraku issues, cp. for example, Amos 2011; The Buraku Liberation and Human Rights Research Institute 1998).

In Japan, where the ideology of blood is still persistent, descent serves as a key factor constituting the idea of race as it is believed to be inherited from generation to generation. While having deep historical roots, this ideology was explicitly reconstructed after the Meiji period started in 1868, when sovereignty was transferred from the samurai to the emperor. The discourse that the emperor has sacred blood that has persisted since ancient times and represents the Japanese nation was developed, which in turn reinforced the myth that the Burakumin have polluted blood; as Jiichiro Matsumoto, a leader of the Buraku liberation movement left very famous words: "Where the High is, there is the Low". The 'sacred' and the 'polluted' were linked through an inseparable relationship constructed around the axis of the blood ideology in the hurried nation-building process.

Scholars have agreed that there is continuity in the discourse of the alien racial origins of the Burakumin from the medieval (until the end of 16th century) to early modern (from the 17th century through the mid 19th century) and modern (since the mid 19th century) periods. There are also historical sources that indicate that discrimination was institutionalized in statuary form by the 16th century. During the Age of Civil Wars in medieval Japan (from the late 15th century through to the end of the 16th century), the contact between *eta*, who handled animal slaughtering and leather production, and the rest of the society increased due to a greater demand for leather, the raw material for the samurai panoply. In the Edo period (1603-1867), *eta* was further fixed as a status (Harada 1973).

In China, there is a group among the Yi (the name of an ethnic group recognized by the state) living in Liangshan in Sichuan province who call themselves the Nosu. Intermarriage between the high-caste *nuoho* (black) and the low caste *quho* (white), who are considered to be polluted, is avoided even today. Domestic labor slaves until the beginning of the 20th century, the *quho* are considered to be of different descent and identifiable through outward appearance (Hill 2001).

race in the lower-case sense still persists in contemporary societies. Today, the targets of what E. Balibar called new racism in Europe, such as immigrants from South Asia, Africa and the Caribbean, as well as migrant workers in Japan and Korea, can be understood as one form of race in the lower case.

RACE IN THE UPPER-CASE SENSE

Race in the upper-case sense refers to a (quasi-) scientific concept, constructed through the mapping and classification of the people of the world. It has been believed to be possible to classify people of the world and make visual 'specimens', in terms of universal language and universal principles, in the name of science. For this reason, the theories proposed circulate and are accepted in many regions of the world. However, classifications do not spread to various regions of the world merely as imported concepts from the West. They have their own unique development in a specific sociopolitical context of nation-building or colonialism.

Among others, Johann F. Blumenbach (1865), who is often referred to as the Father of Anthropology, is probably most influential with his classification of human beings into five categories in the 1795 version of his thesis, but was followed by numerous scientists engaged in the classification of humans. The introduction of European theories of race in the name of science around the mid-19th century had enormous impact almost everywhere in the world. Racial classification theories became a new tool of authority for European colonizers and Asian leaders alike. To name a few: *Races of Britain* (1885) by John Beddoe (British); *Anthropologie* (1888) by Paul Topinard (French); *The Mediterranean Race: a Study of the Origin of European Peoples* (1901) by G. Sergi (Italian). By the mid-19th century, colonial Europeans were employing techniques such as ethnographic research, mapping, and census-taking to describe Asia's various 'races'.

Western racial characterizations spread to other parts of Asia in the latter half of the 19th century. These classifications not only justified the superior social position of European colonizers with regard to Asian subordinates but also evolved into detailed subdivisions between the colonial subjects themselves, wherein the elite characterized 'tribes' and other marginalized groups as 'barbarian' and 'primitive'. In Japanese school textbooks during the Meiji period (1868-1912), the views of representative proponents of racial classification of the Enlightenment period such as Blumenbach and Cuvier were repeatedly introduced (Takezawa 2015).

In colonial India the British anthropologists who conducted ethnographic research built reciprocal relationships with Indian elites and went so far as to construct a defense of the country's caste system (e.g. Risley 1891; Deniker 1900). This defense was based on the 'scientific' analysis of cranial differences between members of different castes. The findings indicated that Bengali upper castes were Aryan in origin and that the lower castes, such as foragers and pastoralists, were, under the precepts of social Darwinism, destined to die out.

From the latter half of the 19th century to the early 20th century, American society was unsettled by the debate over the abolition of slavery and the acceptance of 'unassimilable' immigrants from Eastern and Southern Europe and Asia. Internal colonialism in the U.S., along with the colonialism of the British Empire in the Victorian era, provided the greatest receptacle for *Race* in the upper-case sense. Let us consider the following cases of transformation:

Samuel George Morton, known for the collection and measurement of skulls in the mid-19th century, disseminated the idea of Blumenbach's five-fold classification (Blumenbach 1865 [1775]) in America with his first book, Crania Americana (Morton 1839). Morton described the characteristics of each category based on Blumenbach's five-fold classification, and inserted the following note: "It will be observed, however, that the word race is substituted for variety" (ibid 1839: 5, emphasis original). In spite of Blumenbach's emphasis that clear boundaries cannot be drawn within it, Morton changed the wording from 'variety' to 'race', which implies fixity and definite difference (Brace 2005). As Stephen Jay Gould demonstrates, the differences between races, with 'whites' positioned at the top of a hierarchical system and 'blacks' at the bottom, were fabricated and exaggerated by intentional and unintentional mismeasurement (1981). As is well known, Morton's research on human skulls was adopted by defenders of slavery and of racial segregation as scientific proof of the inferiority of body, ability and character of black people in the historical context of his time.

Brazil has been historically credited as a country with little racial prejudice (e.g. Freyre 1933; Degler 1971), as miscenegation has constructed the basis of its national character (Telles 2004; Silva/Paixão 2014). However, during the period between the two World Wars, it used the idea of *Race* and Social Darwinism as a pretext for the formation and development of the nation state. The leaders of Brazil sought the answer to the question of how to become like the civilized countries of Europe in making its people 'whiter' by welcoming immigrants from Europe and restricting or excluding those from Asia and other regions (e.g. Skidmore 1990). Also in colonial Southeast Asia and India, *Race* in the upper-case sense, which had not existed in traditional local societies, was introduced when the census began around the 1870s. While language, religion and customs had previously been employed as classificatory measures, the introduction of *Race* reorganized the system of classification, incorporating various groups such as people living in the hinterlands, who came to be called 'tribes' (e.g. Guha 1998; Keyes 2002).

The examples above are all from the modern period, but *Race* is also a contemporary problem in the age of the human genome. Various studies have attempted to find genes connected with propensity toward drug use, violence, and other criminal behavior, often linked to racial profiling (Ossorio/Dustor 2004). Some scientists, though by now a minority, maintain that there are meaningful biological differences between what they call races and/or between peoples in different continents (e.g. Risch et al. 2002; Jorde/Wooding 2004).

In Japan a couple of years ago a few tabloid magazines published articles about the Mayor of Osaka, Toru Hashimoto, one of the most influential politicians in Japan, and disclosed his father's Buraku identity and his mother's Korean identity. Later Hashimoto sued these publishers and won. Among the catchy phrases in these articles were "traces Hashimoto's DNA", and "identifies his blood lineage" (Shukan Asahi 2012).

All these examples show how *Race* in the upper-case sense remains deeply rooted even as it shifts its appearance in line with new scientific developments.

RACE AS RESISTANCE (RR)

The third dimension of the idea of race is *Race as Resistance*, or *RR*. The subjectivity of the racialized groups is often awakened in the proactive resistance of race/Race, and is realigned through solidarity. *Race as resistance*, a concept with newly positive meanings, is constructed as a result. There are many forms of *RR*. Some appear as an inverse of race/ Race, and others emphasize identity politics. *RR* indicates the use of race as a discursive strategy to expose existing (or contemporary) racial discrimination, to refuse assimilation promoted by mainstream society, and to put identity politics into operation. In such contexts, racial identity is consciously employed despite its being complicated in reality by the existence of several multilayered and plural identities.

When W. E. B. DuBois organized the first Pan African Congress in 1900 in London, he was already aware that the construction of what is today called transnational African solidarity was a key to progress in rectifying discrimination against people of African descent. There, he made a famous speech calling for whites to give up the rule which had led to European expansionism. Pan Africanism, with DuBois at the head, became a major movement after World War I aimed at a kind of transnational RR. Resistance by non-whites against white rule is another domain of RR. Early international organizations run by non-whites as resistance against whites included the Pan African Congress (1900, 1919, 1921, 1923, 1927, 1945) and the Universal Races Congress (1911), while in the scientific field there was the academic argument by the Boas school against the theory of biological superiority of the white race (Preiswerk 1970).

Race as resistance to white hegemony also developed in East Asia at the beginning of the 20th century. The 'Yellow Race' began to be perceived as a threat to 'White civilized countries', particularly after Japan's victory in the Russo-Japanese War of 1904–05. Resistance to the mounting European invasion of China and other parts of Asia, and Euro-American racism toward the burgeoning Asian population, grew and intensified. The notion of the 'Yellow Peril' had spread sensationally throughout the West Coast region of the U.S., and the exclusion of Japanese immigrants was intensified after the Japanese victory in the Russo-Japanese War. Japan took the establishment of a succession of racist laws, mainly targeting Japanese immigrants on the West Coast, very seriously, and tried to denounce racism in the U.S. by putting the problem of the exclusion of Japanese immigrants on the international agenda. However, Japan's hope to include the article for abolishment of racial discrimination at the peace conference at Versailles after World War I (1919) did not materialize due to strong opposition from the U.S. and its allies. This was a most important turning point for Japan. Having experienced a great setback, it abandoned the ideology of leaving Asia and joining Europe. Later, as is well known, it moved instead towards the plan of the Great East Asian Co-Prosperity Sphere on the pretext of securing the natural resources of the southern seas.

In the period following World War II, as Asian countries embarked on a course of nation-building, perceptions of race have played essential roles in defining their national identities and shaping their external relations, particularly with Europe and America. The advancement of Westernization and the strong presence of U.S. military bases in Asia have significantly affected aesthetic ideals among Asian peoples (Glenn 2009). In different regions of contemporary Asia, lighter skin and other phenotypes that are traditionally considered traits of Europeans are now regarded as more desirable.

CONCLUDING REMARKS

The three dimensions of the idea of race discussed above are linked with one another, and one dimension is able to change into another according to social conditions. Even if *RR* is sometimes seen as a threat to social integration, and some advocate a 'color blind' society in which racial frameworks do not exist, at least at the institutional level there will be always difficulties as long as *Race* in the upper-case and *race* in the lower-case sense are not socially resolved. *RR* has also become a powerful conceptual tool for identifying racism, and for the identity politics of minorities. As long as essentialism based on *race* and *Race* does not disappear, it remains a concept indispensable for understanding the politics of anti-discrimination struggles.

REFERENCES

Amos, Timothy D. (2011): Embodying Difference: The making of burakumin in modern Japan, Honolulu: University of Hawai'I Press.

Blumenbach, Johann Friedrich (1865): "Natural Variety of Mankind." In: Thomas Bendyshe (trans. and ed.), Anthropological Treatises of Johann Friedrich Blumenbach, London: Longman, Green, Longman, Roberts & Green, pp. 65–144.

Brace, C. Loring (2005): 'Race' Is a Four-Letter Word: The Genesis of the Concept, New York: Oxford University Press.

Buraku Liberation and Human Rights Research Institute (1998): Discrimination in Japan from the perspective of the International Covenant on Civil and Political Rights: counter-report to the fourth Periodic Report by the Government of Japan, Osaka: Kaiho Shuppansha.

Chappell, David A. (1998): "Pacific Island Societies." In: Paul Finkelman/Joseph C. Miller (eds.), Macmillan Encyclopedia of World Slavery, Vol.2, New York: Simon & Schuster Macmillan, pp. 665–666.

Degler, Carl N. (1971): Neither Black nor White: Slavery and Race Relations in Brazil and the United States, New York: Micmillan.

Deniker, Joseph (1900): The Races of Man: An Outline of Anthropology and Ethnography, London: Charles Scribner's and Sons.

Freyre, Gilberto (1933): The Masters and the Slaves: A Study in the Development of Brazilian Civilization, Berkeley: University of California Press.

Glenn, Evelyn Nakano (2009): "Consuming Lightness: Segmented Markets and Global Capital in the Skin-Whitening Trade." In: Evelyn Nakano Glenn (ed.), Shades of Difference: Why Skin Color Matters, Stanford: Stanford University Press, pp. 166–187.

Gould, Stephen J. (1981): The Mismeasure of Men, New York: W. W. Norton & Company.

Guha, Sumit (1998): "Lower Strata, Older Races, and Aboriginal Peoples: Racial Anthropology and Mythical History Past and Present." In: The Journal of Asian Studies 57/2, pp. 423–441.

Harada, Tomohiko (1973): Hisabetsu buraku no Rekishi (A History of Buraku), Tokyo: Asahi-Shimbun.

Hill, Ann Maxwell (2001): "Captives, Kin, and Slaves in Xiao Liangshan." In: The Journal of Asian Studies 60/4, pp. 1033–1049.

Jorde, Lynn B/Wooding, Stephen P (2004): "Genetic variation, classification and 'race'." In: Nature Genetics 36, pp. 28–S33.

Keyes, Charles (2002): "Presidential Address: 'The Peoples of Asia'--Science and Politics in the Classification of Ethnic Groups in Thailand, China, and Vietnam." In: The Journal of Asian Studies 61/4, pp. 1163–1203.

Kim, Joong-Seop (2013): The Koran Paekjong Under Japanese Rule: The Quest for Equality and Human Rights, London: Routledge.

Morton, Samuel George (1839): Crania Americana; or, A Comparative View of the Skulls of Various Aboriginal Nations of North and South America, to Which is Prefixed an Essay on the Varieties of the Human Species, Philadelphia: Dobson.

Ossorio, Pilar/Dustor, Troy (2004): "Race and Genetics: Controversies in Biomedical, Behavioral, and Forensic Sciences." Paper presented at the AAA Race and Human Diversity Conference.

Preiswerk, Roy (1970): "Race and Colour in International Relations." In The Year Book of World Affairs, 1970, London: Stevens and Sons, pp. 54–87.

Reid, Anthony (1983): Slavery, Bondage and Dependency in Southeast Asia. St. Lucia: University of Queensland Press.

Risch, Neil/Burchard, Esteban/Ziv, Elad/Tang, Hua (2002): "Categorization of humans in biomedical research: genes, race and disease." In: Genome Biology 3/7, pp. 1–12.

Risley, Herbert H. (1891): The Tribes and Castes of Bengal, New Delhi: Rupa and Co.

Silva, Graziella Moraes/Paixão, Marcelo (2014): Mixed and Unequal: New Perspectives on Brazilian Ethnoracial Relations. In: Edward Telles/ PERLA (eds.) (2014), Pigmentocracies: Ethnicity, Race, and Color in Latin America: Chapel Hill: University of North Carolina Press.

Skidmore, Thomas E. (1990): "Racial Ideas and Social Policy in Brazil, 1870-1940." In: Richard Graham (ed.), The Idea of Race in Latin America, 1870-1940, Austin: University of Texas Press, pp. 7–36.

Stevenson, Agnus (2010): Oxford Dictionary of English, Oxford/New York: Oxford University Press.

Shukan Asahi (2012): "Shukan Asahi magazine suspends series on Osaka mayor", October 10, 2012 (http://ajw.asahi.com/article/behind_news/social_affairs/AJ201210200042).

Takezawa, Yasuko (2011): "Toward a New Approach to Race and Racial Representations: Perspectives from Asia." In: Yasuko Takezawa (ed.), Racial Representations in Asia, Kyoto: Kyoto University Press, pp.1–6.

Takezawa, Yasuko (2015): "Translating and Transforming 'Race': Early Meiji Period Textbooks." In: Japanese Studies, Special Issue: Rethinking Race/Racism from Asian Experiences.

Telles, Edward (2004): Race in another America, Princeton: Princeton University Press.

Telles, Edward/PERLA (2014): Pigmentocracies: Ethnicity, Race, and Color in Latin America: Chapel Hill: University of North Carolina Press.

Ushijima, Iwao (1987): Yapputo no Shakai to Kokan (Society and Exchange in the Yap Islands), Tokyo: Kobunkan.

Ethnicity as social deixis

THOMAS WIDLOK

Ethnicity and ethnic identity appear to be human universals (Antweiler 2007: 190). Ethnic autonyms, the names that people give to themselves, often translate as 'humans' or 'true people', which renders the status of members of other ethnic groups either as not truly human or at least of dubious standing. Across case studies, human communicative interaction seems replete with ascriptions of ethnic status, both in so-called pre-modern times and places and in the current situation of globalized and mediatized politics (cp. Eriksen 1993). In view of the ubiquitousness of reference to ethnic identity I take a lead from two sources, firstly linguistics (specifically speech act theory and pragmatics) and secondly practice theory (specifically as influenced by Pierre Bourdieu). The more general interdisciplinary strategy that I propose is not a simple transfer of a conceptual framework from one discipline to another, but a two-way approach whereby a concept is transferred, but then transformed and offered for re-import, as it were. I shall outline why it is useful to think of ethnic ascription as a form of *deixis*, a linguistic notion that is still foreign to most social scientists. In linguistics, deictic meanings (referred to in philosophy as 'indexical' meanings) are those that are effective only at a particular place and time. In brief, the argument will be that understanding a notion such as 'being indigenous' or 'being black' or 'being a member of ethnic group x' is as much dependent on who uses the notion (and when and where they do so) as is a prototypical deictic sentence such as 'I want her to come here today', which depends on a context of specific persons, on a specific time and place. As Levinson (1983) has pointed out in detail, the concept of deixis/indexicality has had a remarkable career. Initially it seemed to be a property of marginal utterances that required contextual coordinates to be properly understood, but today the question is rather whether there are any utterances at all that are truly context-independent. Here, I use the linguistic terms 'deixis/deictic', rather than the philosophical term 'indexicality' because the use of ethnonyms – linguistic speech acts that classify people ethnically – are central features of ethnicity as a social and political phenomenon. At the same time, I shall add that the original linguistic notion of deixis has to be redefined, as *social deixis*, in a manner quite different from that in which deixis is understood in mainstream linguistics, in order to account for empirical observations. I argue that the main benefit of including notions such as deixis and social deixis in our analysis is that it allows us to take into account both the universal aspects of ethnic ascriptions and the variation that also exists therein. In this contribution I shall illustrate these theoretical points with reference to groups of people in southern Africa with whom I have carried out field research.

ETHNICITY AS DEICTIC REFERENCE

The idea of ethnically defined groups was for a long time a constitutive element of the discipline of 'Ethnology' at universities in Germany and neighboring countries. While ethnic community sentiments were instrumental for building national identity in many European countries they were considered detrimental elsewhere, in particular in Africa, from where I draw the empirical data for this contribution. Since most African countries gained their independence in the 20th century, the focus on ethnic identity has had negative effects for the discipline, because the emergence of nation states and nationalism has often conflicted with notions of ethnicity. As a result, very few research institutions in the independent countries of Africa – and, similarly, in the few newly founded universities in Germany – have departments of 'Ethnology'. It was felt that anything 'ethnic' was backward, and that focusing on such disciplines would highlight ethnic identity at the expense of nation-building. In the meantime, the discipline has increasingly adopted the label Anthropology, and its units of analysis are no longer ethnic groups, but rather may be constituted by any set of social or cultural relations and by the social situations in which people are involved. Conversely, the crises faced by many ethnic groups, and the political (ab)use of ethnic identity has become a recurrent research theme far beyond 'Ethnology' in all major social sciences.

While it may initially seem as if researchers who have converted to the denominations of Social Anthropology or Cultural Anthropology might have little to say about ethnicity, I shall argue that a reintegration of the subject of ethnicity into the wider spectrum of human social relationships, as studied by anthropologists today, has considerable benefits. To begin with, it allows ideas from other domains of anthropological research to be imported into the study of ethnic identities. Consider the transferring of key ideas from the study of kinship relations to research on ethnic relations. After all, there are apparent similarities between these two domains. As I have alluded to above, the study of community formation has for a long time been biased towards ethnicity. Similarly, kinship studies were, up to the last century, firmly based on (European) ideas of biological genealogy, and have only recently been freed from their bias toward genealogical descent (Schneider 1984; Jones/Milicic 2012; Holland 2012). What can the investigation of the problems of ethnicity gain from kinship studies? From a long (and ongoing) discussion in comparative anthropology, it has become clear that kinship is, above all, an *idiom* for talking about social relations. Debate continues as to the narrowness or breadth of the confines within which this idiom can unfold in diverse ways, but modes of addressing others and referring to others as kin continue to be a central part of kinship studies. Transposed to the study of ethnic relations, this could provide us with a fairly easy and reliable guide for defining ethnicity and for recognizing it when stumbling over it during field research: Ethnic relations, according to this lead, are above all references to ethnic status, which make up a large part of the practices of ethnicization. This referencing can take the form of ordinary discourse, for instance when applying ethnic labels in conversation (see below), but other forms of referencing are also common, for instance boxes to tick on a form at a clinic, in an office or school, or as part of a census when being asked for self-identification. The same applies to non-linguistic forms of reference such as exhibiting iconic pieces of dress or body decoration or body modification. Whereas the idiom of kinship typically makes use of references to genealogies, marriage and neighborhood, the idiom of ethnic identity goes beyond that. For ethnic references the shared descent is typically not traceable through individual links and lines, and it involves a much larger group of people, most of whom never encounter one another face-to-face.

Moreover, by treating ethnicity first and foremost as a form of referencing we can benefit from sophisticated tools of analysis that have been developed elsewhere. In this contribution I want to illustrate this with regard to the notion of deixis, i.e. treating ethnicity not only as a reference to ethnic identity, but as an instance of *deictic reference*. Typically, deictic or indexical references include heavily context-dependent notions expressing place ('here'), time ('now') and person ('we') – that is, utterances or actions that *necessarily* change their meaning as they are used in different circumstances. The suggestion, therefore, is to treat ethnic deixis as a form of of social deixis. I shall discuss four main advantages of importing the notion of deixis to ethnicity studies:

- A better understanding of when, how and why people switch between ethnic and alternative modes of referencing;
- An approach that integrates both instrumentalist and primordialist ideas of ethnicity;
- The possibility of analyzing both universal and culturally relative aspects of ethnic reference within a single framework;
- A better understanding of the process whereby situational references to ethnic identity become 'canonized' into ethnicity.

At a more general level the adaptation of linguistic micro-analysis forces us to firmly anchor our theories of ethnicity in human practice and empirical evidence. In order to achieve the four goals set out above, however, it is not enough to simply import the notion of deixis from linguistics. As Bourdieu (2012 [1982]: 42) has pointed out, there is a tendency in linguistics to restrict the consideration of 'relevant' circumstances that affect the meaning of words to the immediate environment of an utterance in a conversation or text. This would restrict the investigation to the language-based parameters that generate a particular deictic reference and that make it acceptable to listeners. By contrast, social and ethnic deixis, as a re-import from political anthropology into linguistics, will look specifically at the social and political positioning of agents and utterances, their differences in power, and the effect that these have in human social settings.

MOVING IN AND OUT OF ETHNICITY

It is part of the political strategy used by both ethnic fundamentalists and their opponents who advocate 'civic' or national group membership, to emphasize how very different ethnic identity is from other forms of identity. The empirical data on reference suggests something different: On the ground we find frequent shifts between ethnic and other forms of reference, and we find a seamless shading in and out of ethnicity instead of a rigid dualism. To give an example: in southern Africa, the most elaborated ethnic difference in discourse is that between so-called 'Khoisan hunter/herder/gatherers' and 'Bantu agropastoralists', categorizations used in both academic and everyday discourse. In northern Namibia and southern Angola this split is manifest between ≠Akhoe Hai//om on the one hand and *Kwanyama Owambo* on the other (cp. Widlok 1999). However, when talking about one another, very few people in the region use the autonym of the respective other group. Instead, Kwanyama mostly refer to Hai//om as *kwankala* and Hai//om refer to Kwanyama as /naben. Both these terms not only have ethnic connotations but also distinguish economic status, i.e. *kwankala* (also) means 'poor person' and */naben* (also) means 'rich person'. To the extent that ethnic group membership in this region is closely tied to ownership of material assets (lifestock, homesteads, etc.) the two meanings are often indiscriminable and may be treated as synonyms. However, there are contexts in which Owambo people use the term *kwankala* within the bounds of their own ethnic group, and at times Hai//om extend the term */naben* beyond their Owambo ethnic neighbours. Even in apparently clear-cut usages, the 'other' meaning is latently present, e.g. when calling someone *kwankala* not only highlights his or her poverty but also latently suggests that he or she is not a 'genuine Owambo'. Furthermore, the ethnic/economic references are often linked to the idiom of kinship. I have met Owambo patrons who downplayed the ethnic difference between themselves and Hai//om living on their farm by referring to themselves as the 'fathers' of the Hai//om 'children', which avoids using ethnic labels that nevertheless remain in the background. A similar process can be observed between Hai//om and other Khoisan-speaking hunter-gatherers like the *!Xũ*, whom they sometimes consider to be relatives 'of one blood' and sometimes as clearly ethnically separate. These examples illustrate a more general point that has been made with regard to the emergence of ethnic boundaries in Africa (cp. Southall 2010[1970]) and the strategic flexibility that exists, not only in terms of ethnic deixis but also with regard to actual group membership. The more general point to make is that our record of ethnic deixis indicates that it is a subset of social or person deixis which allows speakers to creatively link (or separate) the ethnic idiom with other idioms such as kinship or nationality. Ethnicity therefore emerges not as a natural opposite to nationality or family but rather as another variant in a larger repertoire of possibilities. In terms of a future research agenda it is exactly these bridges and shifts between idioms that need particular attention, since these switches constitute a rich political resource. The study of ethnicity, it seems, requires less a theory of its own than a reintegration into the larger field of social referencing.

INSTRUMENTALISM AND PRIMORDIALISM

A lot of ink has been spilled over the conflict between instrumentalist and primordialist approaches to ethnic identity (cp. Eriksen 1993 for a summary). When considering ethnicity in terms of deixis this debate proves to be based on a somewhat bogus distinction. Or, to put it differently, ethnic deixis allows the incorporation of diverse phenomena that may be generally identified solely with either the primordialist or the instrumentalist approaches to ethnicity. Consider the following example, again from my field research in Namibia: This is the account of a young man who had grown up with Owambo-speakers and who did not necessarily strike outsiders as a Hai//om, either in outward appearance or in the personal name he used for himself (for more details cp. Widlok 1996). As a consequence, when he was imprisoned he was put in a cell together with four Owambo men by police officers (of European descent) who took him to be ethnically Owambo. This is what he said happened:

"One of the men told me to go away because, he said, I was spreading diseases like all Kwankala. I told him that we are not like that and that to be a Hai//om was not as bad as being an Owambo. Then one of them men attacked me and I hit him with my fist. But the Owambo men all stuck together and beat me up."

It is easy to recognize the instrumental use of ethnic references here. Hai//om can report many incidences where they are addressed or referred to as 'San' 'Bushmen' or *kwankala* with the aim of discriminating against them, making them act as servants, pressurizing them to accept a low position, and preventing them from being equals in power. Precolonially, the label *kwankala* was used, then during colonial times the term 'Bushmen' was used; since independence 'San' is the official designation in Namibia ('Basarwa' in Botswana). On being asked which of these ethnonyms they like or dislike, Hai//om occasionally disagree, but they all agree that it is the fact that these terms are typically used in conjunction with adjectives such as 'stupid' or 'dirty' that is the problem, not any of the ethnic labels as such. Thus, the instrumentality in these references is very clear, as it is in all deixis. People use deictic terms as speech acts, to achieve something, to address or to discriminate, or simply to distinguish. Instrumentality is inherent in the process. At the same time, deictic expressions only work with reference to a shared background of empirical knowledge. As alluded to above, knowledge of place, time and relative position of speakers (and hearers) is necessary to understand deictic terms like 'here' and 'now'; the same applies to social deixis. The instrumentality of the speech act would not work if there was no shared cultural knowledge. Ethnic deixis 'works' because it refers to a shared world in which, for instance, people have perceivably different outward appearances, speak differently, have different economic status and different family backgrounds, exhibit different ways of doing things, and so forth. I have heard Hai//om jokingly addressing a child: 'Hey !Xũ', and referring to another child as 'little Owambo', and the speakers knew the reference was intelligible to those listening because the first child had more 'peppercorn hair' than others and because the second child was known to have an (absent) Owambo father. In other words, the given state of the world – or 'primordial' state, if you will – is relevant, and it places limits on what can be said (instrumentally) and defines which utterances are not acceptable or intelligible. Background knowledge includes imagined differences as much as experiential ones; the key point is that such knowledge is shared. Since the background knowledge is often diffuse and multivariant it is in turn open to instrumental manipulation. What you are as a particular kinsperson or as a member of an ethnic group is partly produced by the repeated patterned references in particular situations. Far from being opposites, it seems that instrumental and primordial aspects are not only not mutually exclusive, they even condition one another and imply one another.

Deictic statements are therefore part of larger speech acts that are employed to achieve certain goals. The instrumental aspect is part and parcel of an analysis of ethnic deixis. These speech acts only work because they refer to social facts outside the situative discourse as such. They have to refer to the known and (at least partially) shared background of speaker, listener and bystanders in order to be effective.

UNIVERSALISM AND RELATIVISM

Deixis is a universal feature of language and there is sufficient indication to suggest that ethnic deixis is universal, too. Having said that, person deixis also provides a good illustration for showing that there is variation with regard to ways of expressing deixis and, conversely, that there are limits to this variation. For instance, common personal deixis for the first person singular 'we' in many languages allows differentiation between an 'inclusive we' and an 'exclusive we'. In ≠Akhoe Hai//om and other Khoisan languages this distinction is expressed through personal pronouns (cp. Vossen 2013). Instead of one 'we' there is an 'all male we', an 'all female we', and a 'mixed we', and speakers are able to distinguish not only singular from plural but also a dual (the two of us). Moreover any of these forms of 'we' can be expressed either exclusively (e.g. *sida*, 'we', but not including the addressee) or inclusively (e.g. *sada*, 'we', including the addressee). Other qualifications of the deictic 'we'" are possible, relating to whether participants have been previously mentioned or not, whether they are human or not, and whether their communicative status is definite or not. In other words, languages differ in the ways in which they allow speakers to include or to exclude people who are present in a 'we'-construction. As indicated earlier I suggest following this lead and applying it to contexts beyond the narrow speech situation. Bourdieu's reminder of the importance of including the political position of the speaker (and listener) is very relevant here (cp. Bourdieu 2012[1982]). A 'we' uttered by someone in power is different from a 'we' used by a subordinate, even when applied to the same group of people. In the first instance it may be 'granting community' in the second it may be 'claiming community' (or, in rare cases, vice versa, e.g. when politicians want to claim to be 'one of us' among ordinary people). State representatives commonly speak in the name of an absent (but contextually implied) social entity when they say 'I' or 'We', in a way in which other speakers without a mandate cannot (cp. Bourdieu 2014: 93).

The use of ethnonyms does not automatically include or exclude, nor does it necessarily do so in the same way across situations and speakers. Among ≠Akhoe Hai//om I have often observed that the same ethnonym for the neighboring !Xũ is at times used in order to be inclusive ('we are one') or in order to differentiate (from ≠Akhoe). Again, there is evidence that in many settings ethnonyms can be applied in a wider sense (including named subgroups) or in a more narrow sense (the 'xy proper') (cp. Southall 2010 [1970]). In parallel to what I described above in terms of moving in and out of ethnic deixis, here we may speak of upscaling and downscaling strategies within ethnic referencing. Moreover, the two strategies may be combined. Here I slightly part ways with Bourdieu (2014 [2012]: 608) who rightly points at differences in the ways in which citizenship is referenced in Germany and France, at least up to recently, namely ethnically in the German case and universally in the French case. Bourdieu notes that despite this difference in state philosophy and immigration policy the actual treatment of immigrants in France and Germany is strikingly similar (2014 [2012]: 612), but he does not provide an explanation for this. I suggest that this is so because 'being a citizen on universal grounds' and 'being a citizen on ethnic grounds'" are both subject to upscaling and downscaling. As Donnelly (2013: 93) has recently pointed out, universality is always relative to a particular 'universe' of application. Things like 'universal healthcare' (or education, voting rights, rights to move, to work etc.) are typically only available to recognized citizens of a particular country, not to those of other countries, even if they are local residents, let alone for everyone on the planet. The same applies to the status of 'eligibility to become a citizen'. The French civic universality that Bourdieu describes is *in principle* independent of ethnic background, but it is still relative to a universe with particular bounded extensions. In any particular political context it may be downscaled and may exclude for instance those who cannot prove (due to lack of papers) that they do not enjoy citizenship elsewhere or that they have not committed crimes. Similarly, the 'ethnic' criterion for German citizenship can (and has been) upscaled in particular historical settings to include family relations with those already recognized as German citizens (irrespective of their ethnic identity) or those who have previously been deprived of their German citizenship (e.g. when of Jewish descent). In other words, just as 'universality' is defined in relation to a domain, 'relative' by definition is not a general notion but immediately "calls forth the question 'Relative to what?'" (Donnelly 2013: 94), and thus depends on something else. Granting citizenship, just like granting affirmative action based on ethnic grounds, is dependent on a framework to which it relates. Typically this is a temporal framework, a privilege granted for a specific time, in order to compensate for disadvantages during a particular past time frame, or with regard to other conditions that have to be present for such 'positive discrimination' to be maintained. The rights of indigenous people in southern Africa are a case in point: such 'positive discrimination' is not a special right reserved for one ethnic group but a 'universal' right for those who have suffered special marginalization as a group in the past (cp. Zips-Mairitsch 2009: 97). The parallels with the linguistic notion of deixis makes it easier to recognize the relative universality (or universal relativity) of different forms of deixis, including ethnic deixis. However, this needs to be complemented by drawing in the wider political and historical context in the way I have alluded to in the examples above.

CANONIZED DEIXIS

So far, I have highlighted the similarities between ethnic referencing and other forms of deixis. However, the parallel also invites us to be specific with regard to how ethnic deixis may differ from other forms of deixis in general, and from other related forms of social deixis in particular. What marks forms of social deixis off from other forms of deixis is that typically here, humans have found it useful to derive more stable meanings from situational contexts and to 'freeze' meanings across different contexts – in other words, to 'canonize' utterances and actions. This is true for social roles ascribed, for instance, to 'mothers' or 'children', as much as for membership in 'lasting' collective social groups such as clans and lineages, but particularly so with regard to ethnic groups and nations. One of the main research requirements in this approach is therefore to document ethnicity as cases of ethnic deixis, and to retrace the process whereby ethnic classifications become 'canonized' across time and space, thereby limiting their inherent flexibility.

With specific regard to the domain of my research region, southern Africa, but probably also more widely, the main agent that provokes this intensification of 'canonization' across contexts is the state and its representatives. Why is ethnic deixis less flexible than other forms of deixis, e.g. deixis involving personal pronouns, spatial descriptions or, possibly, references to time? It is because the referencing in this domain is not only carried out by 'natural' persons in face-to-face interaction but also, to a very large extent, by agents who represent 'fictitious' (i.e. legally constructed) but at the same time very powerful corporate agents. This power is distilled, for instance, in bureaucratic forms that provide a limited choice of ethnic self-identifications, and in the power of state administrators to specify ethnic membership for state subjects. In pre-independence Namibia this was very crudely visible through the encoding of ethnic identity on the national identity cards (cp. Figure 1, '03' indicating the category 'San/Bushmen'). During apartheid legislation this categorization would specify eligibility to vote (for ethnic representatives only), to marry, and to be resident in a certain area. After independence the ethnic classification was dropped and replaced by proxies such as 'language spoken at home' (during the first national census), or 'born in Namibia' (also encoded on the ID). Most recently the 'invisibility' of ethnic identity has become a matter of concern because of a systematic underrepresentation of some groups in government positions (cp. Widlok 1996). Similar concerns against discrimination have led government agencies (of education, labor, health) in Western, formally 'non-ethnic' democracies to introduce ethnic classification for applicants. When applying for a job in the US or when being admitted to a clinic in the UK, one is routinely asked to self-identify ethnically according to a schema that may or may not coincide with the ethnic deixis one practices in everyday life, but which was designed from a position of power. My argument is that these schematic categorizations are not 'deixis-free', despite the fact that they do not allow situational factors to be brought in. Rather, we are dealing with channelized deixis that structures the social and political environment in such a way that only a limited choice of deictic references remain possible. This is very much like delimiting the temporal deixis of 'now' and 'later' into exactly measured time intervals – a process which is not alien to legal practitioners and their language – or like delimiting the spatial deixis of 'here' and 'there' into the mapped universe of the surveyors and the authority they derive from states to carve up the land.

Conclusion

In this contribution I have suggested an interdisciplinary import from linguistics into anthropology in the form of introducing the notion of deixis. I have also suggested the re-importing of a notion of ethnic deixis that is enriched by having been interpreted through both the social science perspective of political agency and the fieldwork-based perspective of ethnography, in this case of southern Africa. The resulting model provides a number of theoretical benefits: We are able to see, and investigate in more detail, the bridges between ethnicity and other forms of social deixis, of references and relations moving seamlessly into and out of the domain of ethnic identity. We have also been able to reconcile aspects of instrumentalism and primordialism, and we have gained a better understanding of universality and relativity with regard to the phenomena of ethnic identity and ethnic reference. Finally, considering deixis as an activity has directed our attention to the agents engaged in this activity, and in particular to the contrast between 'natural' persons (individual humans) and the often more powerful but 'fictional' corporate agents of the state. The most far-reaching conclusion that one might choose to draw from this is that ethnicity no longer appears to be a domain sui generis, but rather an epiphenomenon of underlying social processes of social deixis and the social positioning that it implies. Ethnicity may be critical in many political constellations, yet not be anything special in itself.

Figure 1: Identity card in pre-independence Namibia.
The second block of figures encodes ethnic identity

Source: Photo by Thomas Widlok

References

Antweiler, Christoph (2007): Was ist den Menschen gemeinsam. Über Kultur und Kulturen, Darmstadt: Wissenschaftliche Buchgesellschaft.

Bourdieu, Pierre (2012): Was heißt sprechen? Zur Ökonomie des sprachlichen Tausches, Wien: New Academic Press.

—— (2014): Über den Staat, Frankfurt/Main: Suhrkamp.

Donnelly, Jack (2013): Universal Human Rights in Theory and Practice, Ithaka: Cornell University Press.

Eriksen, Thomas Hylland (1993): Ethnicity and Nationalism. Anthropological Perspectives, London: Pluto Press.

Holland, Maximilian (2012): Social Bonding and Nurture Kinship: Compatibility between Cultural and Biological Approaches, North Charleston: CreateSpace.

Jones, Doug/Milicic, Bojka (2012): Kinship, Language and Prehistory. Per Hage and the Renaissance in Kinship Studies, Utah: The University of Utah Press.

Levinson, Stephen (1983): Pragmatics, Cambridge: Cambridge University Press.

Schneider, David (1984): A critique of the study of kinship, Ann Arbor: University of Michigan Press.

Southall, Aidan (2010): "The Illusion of tribe." In: Roy Grinker et al. (eds.), Perspectives on Africa, Malden: Wiley-Blackwell, pp. 83-94.

Vossen, Reiner (ed.) (2013): The Khoesan Languages, London: Routledge.

Widlok, Thomas (1999): Living on Mangetti. 'Bushman' autonomy and Namibian Independence, Oxford: OUP Press.

—— (1996): "Ethnicity in the post-apartheid era: A Namibian 'San' case study." In: Louise de la Gorgendière et al. (eds.), Ethnicity in Africa. Roots, Meanings and Implications, Edinburgh: Centre of African Studies, University of Edinburgh, pp. 214-266.

Zips-Mairitsch, M. (2009): Verlorenes Land? Indigene (Land)-Rechte der San in Botswana, Berlin: Reimer.

Ethnicity as a political resource
in different regions of the world

Introduction: Ethnicity as a political resource in different regions of the world

MARIO KRÄMER

Consider the following political events and developments in recent years: the riots and xenophobic violence against African immigrants in Post-Apartheid South Africa; violent ethnic mobilizations in former Yugoslavia, and the genocide in Rwanda in 1994; nativist right-wing politics in today's Europe and their demands for an end to multiculturalism; Scotland's and Catalonia's claims to independence; indigenous mobilizations in India and Latin America; and the resistance of some African and Latin American governments to agreeing to classify ethnic minorities as 'indigenous', in order to prevent the emergence of plurinational states.

Is it possible and analytically fruitful to compare these different uses of ethnicity as a political resource across different regions of the world? What dimensions and levels of comparison might be useful, and what may be accomplished with a comparative perspective? What are the similarities and differences between 'comparison as scientific task' on the one hand and 'comparison as political practice' on the other? Is it possible to neatly separate the two, or do they go hand in hand when it comes to the use of ethnicity as a political resource?

The four contributions in Section B examine these and other questions from different methodological angles: while Dereje Feyissa and Meron Zeleke, and Li Xi Yuan focus on case studies of specific ethnic minorities and their relationships with their respective nation states, Michaela Pelican makes use of an intra-regional comparison of the political trajectories of three 'indigenous peoples' in Africa. Christian Büschges in turn distinguishes between macro- and meso-/micro-levels levels of comparison and illustrates his arguments with selected examples from different world regions.

At the outset of his contribution on the 'ethnicization of politics', *Christian Büschges* compares the war in former Yugoslavia in the early 1990s with political protests by various ethnic organizations in Ecuador at about the same time: the protests in Ecuador led to political debates between indigenous organizations and the government, and a new constitution was adopted in the late 1990s. Levels of violence remained low, although the extent of autonomy rights is still fiercely debated today. On the other hand, most Europeans are aware of the terrible consequences the war in former Yugoslavia had for human lives and societies in the Balkan states. With regard to our thematic interest, Büschges argues that both cases are comparable and are expressions of a phenomenon he names the 'ethnicization of politics', which he understands as a global development evident since the 1990s. However, the outcomes of specific instances of the 'ethnicization of politics may be very different, from political violence and even war to comparably peaceful democratic negotiations.

Büschges proposes that we analyse situational actions, discursive frames, organizational routines and political projects in order to understand the relationship between ethnicity and politics. From a social science point of view, nations or ethnic groups are not fixed, homogenous entities as national or ethnic entrepreneurs often claim. References to national and ethnic identities serve as a political strategy that is used to gain or consolidate political power. Büschges argues in favour of a comparative approach to look for both differences and similarities in the use of ethnicity as a political resource – although comparative studies often focus on only one of the two. On a macro-level of comparison, Büschges claims that "we can analyze for example how the perception of ethnic differences helped to define the borders and inner differentiation of sovereign political communities in different time periods and areas, giving birth to different models of political organization, ranging from (early) modern empires to nation states and multicultural or pluriethnic states". According to Büschges, the ideology of the nation state is based on an ethnically defined political community, and this 'ethnic core' has met increasing resistance from ethnic or national minorities in the late 20th century. In his view, "the notion of the culturally homogeneous nation state has definitively proven to be fiction", and he asks whether it is just a historical *Sonderweg* "situated between pre-modern imperial heterogeneity and postmodern diversity". On a meso-/micro-level of comparison, he suggests, we should focus on "how ethnically legitimized political agendas are communicated, negotiated, and implemented". Regarding pluriethnic policies there are two key strategies adopted to further the aims of national and ethnic minorities: i) specific measures to guarantee political participation, and ii) regional autonomy statutes.

What about the limits of or challenges related to comparative research on ethnicity as a political resource? According to Büschges, it is impossible to understand the similarities and differences between different world regions without taking into account the transnational flow of actors, institutions and discourses. In his view, the ethnicization of politics always has a transnational dimension. One recent example is the notion and discourse of indigeneity: there are a growing number of indigenous organizations and institutions worldwide dealing with indigenous affairs. These organizations not only act on a local or national level but also operate transnationally in cooperation with civil society organizations.

Büschges concludes with a brief but significant comment: that (social) scientists are not the only ones who know how to compare (at least, when they consider a comparative approach to be relevant), and indeed, ethnopolitical activists and organizations may be even better at doing so in the interests of achieving political power and legitimizing the use of ethnicity as a political resource. Furthermore, and as the contribution by Feyissa and Zeleke illustrates, it is not only local political activists or ethnic entrepreneurs who push on with the ethnicization of politics. In some instances international NGOs lay the foundations for the politics of ethnicity – for example, by labelling and advertising certain groups as 'indigenous' and thus giving such 'indigenous groups' the opportunity to start and enforce their struggles for power and resources.

Dereje Feyissa and *Meron Zeleke* examine the notion and discourse of indigeneity, which Büschges understands as a transnational aspect of the ethnicization of politics. The authors compare, in terms of both the 'original' indigenous movement in North America with similar movements in the African context. Their main focus, however, is on a detailed case study of the Anuak indigenous movement, and of the Ethiopian government's reactions to the discourse of indigeneity. Feyissa and Zeleke point to the potential problems and conflicts that may arise if one model or concept is uncritically transferred from one regional context to the other. They argue that the indigenous movement's claims are less contested in the Americas as compared with Africa, mainly due to a different settlement history with more clear-cut cleavages between native populations and European settlers. Indigenous movements in the Americas were able to put pressure on the United Nations, which adopted the Declaration on the Rights of Indigenous Peoples in 2007. This also had an impact on several African states and various groups of people: they adopted and applied the powerful term 'indigenous' in order to improve their political, economic, and social situations.

Feyissa and Zeleke make clear that the application of the term 'indigenous' in Africa is not only contested by the political actors and institutions involved but also among scholars from different disciplines. Whereas some argue that indigeneity is an empowering discourse for marginalized groups, others criticize or even condemn the notion of indigeneity and its use as a political resource. Their critique has at least three aspects; they argue: i) that Africa is different from other world regions due to its more complex and ongoing "histories of migration, assimilation and conquest" (referring to Pelican; see also below); ii) that the concept of indigeneity as it is defined by the African Commission on Human and Peoples' Rights is "too broad to be useful", at least in the Ethiopian context; and iii) that the notion of indigeneity and the related political claims are largely "externally driven" – that is, that the discourse of indigeneity is "imported" by NGOs and applied to specific hunter/gatherer and/or pastoralist groups in various African countries, and that these groups are thus "essentialised" as so-called indigenous peoples.

In order to study the politics of indigeneity in Africa, Feyissa and Zeleke suggest two comparative approaches: the first involves investigating why most African governments resist it, while the second involves research into how local actors in Africa appropriate the concept and internationally legitimized discourse of indigeneity so as to reframe claims to power and resources. With regard to the resistance put up against such actions by African governments, Feyissa and Zeleke distinguish three general objections: i) many African governments refer to the "dynamic population movement in all directions at various times". and thus argue that *all* Africans are indigenous; ii) some governments have adopted a modernist perspective and label indigenous claims as a form of cultural essentialism; and iii) several others again are concerned about "the conflict-generating potential of the term 'indigenous' when it is used in the historical and exclusive sense". The Ethiopian government is one of the most vocal in its critique of the concept and discourse of indigeneity, and also puts forward an additional objection: the concept is seen as irrelevant in the new federal order of the Ethiopian state. The government has recognised the rights of ethnic groups to self-determination, and has thus gone beyond the demands of the global indigenous movement – at least on paper. According to Feyissa and Zeleke, the problem is not the legal framework but the federal encroachment into regional and local autonomy. The Ethiopian government has adopted an alternative terminology – that of 'Nations, Nationalities and Peoples' – which, from its perspective, renders the term 'indigenous' irrelevant.

If we look at the local appropriation of the notion and discourse of indigeneity, the Anuak case study illustrates how an NGO (with the programmatic name 'Cultural Survival') defined this group as indigenous in several publications in the 1980s. Only about a decade later, this label was then used by Anuak political actors as a tool in their struggle for power and resources in the Gambella region. The establishment of the Gambella regional state in 1991 "has put a new premium on the regional politics of number". In comparison to their more numerous Nuer neighbours, the Anuak are in a minority position, and use their supposed status as 'first-comers' to legitimate their claims as indigenous people. With the assistance of the Anuak diaspora, they "insert Anuak politics into global civil society" and thereby challenge the modernist paradigm of the Ethiopian state. The discourse of indigeneity also enabled the Anuak to achieve a dominant political status in the Gambella region until a power-sharing arrangement was introduced in 2005. Feyissa and Zeleke show that the application of the notion of indigeneity fuelled existing tensions between Anuak and Nuer, since the latter also claimed to be indigenous peoples of the region and were recognized as such by the by the African Commission on Human and Peoples' Rights.

The authors conclude by rejecting the concept of indigeneity with regard to the Ethiopian context because of its lack of usefulness and because of the inherent potential for (violent) inter-group conflict; they rather view a functioning federal system with a robust minority rights regime as a better way to promote specific cultural rights and the common good.

The contribution by *Michaela Pelican* also focuses on the concept and discourse of indigeneity, and particularly on the political dimensions as exemplified in the international indigenous peoples' movement. A comparison of the way that the concept and discourse of indigeneity is interpreted in different regions of the world reveals the strongly politicized character of indigenous identities and indigenous rights movements in Africa, which differentiates them from some of their counterparts in other regions of the world, such as the Americas and the Pacific, where indigenous identities have a much longer history and, besides their political uses, may be filled with historical memories, cultural practices and emotional attachment.

Pelican argues that indigeneity has been a highly contested concept, particularly in Africa and Asia, where indigenous rights movements have only recently gained significance. Within the past twenty years, many ethnic and minority groups in Africa have laid claim to indigeneity on the basis of their political marginalization and cultural distinctiveness in their country or region of residence. They have drawn inspiration from the United Nations definition of indigenous peoples as a legal category with collective entitlements, and have linked up with the global indigenous rights movement. With the adoption of the United Nations Declaration on the Rights of Indigenous Peoples in 2007 many

African governments have made attempts to integrate the indigenous rights discourse into their policies and development programs – with varied outcomes.

To give an idea of the varied experiences and political trajectories of indigenous peoples in Africa, Pelican draws on three case studies: Mbororo pastoralists in Cameroon, Maasai pastoralists in Tanzania, and San hunter-gatherers in Botswana. She outlines commonalities and differences and argues that there is no single, coherent indigenous rights movement in Africa, but rather a variety of movements which are shaped by their divergent national and local contexts. The three cases have in common that the groups were able to use indigeneity as a political resource. The movements went through various phases: from expectation and success to disillusionment and pragmatism. As part of this process, they adopted changing and alternative strategies to deal with the adverse consequences of their claims and to improve their respective situations. While in the Mbororo case indigeneity has remained a viable category of identification, the Maasai in Tanzania have shifted from an indigenous rights discourse to a livelihoods discourse, and the San in Botswana have largely withdrawn from the political sphere, concentrating on daily coping strategies at the local level.

Relevant factors shaping the different outcomes of the three indigenous rights movements include the groups' historical and economic situations within their national frameworks, as well as the divergent approaches of the specific national governments in relation to indigenous and minority rights discourses. Here it is important to distinguish between governments that promote a multicultural vision of their respective nations (e.g. Cameroon), and those that promote national identity over regional or ethnic identities and prefer to provide differential treatment on the basis of economic rather than cultural differences (e.g. Botswana, Tanzania). From this point of view, the use of indigeneity as a political resource has proven most effective and lasting in the Cameroonian case, while within the Mbororo community it has engendered disagreement over the cultural and social appropriateness of identifying as an indigenous people. In this sense, for most Mbororo, indigeneity has remained only a political identity, and has not (yet) become a source of shared meaning and belonging; indeed, it is doubtful if it ever will.

Finally, the contribution by *Li Xi Yuan* discusses the minority policy in contemporary China and its impact on ethnic conflict between ethnic minorities and the Han majority population. The case study of Uyghur (and African) migrants in the Xiaobei quarter of Guangzhou illustrates the articulations of ethnic identities and their use as a political resource. Li Xi Yuan argues that the Chinese minority policy shapes ethnic identifications and boundaries on the one hand and the relationship between majority and minority populations on the other. However, she claims that the central government's minority policy "no longer matches the current ethnic diversity of China's urban centers that has resulted from the past twenty years of economic opening-up coupled with internal and international migration". The minority policy was first implemented in the 1950s in order to address the imbalance between the Han majority and other minorities (*minzu*). More precisely, the policy was implemented within the *minzu* autonomous districts and was thus bound to specific territories.

Xiaobei is a multiethnic quarter, with Uyghurs and Africans being the most numerous immigrant communities. They occupy separate economic niches, and most Uyghurs settled in Xiaobei after several instances of ethnic conflicts in 2009. In one of these violent conflicts, Uyghur and Han workers clashed in June 2009 in a factory, leaving two Uyghur workers dead and about 120 injured. It was the beginning of a series of ethnic conflicts between Uyghur and Han in the months to come. The impact of these conflicts on Uyghur migrants in Guangzhou was significant: the working and living conditions deteriorated and many Uyghur moved to Xiaobei quarter. Furthermore, the self-identification of Uyghurs shifted, from an identity as one of numerous Chinese ethnic minorities to a more deliberately emphasized religious identity as Muslims.

In order to explain the origins and outcomes of the ethnic conflicts in 2009, Li Xi Yuan points to the so-called Western Development Plan that was implemented in 2000. It poured billions of US dollars into Xinjiang (the Uyghur autonomous district) and created distribution conflicts between Uyghurs and Han, who were seen as 'invading' the regional and local economies. The plan thus increased (instead of decreased) ethnic competition and conflicts in Xinjiang. The Guangzhou government enforced control over Uyghur migrants in the aftermath of the ethnic conflicts in 2009, and the migrants moved to Xiaobei to avoid the increasing pressure that was put on them. According to Li Xi Yuan, the Uyghur migrants in Guangzhou also started to use religion as a political resource in a hostile political environment, and the strengthening of a Muslim identity served as a shield to protect the Uyghur migrant community from the Chinese state.

Li Xi Yuan concludes that the Chinese minority policy, which "could once maintain a balance between the majority and the minority in the relatively homogeneous society that existed before", has reached its limits due to migration, urbanisation and diversification in contemporary China. Ethnicity and ethnic conflicts remain a sensitive topic, and the Xiaobei case demonstrates that people continue to make use of ethnicity as a political resource and that "the frontier has now moved from marginal ethnic regions to central city areas".

Politicizing ethnicity – ethnicizing politics
Comparisons and entanglements

CHRISTIAN BÜSCHGES

When in the course of the year 1990 democratic elections were held for the first time in all republics of the Socialist Federal Republic of Yugoslavia, political parties with nationalist programs prevailed all over the country. The result of this electoral success was that only a year Slovenia, Croatia, Bosnia-Herzegovina and Macedonia had all declared their independence, while Serbia and Montenegro joined to form the new Federal Republic of Yugoslavia the following year.

An initial military conflict between Slovenian forces and the Yugoslav People's Army in June 1991 was soon followed by an invasion of Serbian forces in Croatia, which resulted in a brutal war that expanded to involve large parts of ex-Yugoslavia until its end in 1999. About 250,000 people died, sometimes as a consequence of a so-called 'ethnic cleansing'. The massacre at Srebrenica in 1995, when Bosnian Serb army and police units killed some 8,000 Bosnian Muslims, was declared a genocide by the International Court of Justice in The Hague in 2007.

By 2008, the former multi-ethnic state of Yugoslavia had disintegrated into the successor states of Slovenia, Croatia, Bosnia-Herzegovina, Serbia, Montenegro, Macedonia and Kosovo. Since 1991, about four million people had been forced to leave their homes, in order to meet the stated goal of many politicians and combatants, who hoped to make ethnic and territorial boundaries match in the area of former Yugoslavia. Nevertheless, the frontiers of the new nation-states still remain controversial.

In June 1990, the South American country Ecuador was struck by multi-day strikes, roadblocks and demonstrations. During these events, various ethnic organizations demanded official recognition of the cultural identity, economic interests and political claims of the country's indigenous population. The protests were aimed at the transformation of a nation-state, which was dominated until the 1980s by a national discourse oriented exclusively toward those members of the population that were considered 'whites' or *mestizos* (people of 'ethnically mixed ancestry'). During the following years political debates and conflicts between indigenous organizations and the democratic governments of the country continued, finally leading to the adoption of a new constitution in 1998, which defined the Ecuadorian state as democratic, pluricultural and multiethnic.

The remarkable thing about the recent Ecuadorian political process is the fact that the level of violence remained low, and no claims or demands for secession were brought forth. On the contrary, during the Ecuadorian-Peruvian border conflicts of the 1990s the Ecuadorian local indigenous population of the affected areas in the southern Amazon region participated in the military defense of the territorial integrity of the nation state.

The political landscape of Ecuador has changed greatly since the 1990s. Today there are numerous civil society organizations, an indegenous political party (Pachakutik Plurinational Unity Movement – New Country) and various indigenous office bearers serving as ministers, constitutional judges, members of parliament, mayors, and provincial governors. In addition, various local and regional autonomy statutes for state-recognized indigenous groups were defined according to the constitutional provisions of 1998 and 2008. The extent of these autonomy rights, and the question of extending such statutes to the Afro-Ecuadorian population are, however, fiercely debated to this day.

The geographical distance between Ecuador and the former Yugoslavia, like the social and political differences between the two, could hardly be greater. However, both cases are comparable as much as they are expressions of a politicization of ethnicity that has become a global phenomenon during the 1990s (Büschges/Pfaff-Czarnecka 2007). The reference to ethnic differences between human groups has become a common starting point for political debate. The justification of political viewpoints, actors and practices using ethnic arguments has led to lasting changes in the political sphere. This ethnicization of politics is reflected in discrimination against and – often violent – exclusion of individual social groups (often called 'ethnic minorities' or 'national minorities') from the political community of the nation-state or, on the other hand, in the enforcement of political participation by ethnically defined groups, using quota systems, claims to regional autonomy, or the creation of new independent states.

The cases of Ecuador and the former Yugoslavia also exemplify the Janus-faced character of the ethnicization of politics, which can provoke democratic negotiation as well as political violence. Between these two extremes a variety of shades, mixed forms and transitions can be observed. The recent immigration debates in Germany, highlighting differing concepts of a 'dominant culture' and multiculturalism, have shown that even in countries that traditionally do not see themselves as multi-ethnic states or countries of immigration, the question of how to deal with ethnic identity and difference has become one of the central global political issues today.

The link between ethnicity and politics is not a historically new phenomenon. The question of whether ethnically based claims should be considered socially important, and, if so, how this should be achieved and regulated, is a fundamental political question, and has undergone several conjunctures and variations throughout history. An important break in this history of the intertwining of ethnicity and politics is the birth of modern nationalism. During the late 18th and early 19th centuries the creation of the nation state was accompanied by the "invention of the ethnic paradigm" (Kaschuba 2006: 139–143).

For over a century, it was taken for granted, first in Europe and then in America, that the territorial unity of the nation-state should be based on the correspondence of ethnic and political boundaries. But in other parts of the world too, the entanglement of ethnicity and politics was the model for the founding, political design, and reform of states. In the decolonization process in Africa and Asia during the 1960s, the last global boom of this political doctrine can be observed (Smith 1983).

But since the 1970s, the ideal of the ethnic homogeneity of the nation-state was increasingly questioned by various social movements worldwide. By the 1990s, the protection of minorities, multiculturalism, and pluriethnicity had become key concepts within global political debates.

Following Max Weber (1976) the concept of ethnicity refers to the belief that the cultural identity of a person or a group is based on the idea of belonging to a specific community of descent. It should be emphasized that ethnic and other social identities are essentially based on a combination of self-perception and external attribution. While older, essentialist interpretations have focused mainly on the supposed objective characteristics (language, religion, etc.) of 'ethnic groups', more recent constructivist approaches, following Fredrik Barth, have stressed the situational and relational design and changeability of ethnic identities. It has to be noted that, even without sharing the primordial perspective of Clifford Geertz (1994), these constructions or imaginations, and the inventions of tradition that they produce (Hobsbawm/Ranger 1993), are neither self-evident nor arbitrary, but are rooted in concrete historical and social contexts, and give birth to traditions of invention that, more often than not, survive long-term historical changes (Sheehan 1996).

The constructivist approach of the current research on ethnicity is also reflected in more recent studies on modern nationalism. The concepts of nation and ethnic group have in common the idea of a culturally homogeneous collective. If both ethnic groups and nations can be understood as "imagined communities" (Anderson 1988: 15), the discourse of the nation is generally characterized by its central reference to an existing or desired state.

Since identity politics based on ethnic arguments bind the presence of a group-specific culture to the criterion of descent, they contribute significantly to the production and consolidation of social and political boundaries. From today's scientific perspective, however, nations or ethnic groups are not fixed social groups, as nationalists and ethnic activists like to claim. Rather, the reference to an ethnic or national identity can be seen as a political strategy, or a "strategic essentialism" (Spivak 1988: 13) that social actors use in their struggle for the recognition and enforcement of concrete political goals.

The sociologist Rogers Brubaker (2004: 10) pleads for a distinction between the reifying categories of ethno-political and national activism and the categories of scientific analysis, and for scientists to abstain from involvement with the 'groupism' of ethnic or national movements. Ethnic groups and nations should not be understood as social groups, but as patterns of interpretation of reality. From these patterns of social identification and delineation, ethnic or national movements or organizations may emerge – that is, "groups whose members develop a sense of belonging [...] and communicate over a relatively long period of time and continuously interact to achieve a common goal" (Elwert 2003: 263). With regard to the question of the relationship between ethnicity and politics considered here, our analysis should focus on the "practical categories, situational actions, cultural languages, cognitive schemas, discursive frames (frames), organizational routines, institutional forms and political projects" (Brubaker 2004: 27) with which social actors engage in different historical and regional contexts in political debates and practices. This is why and how we can speak of ethnicity as a political resource.

From this perspective a wide range of comparative approaches can be defined that cannot be summed up here in a satisfying manner. In historical science, the comparative approach is used to analyze systematically two (or more) historical phenomena with regard to their similarities and differences, in order to reach a deeper understanding of actions and experiences, historical structures and processes (Haupt/Kocka 1996). While the focus on differences helps us to understand individual historical phenomena, analyzing the similarities allows us to reach a more general view of large historical structures, processes, and practices. It can be said that every comparative study is looking for both differences and similarities, but often we find a special emphasis on one of the two. This depends both on the interests of the researcher and the object of analysis. We can distinguish between comparative studies, for example, using the criterion of the relative geographical or temporal distance between the analysed historical phenomena in different studies.

According to Magnus Mörner (1992), comparative studies dealing with historical phenomena that are close to each other with regard to space and/or time, and that share a common or similar historical context for the same reason, focus especially on differences. In contrast, a comparison between historical phenomena that are distant in space and/or time, usually emphasizes their similarities.

With regard to our understanding of ethnicity as a political resource, on a macro level of comparison we can analyze for example how the perception of ethnic differences helped to definine the borders and inner differentiation of sovereign political communities in different time periods and areas, giving birth to different models of political organization, ranging from (early) modern empires to nation states and multicultural or pluriethnic states (Büschges 2012).

Regardless of the numerous specificities of the great empires, one of their common key features is the political differentiation and – peaceful or violent – integration of different peoples or ethnic groups (Darwin 2010). In contrast to 19th- and 20th-century nation states, pre-modern empires and their modern successors did not derive their political legitimacy and organization from the cultural homogeneity of the population. On the contrary, imperial political "integration by difference" (Pfaff-Czarnecka 2005: 4) normally exceeded the limits of different ethnically distinguished social and political communities, and on the other hand, these communities were bound, by different, traditional or newly established institutions and practices of domination, to submit to centralized rule.

With the relocation of the source of sovereignty from the ruler or the ruling dynasty to the nation, nationalism has directly contributed to the collapse of empires, by supplying the decisive pattern of argumentation with which the opponents of imperial orders have expressed their criticisms and mobilized their supporters. The imagined community of the nation, and the nation state as its political expression, are based essentially on the postulated accordance of cultural and political boundaries (Smith 1986). The claim of cultural unity of the nation ultimately also applies to those nation states whose official legitimation was initially based less on their ethnic identity than on their political organization. This was the case in both France and the United States. Still, even in 1882 the French religious historian Ernest Renan characterized the notion of belonging to a nation as a "plebiscite de tous les jours" (cited by Alter 1985: 61), without any reference to an ethnic community. Nonetheless, contemporary colonialism of the Imperial Republic of France offered not democracy but cultural assimilation to their colonial subjects. Although the United States of America is traditionally considered a country of immigrants – a notion reflected in different historical concepts of integration (i.e. melting pot, salad bowl) – attempts to define and defend a national core culture have accompanied all the history of the 19th and 20th centuries, separating the white, Anglo-Saxon protestants from the 'Indian' and 'black' or 'Afro-American' population on the one hand, and impacting upon debates about immigration from Asia or Latin America on the other (Huntington 2004).

If we compare different cases of national movements and nation-state formations, beginning with the breakdown of the *Ancien Régime* during the late 18th and early 19th centuries, followed by the de-colonization processes in Africa and Asia after World War I and II, and up to the breakdown of the communist regimes in Eastern Europe at the end of the 20th century, we can see that the ideology of the nation state is regularly based on an ethnically defined political community.

The ethnic core of the concepts of nation and nation state have provoked growing criticism during the last decades of the 20th century. At the end of the 20th century many so-called ethnic or national 'minorities' that have survived within the boundaries of the nation state have claimed cultural recognition and political representation. In view of the ongoing global migration flows, the notion of the culturally homogeneous nation state has definitively proven to be fiction, and seems to be just an intermediate step – or a historical *Sonderweg*? – situated between pre-modern imperial heterogeneity and postmodern diversity.

The decisive political program for the recognition of ethnic diversity has been multiculturalism, which was adopted for the first time as official state policy during the 1970s in Canada. The central goal of then-Prime Minister Pierre Trudeau was to strengthen the cultural development and social participation of all social groups defined on the basis of ethnic, religious or linguistic criteria and to promote relations between these different groups (Laczko 1994). In addition to Canada, the USA and Australia are considered the classic examples of countries that pursue an official multicultural policy. In Europe, it is primarily Belgium and Switzerland that are taken as examples, although multiculturalism has been increasingly questioned there during recent times. With regard to its political concept and practical outline, multiculturalism and other related terms and concepts (i.e. pluriethnicity, plurinationality) ultimately remain faithful to the core argument of nationalism concerning the accordance of cultural and political boundaries. For this reason, multiculturalist positions are often formulated in the language of nationalism. In Canada, ethnopolitical activists define both the Francophone population of the province of Québéc and the state-recognized indigenous peoples as 'nations', in this legitimizing way their claims to territorial self-government within the Canadian state (Kymlicka 1998).

The language of self-determination that is used by ethnopolitical activists leads us to the meso- and micro-levels of comparative research on ethnicity as a political resource in different world regions, focusing particularly on how ethnically legitimized political agendas are communicated, negotiated, and implemented. As an example, we might consider the concrete implementation of multicultural or pluriethnic policies. Here we can regularly find two key strategies used to ensure political representation and participation of ethnically defined social groups. On the one hand, we can observe the establishment of specific measures to guarantee the political participation of specific ethnic groups within the national political system; on the other hand, local or regional autonomy statutes are implemented for specific state-recognized ethnic groups.

In Germany the abolition of the five-percent hurdle for the South Schleswig Voters' Association guarantees the political representation of the Danish minority in the state parliament of Schleswig-Holstein (Kühl/Bohn 2005). The implementation of regional administrative autonomy is linked in some countries to historical 'ethnic enclaves', as in the case of the total of 562 'Indian reservations' recognized by the US Government, which can in part be traced back to the 19th century. Similar measures can be observed in Colombia in the 1990s, when fifteen *reservas* or *resguardos indigenas* were established and granted autonomy rights (Kloostermann 1994).

With regard to the limits or challenges of comparative research on ethnic identity politics, one general important point has to be taken into account. We must be aware of the fact that localities, nation-states or hemispheres cannot be understood as closed containers, but that more often than not many similarities and disparities between different world regions reflect a geographically far-reaching entanglement of discourses, actors and institutions that have arisen from the increasing transnational flows of people, commodities, and images.

This can be shown for the 1920s with the example of Lenin's nationality politics, which tried to integrate the various national movements of the late Russian multinational empire into the new political order of the Soviet Union (Kappeler 1993). Lenin's model was meant to be used repeatedly over the course of the 20th century as a template for legitimacy and the practical implementation of a political integration of ethnically differentiated populations. This is true even of the most recent heyday of multicultural or pluriethnic politics and states during the 1990s. In Nepal, in the course of the democratic revolution of 1990, the Maoists contributed early and decisively to ethnic mobilization in the Himalayan state and designed a political model that divided the country into autonomous ethnic provinces intended to guarantee the political participation of the population of the country nevertheless divided in different 'indigenous nationalities' (Hachhethu 2004).

While the strategy of politicization of ethnicity on the part of the Soviet leadership and the Nepalese Maoists mainly served as a temporary strategy of political mobilization which, it was hoped, would lead in the future to a communist society that would overcome all ethnic and national boundaries. Finally, the concept of nationality has also influenced ethnic movements beyond the socialist world. This is so in the case of the Confederation of Indigenous Nationalities of Ecuador (CONAIE), founded in 1986, which adopted the Soviet concept of nationalities to accentuate the indigenous peoples' right to political self-determination within the context of a plurinational Ecuadorian state (CONAIE 1997).

The transnational or global dimension of ethnic identity politics can also be seen in the growing number of international meetings and institutions that are dealing with indigenous affairs. In this context, the World Council of Indigenous Peoples (1975-1996) must be mentioned, as well as the UN Working Groups on 'Minorities' and on 'Indigenous Peoples' set up in the 1990s (Levangie 2008; Kemner 2011). In addition, today's indigenous organizations not only operate on a local or national level, but act globally in cooperation with other civil society actors and organizations.

Finally, the ongoing internationalization of the negotiations and statutes for the protection of 'minorities' and 'indigenous peoples' in the 1990s has been accompanied through a worldwide increase in social movements and political demands based on an increasingly standardized "language of ethnicity" (Pfaff-Czarnecka 2012: 63-76). The increasing global attention paid to indigenous interests can also explain why some ethnic activists from various so-called 'hill tribes' in Thailand and Bangladesh have quite recently chosen to refer to themselves as 'indigenous peoples', although the local cultural traditions do not necessarily include historical references to a particular territory. Comparison seems to be not only a scientific task, but also a political practice of ethnopolitical activists.

References

Alter, Peter (1985): Nationalismus, Frankfurt/M.: suhrkamp.
Anderson, Benedict (1988): Die Erfindung der Nation. Zur Karriere eines folgenreichen Konzepts, Frankfurt/M./New York: Campus.
Brubaker, R. (2004): Ethnicity without groups, Cambridge: Harvard University Press.
Büschges, Christian (2012): Demokratie und Völkermord. Ethnizität im politischen Raum, Göttingen: Wallstein.
Büschges, Christian/Pfaff-Czarnecka, Joanna (eds.) (2007): Die Ethnisierung des Politischen. Identitätspolitiken in Lateinamerika, Asien und den USA, Frankfurt/M.: Campus.
CONAIE (Confederación de Nacionalidades indígenas del Ecuador) (1997): Proyecto Político de la CONAIE, Quito.
Elwert, Georg (2003): "Ethnizität und Nation." In: Hans Joas (ed.), Lehrbuch der Soziologie, 2nd. ed., Frankfurt/M./New York: Campus.
Darwin, John (2010): Der imperiale Traum. Die Globalgeschichte großer Reiche 1400-2000, Frankfurt/M./New York: Campus.
Geertz, Clifford (1994): "Angestammte Loyalitäten, bestehende Einheiten. Anthropologische Reflexionen zur Identitätspolitik." In: Merkur 5, pp 392–403.
Hachhethu, Krishna (2004): "The Nepali state and the Maoist insurgency, 1996-2001." In: Michael Hutt (ed.), Himalayan 'Peoples War': Nepal's Maoist Rebellion, London: Hurst & Co., pp. 58–78.
Haupt, Heinz-Gerhard/Kocka, Jürgen (1996): "Historischer Vergleich: Methoden, Aufgaben, Probleme. Eine Einleitung." In: Heinz-Gerhard Haupt/ Jürgen Kocka (eds.), Geschichte und Vergleich. Ansätze und Ergebnisse international vergleichender Geschichtsschreibung, Frankfurt a.M./New York: Campus, pp. 10–45.
Hobsbawm, Eric J./Ranger, Terence (eds.) (1993): The invention of tradition, Cambridge: Cambridge University Press.
Huntington, Samuel P. (2004): Who are we? Die Krise der amerikanischen Identität, Hamburg/Wien: Europa Verlag.
Kappeler, Andreas (1993): Russland als Vielvölkerreich. Entstehung – Geschichte – Zerfall, 2nd. ed., München: C.H. Beck.
Kaschuba, Wolfgang (2006): Einführung in die Europäische Ethnologie, 3rd. ed., München: C.H. Beck.
Kemner, Jochen (2011): "Lobbying for global indigenous rights: The World Council of Indigenous Peoples (1975-1997)." In: The Forum for Inter-American Affairs (FIAR) 4, p. 2.

Kloosterman, J. (1994): "Indigenous self-government in Colombia: the case of the Muellamués resguardo." In: W J. Assies/A.J. Hoekema (eds.), Indigenous peoples' experiences with self-government, Copenhagen/Amsterdam: IWGIA/ University of Amsterdam, S. 157–176.

Kühl, Jørgen/Bohn, Robert (eds.) (2005): Ein europäisches Modell? Nationale Minderheiten im deutsch-dänischen Grenzland 1945 – 2005, Bielefeld: Verlag für Regionalgeschichte.

Kymlicka, Will (1998): Finding our Way. Rethinking Ethnocultural Relations in Canada, Toronto: Oxford University Press.

Laczko, Leslie (1994): "Canada's Pluralism in Comparative Perspective." In: Ethnic and Racial Studies 17:1, pp. 20–41.

Levangie, Shelagh (2008): Globalized Native Politics. Negotiating the UN Declaration on the Rights of Indigenous Peoples, Saarbrücken: VDM Verlag.

Mörner, Magnus (1992): "Labour Systems and Patterns of Social Stratification in Colonial America: North and South." In: Wolfgang Reinhard/Peter Waldmann (eds.), Nord und Süd in Amerika: Gemeinsamkeiten, Gegensätze, europäischer Hintergrund, Freiburg: Rombach, pp. 347–363.

Pfaff-Czarnecka, Joanna (2012): Zugehörigkeit in der mobilen Welt. Politiken der Verortung, Göttingen: Wallstein.

—— (2005): "Democratisation and Nation-building in 'Divided Societies'." In: Jochen Hippler (ed.), Nation-Building – A Key Concept for Peaceful Conflict Transformation? London/Ann Arbor: Pluto, pp. 28–41.

Sheehan, James J. (1996): "Nation und Staat. Deutschland als 'imaginierte Gemeinschaft'." In: Manfred Hettling/Paul Nolte (eds.), Nation und Gesellschaft in Deutschland. Historische Essays, München: C.H. Beck, pp. 33–45.

Smith, Anthony D. (1986): The Ethnic Origins of Nations, Oxford/New York: Basil Blackswell.

—— (ed.) (1983): State and Nation in the Third World. The Western State and African Nationalism, Brighton; Wheatsheaf Books.

Spivak, Gayatri Chakravorty (1988): "Subaltern studies: Deconstructing historiography." In: Ranajit Guha/Gayatri Chakravorty Spivak (eds.), Selected studies, New York: Oxford University Press, pp. 3–32.

Weber, Max (1976): Wirtschaft und Gesellschaft. Grundriß der verstehenden Soziologie, 5th revised ed., ed. by Johannes Zimmermann, Tübingen: J.C.B. Mohr.

The contestation over the indigenous in Africa
The Ethiopian example

DEREJE FEYISSA/MERON ZELEKE

INTRODUCTION

The discourse and related practices regarding the rights of indigenous peoples is considered 'the last frontier' in the human rights revolution, as it relates to those particular groups who have been left on the margins of development, who are perceived negatively by dominant mainstream development paradigms, and whose cultures and lives are subject to discrimination and contempt (Jackson/Warren 2005). But the big elephant in the room is the issue of definition – who are the 'indigenous people' anyway, and how to find them, and where? The contention surrounding the definition of indigenous people and the criteria used for identification are hugely contested. The applicability in the African continent is even more acute, disputed not only between human rights advocates and African governments, but also among local communities and scholars.

In a highly debated article *The return of the natives*, Kuper deconstructs the concept of the indigenous as a mere rehash of the western quest for the 'native' and the 'primitive':

"The image of the primitive is often constructed today to suit the Greens and the anti-globalization movement. Authentic natives represent a world to which we should, apparently, wish to be returned, a world in which culture does not challenge nature."(2003: 345)

Kuper is also concerned by the dangerous consequence of the indigeneous peoples' movement, so long as it is based on essentialised notions of social identity:

"They are unlikely to promote the common good, and they will certainly create new problems. Wherever special land and hunting rights have been extended to so-called indigenous peoples, local ethnic frictions have been exacerbated. These grants also foster appeals to uncomfortably racist criteria for favouring or excluding individuals or communities." (Ibid.)

However, deconstructing and debunking the discourse does not make the issue go away. Notwithstanding the scholarly debate, a wide variety of actors are already using the discourse of the indigenous and other related, globally recognized legitimising discourses with various degrees of success. Besides, despite strong resistance from governments with regard to the applicability of the term 'indigenous' in the African continent, recently thirteen African countries have grudgingly allowed the World Bank to initiate its indigenous peoples policy, at least in the projects that it funds (World Bank 2010). As such, it is actually more interesting academically to ask why and how governments contest the applicability of the term 'indigenous' in Africa in general and in their respective countries in particular. Equally important is to look at how people embrace the label 'indigenous' than to reflect on its 'real applicability'.

Broadly speaking, two comparative approaches suggest themselves for the study of the discourse and politics of indigeneity in Africa. One is to look into the reasons why nearly all of the African governments resist the discourse of the indigenous. The other is to investigate the appropriation of the 'indigenous people' label by local actors who might use it as a new globally recognized legitimizing discourse that helps reframe the already existing resource- or power claims at the national, regional or local levels. In this contribution we examine these two comparative approaches with reference to the contested nature of indigineity as it plays out in the Ethiopian context, where currently there is a contention between the Ethiopian government and international development and human rights organizations over the applicability of the term 'indigenous people'.

There are some comparable explanations for African governments' resistance to the discourse and politics of indigeneity. One is that of *African exceptionalism*; a settlement history which – in contrast to North America, where the markers signifying the 'indigenous' are not difficult to discern – is characterized by a dynamic population movement in all directions at various times. As such, it is common to hear the statement, 'we are all indigenous' by African governments. Fear of institutionalising what appears to be a "hierarchy of citizenship" (Tucker-Mahl 2008: 23) by recognising the indigenous peoples as if they were "special rights-bearing subjects" (ibid.) is another concern. Most African governments also adopt a modernist perspective, labelling indigenous claims on behalf of some peoples in Africa, particularly by international human rights organisations, as driven by 'primitive romanticism' and exoticism, while as governments they are more interested in changing the lives of the same people towards higher living standards, such as livelihood shifts from mobile pastoralism to a more sedentarized agro-pastoral lifestyle. Many African governments are also concerned about the conflict-generating potential of the term 'indigenous' when it is used in the historical and exclusive sense. The recent politicization of the notion of autochthony (equivalent to indigeneity) and the attendant exclusionary political practices in French-speaking West Africa – notably in Côte d'Ivoire – and its link with the escalation of conflict is a case in point.

However, there are also country-specific objections, which undermine the comparative perspective. In the Ethiopian case that we examine here, for instance, the primary reason why the Ethiopian government is opposing the discourse and politics of the indigenous is in reference to the unique federal political order that it has established – a political order which has instituted cultural pluralism allowing ethnic groups the right to self-determination including and up to secession. This is unlike other African governments who primarily oppose the discourse of the indigenous from the perspective of the 'divisive' nature of institutionalizing cultural difference, though ethnicity is a crucial factor behind the scenes of national politics (Mamdani 1996; Deng 1997). Hence we outline only this case here to stress that the specificity of each case is vitally important and can only be taken into consideration when taking it *as* a particular case, though a reflection on the comparative dimensions mentioned earlier is also made where it is warranted. The Ethiopian government is resisting the discourse of the indigenous people by forwarding an alternative, and what it considers more inclusive terminology, that of 'Nations, Nationalities and Peoples'. This renders the term 'indigenous' not only divisive but also irrelevant, as whatever cause might be served under the indigenous label could also be served through any of the three constitutionally recognized terms. For the second comparative angle – how local actors have appropriated the label 'indigenous' – we provide a case study of the Anuak of western Ethiopia, who have claimed the status of an indigenous people to reframe resource- and power claims in regional politics through a successful advocacy work of their diaspora in North America, and who seek dialogue with the global indigenous movement by drawing on the repertoire of the works of international human rights organisations.

The discussion is divided into three sections. Section one provides background information on the origins of indigenous rights in North America, where the issue is least contested and is more comparable across countries, and on why and how it is contentious when it is introduced into other regions, particularly in Africa. Section two examines how various international organisations have sought to popularize and introduce the politics of indigeneity into Ethiopia, which the Anuak have tapped into in their struggle for identity maintenance and resource- and power claims in regional politics. Section three examines the response of the Ethiopian government and how its resistance is situated within an alternative institutional design – variously referred to as ethnic or multination federalism – to address the issue of social justice for the country's minorities. Section four concludes by outlining the comparative dimensions and the country-specific issues involved in discussing the politics of indigeneity in Africa.

INDIGENEITY– A CONTESTED TERM

The indigenous mass movements that started in the Americas during the 1960s and 1970s gave rise to the international indigenous movement. The claim to being an indigenous people is less contested in the Americas as compared with other regions, primarily because of a clear-cut settlement history between native populations (variously called 'Red Indians', 'Native Americans' or 'First Nations') and the European settlers and colonizers that followed the Colombian 'discovery' of the Americas in the 15th century. This social cleavage was marked by violent conquest with genocidal dimensions and large-scale land dispossession. The history of Latin America's indigenous peoples, for instance, is that of a long struggle that started with the European invasion and conquest in the 15th and 16th centuries, when an estimated 90 to 95 percent of the native populations were wiped out (Van Cott 2007: 129)

Broad-based mass movements also mark the question of the indigenous peoples in the Americas. In North America, gaining indigenous autonomy from the colonial powers of the United States (US) and Canada has involved efforts at state-formation; that is, 'tribal governance'. These nations seek to gain control over their social and political institutions without compromising what they consider to be unique and essential cultural markers. In Latin America, indigenous efforts to combat colonialism have taken a different strategy. These peoples have organized into movements against racialized social hierarchies, and have agitated for increased rights. They have overtly challenged the state and contemporary capitalism, drawing upon an ethical reading of Marxism that calls for improved social rights and economic justice (Curley 2012).

The indigenous peoples' movements in the Americas, in turn, brought pressure to bear on the UN, which led to the Declaration on the Rights of Indigenous Peoples. Within international discourse, new indigenous alliances have found resonance in indigenous claims against the states that act as their colonizers. In response to indigenous movements around the world, even the United Nations (UN) has been compelled to formally recognize indigenous rights. The UN Declaration on the Rights of Indigenous Peoples (2007) has provided indigenous peoples with legal grounds from which to argue for increased autonomy and recognition of their social, cultural, and political practices in places where they have been historically exploited and marginalized. As Pelican has noted, "among its most significant assertions are indigenous peoples' right to self-determination; to lands, territories, and natural resources; and to free, prior, and informed consent" (2009: 52). This new global legal framework makes indigenous peoples special rights-bearing subjects in international law, beyond national laws and possibly even against governments who violate or do not comply with the indigenous peoples' rights.

Engaging with the global indigenous peoples' movement, various groups of people in Africa have already started to apply the term 'indigenous' in their efforts to address their particular human rights situations. The claimants are from various economic systems and include hunter-gatherers, pastoralists, and some small-scale farmers. They practice different cultures, have different social institutions and observe different religious systems (ACHPR 2006; Pelican 2009). According to the African Commission on Human and Peoples' Rights, the overall characteristics of groups identifying themselves as indigenous peoples are that their cultures and ways of life differ considerably from those of the dominant society, and that their cultures are under threat, in some cases to the point of extinction. A key characteristic for most of them is that the survival of their particular way of life depends on access and rights to their traditional lands and the natural resources thereon. They suffer from discrimination as they are regarded as less developed and less advanced than other more dominant sectors of society. They often live in inaccessible regions, often geographically isolated, and suffer from various forms of marginalization, both politically and socially. They are subjected to domination and exploitation within national political and economic structures that are commonly designed to reflect the interests and activities of the national majority. This discrimination, domination and marginalization violates their human rights as peoples/communities, threatens the continuation of their cultures and ways of life, and prevents them from being able to genuinely participate in decisions regarding their own future and forms of development. Moreover, rather than aboriginality, the principle of self-identification is considered to be a key criterion for identifying indigenous peoples. This principle requires that peoples identify themselves as indigenous, and as distinctly different from other groups within the state (ACHPR 2006:9–10).

If some anthropologists and scholars from neighbouring disciplines welcome the global recognition of the rights of indigenous peoples as yet another empowering discourse for marginal and vulnerable groups of people in the sense of strategic essentialism (Spivak 1998), others strongly criticize and even condemn the term in general and its application in Africa in particular (Hodgson 2002; Kuper 2003). One of the main objections is on the basis of settlement history. As Pelican has noted, "whereas in North, Central and South America indigenous activism has a long history and the status of first peoples is generally uncontested, the situation in Africa is different where defining which groups may count as indigenous is much more problematic and controversial, as there are long and on-going histories of migration, assimilation, and conquest"(2009: 53).

The discourse of indigeneity in Africa is also criticized, for it is, largely, externally driven. To start with, the insertion of the African "indigenous peoples' movement into its global mother movement – by invoking experiences of indigenous peoples elsewhere is not a culmination of popular or mass and conscious self-identification by some ethnic groups" (Bojosi/Wachira 2006: 124). Rather it is a product of a long, enduring external mission, and is essentially driven by external funding and certain ideological assumptions (ibid.). These activist NGOs sought to ascribe special rights to a certain pre-determined discriminated cultural groups, those being hunter-gatherers and/or pastoralists. Determining which groups of people belong to the category of African indigenous peoples and claim special legal rights thereby is based on the conceptualization of indigenous peoples, the ideological positions these leading NGOs had/have, and the consequent assumptions and abstractions which follow from the appending of Africa's "indigenous peoples' movement to the global indigenous movement" (ibid.). Many African governments refer to this 'externality' of the discourse of indigeneity in Africa to justify their resistance. In 2010 for instance, the president of Botswana, Seretse Khame Ian Khame, accused Survival International, a powerful international human rights organisation actively engaged in promoting the indigenous peoples' rights in Africa, of trying to keep the San "in a life of backwardness" that "appeals to the racist mentality of having people in Africa live in a primitive life of deprivation" (cited in Sylvain 2014: 257).

It is also our contention that, at least in the Ethiopian context, on which our contribution mainly focuses, the indigenous criterion is too broad to be useful. The criterion of "self-identification as members of a distinct cultural group and recognition of this identity by others" (UN 2004: 2) is non-exclusive in the context of Ethiopia, as is probably the case in most African countries, for nearly all ethnic groups have a distinct sense of self and other. Ethiopia is a very diverse country, with 75 officially recognized ethno-linguistic communities. Even closely related people such as the ethnic groups in South Omo, which have become the focus of indigenous activism by international human rights organisations, exhibit and maintain visible ethnic boundaries. Similarly, the criteria of collective attachments to geographically distinct habitats or ancestral land are non-exclusive in the context of Ethiopia. With the exception of those members of groups who now reside in urbanized areas, all groups have, albeit to different degrees, a strong sense of territoriality, and depend on one or more key natural resources (e.g. forest, river, farming land, etc.) for their livelihoods. The nature of these livelihoods – specifically their very low level of economic diversification – makes the direct applicability of this second criterion in the Ethiopian context very problematic.

Nor are the criteria "customary cultural, economic, social, or political institutions that are separate from those of the dominant society and culture" (ibid.) useful signifiers. Horizontally, a history of population movement has resulted in a dynamic process of cross-cultural fertilization among the four broad linguistic and cultural communities to which all of Ethiopia's ethnic groups belong: The Cushitic, the Semitic, the Omotic and the Nilo-Saharan. In South Omo, for instance, in the encounter between Omotic, Cushitic and Nilo-Saharan cultural traditions, hybrid cultures are evident, though ethnic boundaries are sharply marked. Vertically, the issue of a 'dominant society and culture' was evident only until the 1974 revolution, before which the Amhara, and their kindred the Tigreans, were considered the dominant ethnic groups, and strongly identified with the Ethiopian state, which was principally defined in terms of the Amharic language and the institutions and cultural practices of the Orthodox Church. The revolution has made significant changes in the social make-up of the Ethiopian state, moving towards religious pluralism and redressing the economic grievances of ethnic minorities. The Ethiopian polity has been further restructured since the establishment of the federal political order in 1991, which instituted ethno-cultural justice (cp. the discussion in the sections below). Where a broad distinction can be made, it is between societies built along egalitarian principles on one hand and hierarchical societies on the other. Most of Ethiopia's egalitarian societies are found in the lowland, pastoralist areas, whereas many of the highland societies are built along hierarchical principles.

The criterion "an indigenous language, often different from the official language of the country or region" (ibid.) is also an insufficient marker of indigeneity, especially since 1991, when Amharic lost the status of being a 'national' language. Historically, Amharic has been the dominant language because of its identification with the Ethiopian state. All other languages had faced discrimination during and at the hands of the previous governments. The constitutional recognition of language rights since the establishment of the federal political order has rendered the issue no longer relevant in contemporary Ethiopia. For instance, currently the language of instruction for elementary education is based on the policy of mother tongue. At the federal level too, Amharic is adopted as the working language only for practical reasons.

THE DISCOURSE OF INDIGENEITY IN ETHIOPIA

What makes the discourse of indigeneity in Ethiopia unique is that it was the NGOs who first picked up the discourse of defining some groups as indigenous. As the example from the Gambella region shows, it was only a decade after the NGOs had begun to use the discourse of indigeneity that groups such as the Anuak started using the label in regional politics. The first international human rights organisation to use the term indigenous in the Ethiopian context is Cultural Survival (hereafter CS), a powerful advocacy organisation for indigenous peoples.

CS first used the term 'the indigenous people' in Ethiopia to describe the cultural and political situation of the Anuak of the Gambella region of western Ethiopia, who also live across the border in South Sudan, comprising a total population of circa 100,000. The context within which the term 'indigenous' is applied to the Anuak is related to Ethiopia's colour border and the modernist approach of the socialist government of the 1980s whose villagisation and resettlement program infringed upon local people's land rights and radically changed the regional demographic structure. The Anuak are part of the wider Nilotic society, which occupies a peripheral position within the Ethiopian polity. They form Ethiopia's borderland peoples, who differ from the mainstream Ethiopian population not only in terms of their marked economic marginality but also in their physical features. In the Ethiopian parlance the Nilotes are 'black', darker in their skin pigmentation, and contrasted with the 'red', lighter skin pigmentation of highland peoples. Generically called 'Highlanders', the latter are identified with the Ethiopian state. As such, the Ethiopian state is also 'red'. As the colour black is disdained and associated with an inferior position historically legitimated by the slave trade, which mainly victimized the 'black' Nilotes and other related peoples of the borderlands, the discourse on skin colour suggests the existence and relevance of the 'race factor' in Ethiopia.

The CS first encountered the Anuak as refugees in the Sudan in the 1980s; those who fled the revolutionary violence of the military-socialist Derg regime, violence which included not only the uprooting of local cultural practices in the name of progress and modernity, but also dispossessed the local people of their land in the controversial resettlement and villagisation programs. The 'biblical famine' that plagued Ethiopia in the mid-1980s and which was depicted and popularized by the Live Aid global concert prompted the government to embark on one of its most ambitious humanitarian projects, transferring hundreds of thousands of famine-affected farmers from the northern highlands to the relatively fertile western lowland areas such as Gambella. This transfer of population was not consented to by the resettlers, nor were local communities consulted about hosting this massive influx. Drawing on the narratives of the Anuak refugees who rejected the resettlement program and fled to South Sudan, in 1981 CS published an article calling them "indigenous people" (CS 1981: 3):

"The Anuak cannot survive without their ancestral lands [...] Today the total population is half of what it was a generation ago, but for the Amhara [Highlanders] whose traditional contempt for the Anuak as slaves and property continues, the Anuak are expendable." (CS 1981: 3)

CS published a second article on the Anuak in 1984 entitled *The Anuak – A Threatened Culture*, in which the discourse of ethnic extinction was further spelled out

"The future of the Anuak is in serious doubt. The Anuak are however a tenacious people who have, over the years, been able to keep their language and customs alive in the face of extreme hardship and pressure [They] however must be regarded as an endangered people." (CS 1984: 2)

In its 1986 issue CS published an article entitled *Ethiopia's policy of Genocide against the Anuak of Gambella*, in which the resettlement program was defined as part of a systematic measure taken by the Ethiopian government to exterminate the Anuak:

"The Anuak believe that one of the reasons for the resettlement program is to intermarry the Nilotic Anuak people with the light skinned highlanders and thus breed the Anuak out of existence. They rightly consider this is a form of genocide [...] earlier reports from Cultural Survival indicate that the Derg has attempted to squelch Anuak procreation by confiscating the sacred marriage beads which are used as dowries." (CS, 1986: 3)

Building on the extensive work of CS, many other international human rights organisations, such as Human Rights Watch, have produced volumes of work on the plight of the Anuak as indigenous peoples of Ethiopia. CS has renewed its advocacy practices in the new context of land grabbing. Ethiopia is at the forefront of the land-grabbing phenomenon in Africa, already leasing over three million hectares of land to foreign investors to develop large-scale commercial agriculture to boost export. Within Ethiopia, Gambella is at the centre of the land grabbing debate, where over 300,000 hectares of land have already been leased. Associated with land grabbing is the controversial villagisation program, which the government is justifying as the most effective strategy for delivering social services in lowland areas with dispersed settlement patterns. Critics however point out that the villagisation program is meant as a 'cost-effective' strategy to clear the land of the indigenous peoples, so that investors do not have to worry about consultation or compensation. In 2010 CS wrote about the issue of land grabbing and the related villagisation program in Ethiopia with a special focus on the Gambella region and how this has adversely affected the indigenous Anuak people in the following way:

For over 400 years, indigenous Anuak families have lived along the wide rivers of Ethiopia's Gambella region, cultivating maize and sorghum in the rich alluvial soil. On higher ground, they practice shifting cultivation, and in the forests they gather fruits, nuts, roots, and medicines. These diverse resources have spared them from hunger even in times of drought. But now Ethiopian soldiers are moving nearly all of Gambella's indigenous people – off their lands and farms and into state-created villages where the people fear starvation. Nearly half of Gambella's land is leased or available for lease to investors who are creating vast plantations of agrofuel and food crops, mostly for export. (CS 2010: 4)

Some other international human right organisations have taken the discourse of indigeneity in Ethiopia one step further, translating the discursive struggle into practical action aimed at influencing the actions and decisions of the Ethiopian government, with the understanding that the government is significantly dependent on foreign assistance. As such, some of the organisations, such as Inclusive Development Investment (IDI) have targeted the flow of money to the Ethiopian government from such interventions as the

Protection of Basic Services project, a multi-billion-development assistance package by a coalition of donors such as the World Bank and DFID.

A decade after CS began its advocacy work we now find Anuak political actors embracing the label 'indigenous' while legitimating power- and resource claims in the Gambella region. The term 'indigenous' is strategically deployed in inter-ethnic relations, as well as vertically in their relationship with the Ethiopian state. The Anuak have trouble with their main neighbours – the Nuer in the west and the Highlanders in the east. They have experienced demographic pressure from both sides. The ethnographically celebrated 19th-century Nuer expansion into the east was accomplished at the expense of Anuak territories. This expansion, which still continues, is not only territorial but also demographic. In fact, Nuer territorial expansion has been accompanied by a robust assimilation of their neighbours, including the Anuak; a demographic trend that has accelerated since the outbreak of the South Sudanese liberation movements in the 1960s, which resulted in a massive refugee influx into the Gambella region. Many of the South Sudanese refugees have always been Nuer, who constitute the second largest ethnic group in South Sudan. Equally threatening for the Anuak is the demographic growth of the Highlanders who have come to the Gambella region recently, mainly due to the activities of the Ethiopian state, such as the resettlement of the famine-affected people from northern Highlands that Cultural Survival has referred to in its genocidal account.

The establishment of the Gambella regional state as a constitutive member of the Federal Democratic Republic of Ethiopia since 1991 has put a new premium on the regional politics of number. Cognizant of the rapidly changing regional demographic structure, which has placed the Anuak in a minority position, they have picked up a historical argument for political entitlement to the Gambella region. In doing so they not only refer to settlement history, which accrues them 'first-comer' status but also they now also have begun extensively referring to the writings of Cultural Survival to legitimate their claim as an indigenous people of Gambella/Ethiopia. As Cultural Survival has continued to write about the plight of the indigenous Anuak people with reference to current issues such as land grabbing, the Anuak political actors, especially in the diaspora, have linked indigenousness with land grabbing to successfully insert Anuak politics into global civil society as prominent human rights issue. Armed with a globally legitimated empowering discourse they have recently engaged the Ethiopian state, which has an ambitious modernisation and industrialisation plan that among other things includes large-scale commercial agriculture in the country's lowland regions, where there is "abundant empty land". (Makki/Geisler 2011: 6–7).

Presenting themselves in terms of the discourse of the indigenous people enabled the Anuak political actors to legitimate a dominant political status in the Gambella region, at least throughout the 1990s and up until 2005, when a new power-sharing arrangement was introduced that balances the Anuaks' historical and the Nuers' demographic arguments for political entitlement. In their politics of inclusion the Nuer have sought to deconstruct the Anuaks' claim of indigeneity by referring to a longer historical frame of reference in which the Anuak, too, emerge, as migrants – a reference to the historical migrations of the various Nilotic groups of people back in the first millennium AD (Collins 1971). Moreover, unlike the CS, which recognizes the Anuak as indigenous people of Gambella, the AU/ACHPR, in its list of indigenous peoples of Africa, has identified the Nuer pastoralists as the indigenous people. These divergent schemes of representation by the international human rights organizations have sent conflicting signals about who the indigenous people in the Gambella region 'really' are.

THE RESPONSE OF THE ETHIOPIAN GOVERNMENT TO THE INDIGENOUS CLAIMS

Ethiopia has been most vocal in its criticisms against the African Commission's Working Group of Experts on Indigenous Populations/Communities, to the extent of questioning the very relevance of the Working Group and the validity of its reports (Bojosi 2010: 295). Like his Botswanan counterpart, who we referred to earlier, Ethiopia's late Prime Minister Meles Zenawi denounced international human rights organisations championing indigenous peoples' rights in Africa for being driven by a desire to create "a human zoo" (2011) to provide photo-opportunities for western tourists. Anthropologists were not spared in his condemnations either; he considered them "friends of poverty" (ibid.). The Ethiopian government has shown a strong resistance to the application of the term 'indigenous' in the Ethiopian context, for at least four major reasons:

The term 'indigenous' is primarily understood in its historical sense

The Amharic equivalent of the term 'indigenous' is *nebar hizb*, which means 'firstcomers' and is contrasted with *mete*, which means 'latecomers'. Given the country's history of dynamic population movements in all directions the government rejects the relevance of the term 'indigenous' in the Ethiopian context. As the discussion in the previous section showed, the Ethiopian government is not alone in its perception of the term 'indigenous' in this way. Many African governments vehemently argue that all Africans are 'indigenous'.

The term 'indigenous' is considered to be irrelevant in the context of the new federal political order

The high modernism and political repressiveness of the military-socialist government of Ethiopia (1974–1991) had its malcontents. By the end of the 1980s there were dozens of ethno-national liberation movements, of which the Ethiopian Peoples Revolutionary Democratic Front (EPRDF), a coalition of the country's major ethnic groups, was the strongest militarily. The EPRDF succeeded in defeating the Derg's army, and following its seizure of state power it has radically restructured the historically entrenched unmilitary state into a federation based on the principle of ethnicity. The preferred terminology used in the ethnic discourse in Ethiopia is 'Nations, Nationalities and Peoples' (NNP), a clear indicator of the Marxist legacy of the Tigrean Liberation Front, the dominant political force within the EPRDF.

Ethno-cultural justice is thoroughly recognized in the Ethiopian federation, and the right to self-determination is broadly understood to include: the right of a people to speak and develop its own language; the right to preserve, express and promote its own culture and history; the right to self-determination within a particular territory; and the right to political representation at the regional and federal levels of government. As a result of the new language policy, there are twenty-one languages, excluding Amharic, which are currently used as media of instruction at primary school level. According to Article 39 (1), the right to self-determination even includes the right to secede from the federation, when ethnic groups feel the federal government violates their rights. As such, Ethiopia's new federal political order is unique in generously recognizing group rights. By recognising the rights of all ethnic groups for self-determination up to and including secession, the Ethiopian government even seems to have gone beyond simply meeting the main demand of the global indigenous movement: the self-determination of vulnerable and marginalized communities. The problem in Ethiopia is not the lack of a legal framework to protect the self-determination rights of these communities, but rather the translation of this constitutionally-backed right into a lived reality. Federal encroachment into regional and local autonomy abounds, rendering the exercising of the right of self-determination, particularly, among those with weaker political voice, impossible (Feyissa 2013).

Government categories of marginalized groups

What is progressive about Ethiopia's new federal political order is not only the constitutionally sanctioned ethno-cultural justice and self-determination but also its recognition of the need to redress historically conditioned imbalances that have created inequality among the 'Nations, Nationalities and Peoples' of Ethiopia. Inequality among ethnic groups is recognized as a legacy of historical discrimination by the previous governments. This is reflected, above all, in the livelihood vulnerability of some groups of people, who are constitutionally recognized as "least advantaged" (Demisse 2013) and/or as national minorities. In identifying the 'least advantaged people' the government takes a regional approach, rather than only recognizing named peoples *per se*. Accordingly, the government identifies three categories of marginalised groups, which it calls the "historically least-advantaged" (ibid.) people. These are: the four "developing" (ibid.) regional states of Gambella, Benishangul-Gumuz, Afar and Somali; pastoralists, and national minorities.

The constitutional framework by which the 'Developing Regional States' (hereafter the DRS) are recognized is laid out in Article 89(4): "the Government shall provide special assistance to Nations, Nationalities, and Peoples least advantaged in economic and social development." (FDRE Constitution 1995: 214) As per this article, peoples of the DRS are historically marginalized, with reduced life opportunities than peoples who live in the other regions. The federal government not only identifies peoples of these regions as among the least advantaged but also makes it a constitutional obligation to provide them with special assistance. The requirements set out here form the basis of affirmative action leading to the goal of guaranteeing equal chances throughout the country.

Pastoralists also fall under the category of least advantaged people. The Ethiopian government, for the first time in the history of the country, rightly recognizes pastoralists as one of the most marginalized communities, in need of special support. The marginalisation of pastoralists is an issue, despite their larger demographic size and crucial contribution to the national economy. Pastoralists in Ethiopia occupy 60 percent of the national territory, constitute about 12 percent of the total population, and are responsible for about 42 percent of the total livestock population of the country (Solomon 2002). The government's identification of the pastoralists as vulnerable and in need of a special support clashes with local representations and status claims. In Gambella, for instance, the Anuak, whom CS recognizes as the indigenous people, deeply resent the Nuers' representation by the government, by virtue of being pastoralists, as 'vulnerable' and 'marginalized'. The Anuak political leadership has sought to deny the Nuer recognition as pastoralists, which they managed to do until recently, when the government has officially recognized the latter.

The so-called 'national minorities' also belong to the category of the least advantaged. The legal basis for this is Article 54 (3) of the Constitution: "out of the maximum number of 550 seats in the House of People's Representatives (HoPR), a minimum of 20 seats is reserved for minority nationalities and peoples." (FDRE Constitution 1995: 179) The federal parliament is composed of two chambers: the House of People's Representatives, and the House of the Federation. The representatives of the former are representatives of the Ethiopian people as a whole. They are elected by means of general and direct elections under a first-past-the-post electoral system. In practice, this means that the candidate who gets the most votes in the district wins the single seat in each electoral district. In a state organized on an ethnic basis, the use of such an electoral system runs the risk that the only seat in each electoral district will be won by the candidate who represents the interests of the largest ethnic group in that district. This is particularly problematic for those ethnic groups that are a minority in every electoral district: there is a real risk that those ethnic groups will not have a single representative in the HoPR. To reduce this risk and to guarantee the representation of all ethnic groups in the first chamber of parliament, the federal constitution provides for a guaranteed representation of "minority nationalities and peoples" (ibid: 185). The constitutive units of the Ethiopian federation – Nations, Nationalities and Peoples – are asymmetrical, ranging from ethnic groups with a demographic size of over twenty million (e.g. Oromo and Amhara), to groups with as few as one thousand members (e.g. Brayle and Kwegu).

There is a close fit between regions and peoples recognized by the Ethiopian government as marginalized and in need of special support, and the academic literature on marginalized communities in Ethiopia, as well as the groups that international human rights organisations or development institutions would have readily defined as 'indigenous'. However, the direct application of the term 'indigenous' and the conventional criteria used to identify the indigenous is more problematic, and may even be too broad to be useful.

CONCLUSION

As the discussion in the previous sections indicates, the Ethiopian example shows the limits of the notion of the indigenous as a useful and convenient label to further the social justice agenda for marginalised groups in Africa. When used in the sense of strategic essentialism (Spivack 1998) the term 'indigenous' could be empowering for vulnerable groups of people. But As Kuper (2003; 2005) emphatically and convincingly noted, the term 'indigenous people', used both as an anthropological concept and a political tool for activists, might also do more damage, rather than furthering the social justice agenda. Not least, its application might create new divisions and fuel existing inter-group tensions, as shown in the example from Gambella, where the Anuak claim to the title of 'indigenous people' is contested by the Nuer; claims which are variously validated by international human rights organisations depending on which definitional criteria they emphasize. Alternatively, Kuper argues for individual rights of citizens within liberal-democratic states as a better way of promoting the common good, including redressing the grievances of members of minority communities.

As the comparison between the Ethiopian case study and the origins of the concept of indigeneity in the Americas showed, alternative institutional designs that support a robust minority rights regime, such as the multi-nation federation, might better address the issue of the special recognition of certain cultural communities than the more contested term 'indigenous'. The challenge is how to make the Ethiopian federal political order more federal and help it to deliver on its promises. What Ethiopia needs is not a fourth category of people – the indigenous – in addition to the already bulky appellation 'Nations, Nationalities and Peoples' but rather a robust federal system in which the rights of individuals and collectivites are lived realities, rather than merely ideas inserted into a constitution. Mukundi Wachira argued along the same lines, while reflecting on the issues of indigenous peoples' rights in Kenya:

"It is possible to meet indigenous peoples' claims by adopting general legal measures aimed at redressing past injustices and continuing socio-economic deprivation and inequality [...]. Indigenous peoples' core claim to land rights in Kenya can be accommodated within the mainstream legal framework, including the Constitution, legislation, and judicial decisions." (2008: X)

REFERENCES

ACHPR (2006): "Indigenous peoples in Africa: The forgotten peoples? The African Commission's work on indigenous peoples in Africa. Banjul: International Work Group for Indigenous Affairs" (http://www.achpr.org/files/special-mechanisms/indigenous-populations/achpr_wgip_report_summary_version_eng.pdf).

Bojosi, Kealeboga (2010): "The African Commission Working Group of 95 experts on the rights of indigenous Ccommunities/populations: Some reflections on its work so far." In: Solomon Derso (ed.), Persectives on the rights of minorities and indigenous peoples in Africa, Pretoria: University Law Press.

Bojosi, Kealeboga./Wachira, Margaret (2006): "Protecting Indigenous peoples in Africa: An analysis of the approach of the African Commission on Human and Peoples' Rights." In: African Human Rights Law Journal 6, pp. 382–406.

Collins, Robert O. (1971): Land beyond the rivers: the Southern Sudan 1898-1918, New Haven: Yale University Press.

Cultural Survival (1981): "Anuak decimated by Ethiopian government" (http://www.genocidewatch.org/images/Ethiopia_31_Jul_81_Anuak_Decimated_by_Ethiopian_Government.pdf).

—— (1984): "The Anuak – A Threatened Culture" (http://www.culturalsurvival.org/publications/cultural-survival-quarterly/ethiopia/anuak-threatened-culture).

—— (1985): "Ethiopia's Policy of Genocide Against the Anuak of Gambella" (http://www.culturalsurvival.org/ourpublications/csq/article/ethiopias-policy-genocide-against-anuak-gambella).

—— (2010): "Ethiopia: Stop Land Grabbing and Restore Indigenous Peoples' Lands" (https://www.culturalsurvival.org/sites/default/files/ethiopia_action_alert.pdf).

Curley, Andrew (2012): "The International Indigenous Movement for Self-Determination." In: International Viewpoint IV Online magazine 449 (http://www.internationalviewpoint.org/spip.php?article2671).

Demisse, Ato Daniel (2013) (Secretary of Constitutional Interpretation and Regional Affairs, House of Federation), interview by the author, January 16, 2013.

Deng, Francis (1997): "Ethnicity: An African Predicament." In: The Brookings Review 15/3, pp. 28–31.

Feyissa, Dereje (2011): Playing different games: The Paradox of the Anuak and Nuer Identification Strategies in the Gambella region. New York: Berghahn Books.

Hodgson, Dorothy (2002): "Introduction: Comparative perspectives on the indigenous Rights Movement in Africa and the Americas." In: American Anthropologist 104/4, pp. 1037–1049.

Jackson, Jean/Warren Kay (2005): "Indigenous Movements in Latin America, 1992-2004: Controversies, Ironies, New Directions." In: Annual review of Anthropology 34, pp. 549–573.

Kuper, Adam (2003): "The Return of the Native." In: Current Anthropology 44/3, pp: 389–395.

Makki, Fuad/Geisler, Charles (2011): "Development by Dispossession: Land Grabbing as New Enclosures in Contemporary Ethiopia" (http://www.iss.nl/fileadmin/ASSETS/iss/Documents/Conference_papers/LDPI/29_Fouad_Makki_and_Charles_Geisler.pdf).

Mamdani, Mahmood (1996): Citizen and Subject, Princeton: Princeton University Press.

Pelican, Michaela. (2009): "Complexities of Indigeneity and Authoctony: An African Example." In: American Ethnologist 36/1, pp. 52–65.

Sylvain, Renée (2014): "Essentialism and the Indigenous Politics of Recognition in Southern Africa." In: American Anthropologist. 116/2, pp. 251–264.

Spivak, Gayatri (1988): "Can the subaltern speak?" In: Cary Nelson/Lawrence Grossberg (eds.), Marxism and the Interpretation of Culture, Illinois: University of Illinois Press, pp. 271–313.

The Constitution of the Federal Democratic Republic of Ethiopia, 1995.

Tucker, Richard (2008): "Globalization and Indigenous Peoples in Asia:Changing the Local-global Interface." In: Conservation and Society 6/2, pp. 204–205.

UN (2004): "The concept of the indigeneous" (www.un.org/esa/socdev/.../documents/workshop_data_background.doc).

van Cott, Donna Lee (2007): "Latin America's Indigenous Peoples." In: Journal of Democracy 18/4, pp. 127–142.

World Bank (2010): "Indigeneous peoles, poverty and development." (http://siteresources.worldbank.org/EXTINDPEOPLE/Resources/407801-1271860301656/full_report.pdf).

Zenawi, Meles: "Speech during the 13th Annual Pastoralists' Day celebrations, Jinka, South Omo", January 25, 2011 (http://www.mursi.org/pdf/Meles%20Jinka%20speech.pdf).

Ethnicity as a political resource
Indigenous rights movements in Africa

MICHAELA PELICAN

Three lines of argument have been prominent in the study of ethnicity, depending on the scholarly viewpoint: first, that ethnicity is a collective identity that is based on shared meanings and cultural practices and that engenders a sense of belonging (Geertz 1963); second, that ethnicity is socially constructed and may be used or abused for political purposes (Cohen 1974; Brubaker 2002); and third, that ethnicity emerges from the interplay of different groups and is most pronounced at ethnic boundaries (Barth 1969). All three approaches have their merits, and they have been complemented by a fourth argument – that ethnicity ought to be studied in a historical perspective so as to understand its emergence and transformation over time, as well as the factors that have contributed to it (Comaroff 1995; Lentz 1995).

In this chapter, I will focus on indigeneity as a particular category of ethnicity that over the past decades has gained global relevance and that here serves as an example of ethnicity as a political resource. While indigeneity entails the various aspects of ethnicity outlined above, I argue that its political dimensions – exemplified in the global indigenous rights movement – are its central feature, particularly in the African context.

Unlike ethnic identities that are tied to certain territories and peoples, indigeneity is a rather abstract and relational category. In this regard, it shares similarities with the notion of autochthony, as discussed by Geschiere (2005). Historically, the notion of indigenous peoples emerged in the context of European expansion into the Americas and the Pacific. In the 1960s, it was adopted by the United Nations as a legal mechanism to protect and empower minority groups that had been marginalized on the basis of cultural difference (Niezen 2003; Minde 2008). In this process, it became necessary to conceptualize 'indigenous peoples' in a way that would be applicable to a variety of historical and regional contexts.

Indigeneity has been a highly contested concept, particularly in Africa and Asia, where indigenous rights movements have only recently gained significance (Hodgson 2002a; Uddin et al. forthc.). Within the past twenty years, many ethnic and minority groups in Africa have laid claim to indigeneity on the basis of their political marginalization and cultural distinctiveness in their country or region of residence. They have drawn inspiration from the United Nations definition of indigenous peoples as a legal category with collective entitlements, and many have linked up with the global indigenous rights movement.

Concurrently, there has been an extensive debate within Africanist anthropology on the analytical usefulness of the concept. Moreover, several African governments have questioned its applicability to the African continent, arguing that all population groups may count as indigenous. With the adoption of the United Nations Declaration on the Rights of Indigenous Peoples in 2007 conceptual criticism has abated. While some governments have remained skeptical of ethnicity as a valid basis for differential political and economic treatment, many have made attempts to integrate the indigenous rights discourse into their policies and development programs. This contribution will focus on three case studies, from Botswana, Tanzania, and Cameroon, to outline different uses of indigeneity as a political resource.

CONTROVERSIES OVER INDIGENEITY: ACADEMIC AND POLITICAL DEBATES

In his comprehensive study on the history of the global indigenous rights movement, Niezen (2003; 2010) makes clear the constructed nature of indigeneity; he actually prefers the term 'indigenism', to highlight its character as a political movement. He states that "Indigenous Peoples were first the citizens of an idea before they became members of an international community with distinct rights" (ibid 2010: 135). That is, the term 'indigenous peoples' was initially introduced as a legal category, and only later filled with meaning. Understood primarily as a political notion, the term may refer to different subjects in different historical and regional contexts.

The application of the indigenous rights discourse to the African continent instigated much debate, among both academics and political actors (cp. also Feyissa and Zeleke in this volume). While in the Pacific and the Americas, indigenous activism has a long history and the status of 'first peoples' is generally uncontested, in Africa the situation is different. Here it is much more problematic and controversial to define which groups may count as 'indigenous', as the African continent looks back on long and complex histories of migration, assimilation, and conquest. Furthermore, as Kopytoff (1987) has demonstrated in his classic essay, African societies tend to reproduce themselves at their internal frontiers, thus continuously creating and re-creating a dichotomy between 'original inhabitants' and 'latecomers' along which political prerogatives are negotiated. This recurrent process does not allow for a permanent and clear-cut distinction of 'first nations' versus 'dominant societies', as implied by the universal notion of indigenous peoples. Accordingly, some anthropologists have criticized the concept of indigenous peoples as inapplicable to the African context, and as promoting an essentialist ideology of culture and identity (e.g., Kuper 2003; 2005). Conversely, others have claimed that these complexities have effectively been reflected in the working definitions of the International Labor Organization (ILO) and the United Nations (UN), which emphasize cultural distinctiveness, political marginalization, and self-identification as fundamental criteria. In their view, the above criticism is not only unjustified, but counterproductive both to the anthropological endeavor and to 'indigenous realities' (e.g., Kenrick/Lewis 2004: 8). A conciliatory approach has been suggested by Barnard (2004; 2006), who questions the validity of 'indigenous peoples' as an anthropological concept, while recognizing its utility as a political and legal tool in the struggle for collective rights. I agree with Barnard, and I contend that at this point – more than ten years after the initial debate – the focus has shifted from debating the validity of the concept to studying the social dynamics of the indigenous rights movement in different parts of Africa.

Concurrent to the academic debate of the 2000s, many African governments have been opposed to the concept of indigenous peoples and their entitlement to land, arguing that all Africans are 'indigenous' and should have equal access to natural resources (Lutz 2007). While the deliberative process at the United Nations had its starting point in 1971, it was only in 2007 that it finally culminated in the adoption of the Declaration on the Rights of Indigenous Peoples. A critical moment occurred in 2006, when a group of African states (in particular Namibia, Botswana, and Nigeria) took exception to some formulations of the declaration (Oldham/Frank 2008; Pelican 2009). Subsequently, the African UN member states agreed to maintain a united position and issued a draft aide mémoire, specifying their concerns regarding the definition of indigenous peoples, and the issues of self-determination, ownership of land and resources, establishment of distinct political and economic institutions, and national and territorial integrity. Moreover, they stated that for some member states the declaration might pose fundamental constitutional and political problems, rendering its implementation impossible. Faced with these objections, the African Union and the Global Indigenous Peoples' Caucus engaged in a series of negotiations. Eventually, the African Group agreed on nine amendments to the declaration, two of which addressed the issue of definition and the possible misinterpretation of the right to self-determination. Finally, in September 2007, the Declaration on the Rights of Indigenous Peoples was adopted by the General Assembly with the support of the African group, but with four negative votes from Canada, Australia, New Zealand, and the United States.

As rightly noted by Oldham and Frank (2008), the objections of the African Group take us to the center of the anthropological controversy over the concept of indigenous peoples. As argued by Suzman (2002) and others, the adoption of the Declaration on the Rights of Indigenous Peoples has been particularly problematic for southern African states, such as Botswana and Namibia, which – as a way of distancing themselves from apartheid politics –excluded the provision for differential treatment of their citizens on the basis of race or ethnicity. Conversely, in countries like Cameroon, where ethnic and regional favoritism have long been vital features of national politics (Bayart 1984; Kofele-Kale 1986), the concept of indigenous peoples is much less problematic. However, the Declaration's implementation has not been without problems both in Cameroon and in other parts of the continent.

DIFFERENT TRAJECTORIES OF INDIGENOUS RIGHTS MOVEMENTS IN AFRICA

To give an idea of the varied experiences and political trajectories of 'indigenous peoples' in Africa, I will outline three case studies: San hunter-gatherers in Botswana, Maasai pastoralists in Tanzania, and Mbororo pastoralists in Cameroon. While basing my elaborations on the Mbororo case on my own research (Pelican 2009; 2010; 2015), I will draw on the extensive works of Maruyama (2003; 2010; 2012) and Hodgson (2002b; 2009; 2011) to analyze the situations of the San and Maasai. For the purpose of comparison, I will not go into the details of each case, but will highlight their characteristics as outlined by each author. I argue that there is no single, coherent indigenous rights movement in Africa, but a variety of movements which are shaped by their divergent national and local contexts.

The San of Botswana: Between international advocacy and local coping strategies

The San of Botswana were among the first African peoples to join the global indigenous rights movement. As Maruyama and others have argued, their participation has largely been stimulated by external actors (Hitchcock 2002; Suzman 2002; Maruyama 2010). Furthermore, while claiming indigenous rights has benefited them in terms of access to land, it has engendered political and social tensions that have motivated many San to withdraw from political activism and to focus on local coping strategies.

The San are known as nomadic hunter-gatherers who live in Botswana, Namibia, South Africa and Angola. For a long time, they have experienced displacement and impoverishment as a result of various factors, including the intrusion of Bantu-speaking agro-pastoralists, European colonialism, large-scale infrastructural projects, and land concessions to private companies. Today, they count among the most marginalized ethnic groups in southern Africa. A large part of the San population lives in Botswana, in particular the Central Kalahari region. Their case has attracted much public and scholarly attention because of their displacement from the Central Kalahari Game Reserve (CKGR) and their successful court case against the Botswanan government in 2006 (e.g. Hitchcock 2002; Saugestadt 2011).

Being opposed to the South African apartheid system, Botswana early on adopted the ideal of a non-racial democracy. The Tswana language and culture were promoted as the national norm, and socio-economic disparity (rather than ethnic difference) was defined as the prime criterion for development measures. In the 1970s, the Remote Area Development Program was introduced to provide special support to marginalized minorities, including the San. It encouraged them to adopt a sedentary lifestyle and thus to integrate into mainstream society. In 1986, the government decided to relocate the remaining San residents of the Central Kalahari Game Reserve so as to ensure the protection of its fauna and flora, and to provide them with infrastructural and social services in the nearby government-planned settlements.

Around the same period, the indigenous rights movement began to gain traction in Africa. International NGOs, such as the International Work Group for Indigenous Affairs (IWGIA) and Survival International, became interested in the situation of the San and encouraged them to form their own local and national NGOs. In contrast to the Botswanan government, they emphasized the aspect of cultural uniqueness, and portrayed the San as an 'indigenous people' at the verge of disappearance if no longer allowed to practice a hunter-gatherer lifestyle.

By 2002 some 3,000 people had been relocated. The government decided to stop providing services in the CKGR, such as water and medical care, and to prevent former residents from returning to the game reserve. In response, local and international NGOs rallied in support of the displaced San and eventually filed a case against the government with the Botswana High Court. After a long process, the High Court passed its ruling in December 2006, stating that the government had illegally evicted the San from their ancestral lands and that the San families listed as complainants should be allowed to return to the CKGR.

The ruling was celebrated by the global indigenous rights movement as a victory for the San. However, research by Maruyama (2010; 2012) shows that its implementation caused unforeseen challenges. Instead of resolving the problem, international intervention contributed to unduly politicizing the matter and confronting the San with the choice of either 'tradition' or 'development' – a binary choice that for many was neither desirable nor practicable. Moreover, as the government was not obliged to provide services to residents in the CKGR, many San were unable to return. Finally, Maruyama noticed frictions within the San community over who was entitled or able to return, thus contributing to incipient socio-economic differentiation. As a result, many San were frustrated with their situation and felt that their fate had largely been defined by external actors, whether the Botswanan government or international NGOs. They gradually redrew from the indigenous rights movement and focused on local coping strategies. While living in government settlements, many San have established nearby bush residences as a strategy to utilize both the social services provided by the development program and the natural resources found in the bush. Moreover, they have developed new forms of mobility and exchange relations that connect settlement and bush, and that contribute to converting both the CKGR and the resettlement site into livable environments (ibid 2003; 2012).

The Maasai of Tanzania: From indigenous rights to pastoralist livelihoods

In Tanzania, it is Maasai pastoralists and Hadza hunter-gatherers who have engaged in the indigenous rights movement since the late 1980s. Here I focus on the Maasai, who have experienced a long history of cultural, economic and political marginalization. They live in the country's arid and semi-arid northeast, an area largely neglected by the government. As Hodgson (2002b) argues, Maasai involvement in the indigenous rights movement should be seen against the background of Tanzania's turn toward democracy and neoliberal economy. On the one hand, it opened up new opportunities for Maasai and others to organize themselves collectively and to partake in the country's political and economic development. On the other, it exposed them to heightened competition over natural resources and attempts at land appropriation by the state and international investors. Hodgson (2011: 157) describes Maasai political activism of the past twenty years as shifting from discourses of 'indigenous rights' to those of 'pastoralist livelihoods'. In her view, this shift reflects the need for individuals and NGOs to reposition themselves in response to government pressure and changing national and international development frameworks.

In 1989 the Maasai activist Moringe ole Parkipuny participated in the United Nations Working Group on Indigenous Populations in Geneva, Switzerland. He was one of the few educated and politically well-placed Maasai in Tanzania, and the first African to address the UN Working Group. Together with other Maasai men, he then formed the non-governmental Maasai organization KIPOC (Korongoro Integrated People Oriented to Conservation). Around the same period, a second Maasai NGO emerged. By declaring Maasai pastoralists an 'indigenous people', both organizations aimed to secure international as well as national recognition of Maasai cultural and political rights and, most importantly, their access to land. In the subsequent years, two umbrella organizations were created to represent the interests of not only Maasai but also other pastoralist and hunter-gatherer groups, all of whom considered themselves 'indigenous' and 'marginalized peoples'. Yet, driven by donor agendas and the need to secure their own survival, these organizations gradually distanced themselves from their grassroots constituencies. Moreover, they faced rivalries with government institutions who felt sidelined by the NGOs and the international donors (ibid 2002b; 2011: 137–144).

In the early 2000s, the political climate changed and Maasai NGOs were faced with government disapproval. Similar to many African countries, the Tanzanian state was critical of the UN notion of indigenous peoples, and responded unfavorably to Maasai claims to indigeneity and entitlement to land and resources. In consequence, several organizations re-oriented their focus from the international to the national arena. Moreover, they adopted a more pragmatic approach, forgoing political opposition for collaboration with government institutions. They reframed their political struggles, shifting from the use of the language of 'indigenous rights' to that of 'pastoralist livelihoods', and participated in drafting Tanzania's second poverty reduction strategy and the new National Livestock Policy.

In reassessing the effects of Maasai political activism on the lives of Maasai pastoralists, Hodgson (2011: 181–209) comes to a rather disappointing conclusion. While few individuals have benefited, poverty is still a fact, and the privatization of land is an ongoing issue. At the same, she recognizes that, taking into account the government's enduring neglect of Maasai pastoralists, their organizations faced an enormous challenge in promoting pastoralists' rights and development. Evidently, they could not meet the latter's expectations, and have made limited contributions to reducing the structural inequalities that impact on pastoralists' lives. Furthermore, Hodgson (ibid: 8) draws attention to recent policy changes in the international development establishment which no longer channel funds via NGOs but through government institutions instead. She concludes that despite the global emphasis on civil society and international law, the nation state has retained its position as a crucial player in shaping the realities and development of its populace.

The Mbororo of Cameroon: From 'latecomers' to an 'indigenous people'

The Mbororo are cattle pastoralists who, coming from northern Nigeria, settled in Cameroon in the course of the 19th and 20th century. In this chapter, I focus on the Mbororo in the country's Anglophone northwest who have been at the forefront of Mbororo engagement in the global indigenous rights movement. I argue that while Mbororo identification as 'indigenous' has helped them to strengthen their position within the nation state, it has also engendered disagreement about the meaning of indigeneity both among different population groups and within Mbororo society.

Like Tanzania, Cameroon underwent a democratic transition in the early 1990s which gave room to the formation of ethnic and regional elite associations. At the time, the Mbororo Social and Cultural Development Association (MBOSCUDA) was created, and soon became the most effective organ of Mbororo self-representation to the state and international development organizations. Among its primary activities were programs aimed at Mbororo children's education, women's socio-economic empowerment, and the lobbying for Mbororo political and legal entitlements (Duni et al. 2009). In the mid-2000s MBOSCUDA expanded its advocacy work and actively engaged in the global indigenous rights movement. However, their claims to indigeneity have been ambiguous, as they collide with local conceptions of autochthony (Pelican 2008; 2009).

In Cameroon – as in other parts of Western Africa – notions of indigeneity, autochthony, 'firstcomers', and 'natives' have a long history, and frame local conceptions of political hierarchy and legal entitlement (Bayart et al. 2001; Geschiere 2009). In northwest Cameroon, it is local Grassfields societies that consider themselves 'natives' and 'guardians of the land', as they have settled in the region for several hundred years. Conversely, Mbororo pastoralists arrived only in the early 20th century, and thus have been regarded as 'strangers' and 'latecomers' with limited rights to land and landed resources. On the national level, discourses of autochthony became highlighted in the context of Cameroon's democratization. As stipulated in the country's revised constitution of 1996, priority is given to the protection of the rights of minorities and indigenous populations. In this national political framework, 'indigenous populations' is meant to refer to local groups that consider themselves 'firstcomers', 'natives' or 'autochthones'. It is different from the UN and ILO conception of indigenous peoples, which prioritizes the criteria of self-identification, historical or contemporary experience of marginalization, and cultural difference from the majority population (ILO 1989; Daes 1996).

As confirmed by Tchoumba (2006) in his ILO pilot study on Cameroon, Mbororo pastoralists, as well as Baka and Bagyeli hunter-gatherers of southern and southeastern Cameroon (also known as Pygmies), do fulfil the ILO and UN criteria, and thus may be considered indigenous peoples of Cameroon. Conversely, the Cameroonian government has never officially endorsed the two groups' classification as 'indigenous peoples', but operates with the notion of 'marginal populations'. This complexity of concepts with family resemblance but different political and legal implications has resulted in the puzzling situation in which the Mbororo internationally qualify as an 'indigenous people', while in the local and national contexts they are seen as 'latecomers', 'allochthones', or 'marginalized minority'. We thus have a situation in which international and local interpretations of indigeneity are irreconcilable, and engender new potential for competition and conflict. This has been reflected, for example, in a crisis over leadership in Sabga, one of the most influential Mbororo settlements in northwest Cameroon, in which UN bodies were called in to endorse Mbororo entitlement to self-organization (Pelican 2010). At the same time, critical voices emerged among members of the economically progressive Mbororo elite, who viewed the classification of Mbororo as 'indigenous' as inaptly suggestive of Mbororo backwardness and poverty (ibid 2013).

Thus, similarly to the San and Maasai cases, the Sabga crisis initiated a phase of disenchantment with the indigenous rights discourse. It occasioned the reorientation of Mbororo activists away from overt criticism towards a more pragmatic approach and their collaboration with governmental institutions. Yet, in contrast to Botswana and Tanzania, the Cameroonian government has integrated the indigenous rights discourse in its developmental agenda, albeit under the heading of 'marginal populations'. Thus, Mbororo organizations continue to employ the indigenous rights discourse, while at the same time seeking to engage with government officials. As I have argued elsewhere (ibid), Mbororo have diversified (rather than shifted) their socio-political strategies by integrating advocacy at various international, national, and local levels. That is, they participate in the yearly meetings of the UN Permanent Forum of Indigenous Issues, submit reports to the Human Rights Council, circulate critical information via social media networks, and collaborate with government representatives on development programs. Even though the Cameroonian government has not fully subscribed to the concept of indigenous peoples, or to its legal implementation, the indigenous rights discourse has retained its place in the national and international political domain.

COMPARATIVE ANALYSIS

The three cases have in common that San, Maasai, and Mbororo have been able to use indigeneity as a political resource. Conversely, there are also counter-examples of groups who either did not want to or were unable to convincingly argue for their right to be recognized as an 'indigenous people'. Furthermore, these movements went through various phases; from expectation and success to disillusionment and pragmatism. As part of this process, they adopted changing and alternative strategies to deal with the adverse consequences of their claims and to improve their situation. Yet while in the Mbororo case indigeneity has remained a viable category of identification, the Maasai in Tanzania were obliged to shift from an indigenous rights discourse to a pastoralist livelihood discourse. Meanwhile the San in Botswana have largely withdrawn from the political sphere and have concentrated on coping strategies at the local level.

Relevant factors shaping the different outcomes of the three indigenous rights movements include the groups' historical and economic situations within their national frameworks, such as divergent levels of poverty, historical discrimination, and national integration. Here it is noteworthy that, while all three groups have experienced considerable degrees of social and political marginalization, they differ in terms of economic strength, with implications for their respective political leverage. That is, the San and Maasai have experienced relative poverty as a result of historical, ecological and political factors, which does not apply to the same degree to the Mbororo in Cameroon. Moreover, San and Maasai have been exposed to powerful competitors over land and natural resources (state enterprises as well as national and international investors) whose contribution to the countries' overall economic development has been rated higher than the groups' 'traditional' livelihoods. Here as well, the situation is somewhat different for the Mbororo in Cameroon, who also face competition, but on a much smaller scale.

A second relevant factor affecting the indigenous movements' outcomes concerns the divergent approaches of the specific national governments in relation to indigenous and minority rights discourses. Here it is important to distinguish between governments that promote a multicultural vision of their nation (e.g. Cameroon), and those that promote national identity over regional or ethnic identities and that prefer to provide differential treatment on the basis of economic rather than cultural differences (e.g. Botswana, Tanzania).

In this view, the use of indigeneity as a political resource has proven most effective and lasting in the Cameroonian case. At the same time, it has engendered disagreement within the Mbororo community over the cultural and social appropriateness of identifying as an 'indigenous people'.

Conclusion

In concluding this chapter, I wish to return to my initial argument that indigeneity is a particular category of ethnicity that thrives on its political dimensions. As the three case studies indicate, there has been a waxing and waning of indigenous rights movements in Africa. For many, identifying as an 'indigenous people' has primarily been a political strategy to substantiate legal claims and gain access to development. In this regard, Africa differs from other parts of the world, such as the Americas and the Pacific, where indigenous identities have a much longer and more tangible history, and where indigeneity has also been a source of shared meaning and belonging (cp. Clifford 2013). I therefore believe that it is the abstract and discursive character of indigeneity that constitutes both its strength and its weakness when it is employed as a globally applicable category.

References

Barnard, Alan (2004): "Indigenous Peoples: A Response to Justin Kenrick and Jerome Lewis." In: Anthropology Today 20/5, p. 19.
—— (2006): "Kalahari Revisionism, Vienna and the 'Indigenous Peoples' Debate." In: Social Anthropology 14/1, pp. 1–16.

Barth, Fredrik (1969): "Introduction." In: Fredrik Barth (ed.), Ethnic Groups and Boundaries. The social organisation of culture difference, Oslo: Universitetsforlaget (Scandinavian University Press), pp. 9–38.

Bayart, Jean-François (1984): L'état au Cameroun, Paris: Presses de la fondation nationale des sciences politiques.

Bayart, Jean-François/Geschiere, Peter/Nyamnjoh, Francis (2001): "Autochtonie, Démocratie et Citoyenneté en Afrique." In: Critique Internationale 10, pp. 177–194.

Brubaker, Roger (2002): "Ethnicity without Groups." In: European Journal of Sociology 43, pp. 163–189.

Clifford, James (2013): Returns: Becoming Indigenous in the Twenty-First Century, Cambridge, Mass.: Harvard University.

Cohen, Abner (1974): "Introduction: the lesson of ethnicity." In: Abner Cohen (ed.), Urban Ethnicity, London et al.: Tavistock Publications, pp. 9–24.

Comaroff, John (1995): "Ethnicity, nationalism and the politics of difference in an age of revolution." In: John Comaroff/Paul Stern (eds.), Perspectives on Nationalism and War, Luxembourg: Gordon and Breach Publishers, pp. 243–276.

Daes, Erica (1996): "Working Paper on the Concept of Indigenous Peoples. UN doc. E/CN.4/Sub.2/AC.4/1996/2", January 15, 2015 (http://ap.ohchr.org/documents/alldocs.aspx?doc_id=7620).

Duni, Jeidoh/Fon, Robert/Hickey, Sam/Salihu, Nuhu (2009): "Exploring a Political Approach to Rights-Based Development in North-West Cameroon: From Rights and Marginality to Citizenship and Justice." In: BWPI Working Paper 104, Manchester: Brooks World Poverty Institute.

Geertz, Clifford (1963): "The integrative revolution: Primordial sentiments and civil politics in the new states." In: Clifford Geertz (ed.), Old Societies and New States: The Quest for Modernity in Asia and Africa, London: Free Press of Glencoe, pp. 105–119.

Geschiere, Peter (2009): The Perils of Belonging: Autochthony, Citizenship, and Exclusion in Africa and Europe, Chicago: University of Chicago Press.

—— (2005): "Autochthony and citizenship. New modes in the struggle over belonging and exclusion in Africa." In: Quest: An African Journal of Philosophy 18, pp. 9–24.

Hitchcock, Robert (2002): "We are the First People: Land, Natural Resources and Identity in the Central Kalahari, Botswana." In: Journal of Southern African Studies 28/4, pp. 797–824.

Hodgson, Dorothy (2011): Being Maasai, Becoming Indigenous: Postcolonial Politics in a Neoliberal World, Bloomington: Indiana University Press.

—— (2002a): "Introduction: Comparative Perspectives on the Indigenous Rights Movements in Africa and the Americas." In: American Anthropologist 104/4, pp. 1037–1049.

—— (2002b): "Precarious Alliances: the Cultural Politics and Structural Predicaments of the Indigenous Rights Movement in Tanzania." In: American Anthropologist 104/4, pp. 1086–1097.

—— (2009): "Becoming Indigenous in Africa." In: African Studies Review 52/3, pp. 1–32.

ILO (International Labor Organization) (1989): "Convention (No. 169) Concerning Indigenous and Tribal Peoples in Independent Countries", October 13, 2014 (http://www.ilo.org/wcmsp5/groups/public/---ed_norm/---normes/documents/publication/wcms_100897.pdf).

Kenrick, Justin/Lewis, Jerome (2004): "Indigenous Peoples' Rights and the Politics of the Term 'Indigenous'." In: Anthropology Today 20/2, pp. 4–9.

Kofele-Kale, Ndiva (1986): "Ethnicity, Regionalism, and Political Power: A Post-mortem of Ahidjo's Cameroon." In: Michael Schatzberg/William Zartman (eds.), The Political Economy of Cameroon, New York: Praeger Publishers, pp. 53–82.

Kopytoff, Igor (1987): "The Internal African Frontier. The Making of African Political Culture." In: Igor Kopytoff (ed.), The African Frontier. The Reproduction of Traditional African Societies, Bloomington: Indiana University Press, pp. 3–84.

Kuper, Adam (2005): The Reinvention of Primitive Society: Transformations of a Myth, London/New York: Routledge.

—— (2003): "The Return of the Native." In: Current Anthropology 44/3, pp. 389–395, 400–401.

Lentz, Carola (1995): "'Tribalism' and ethnicity in Africa: a review of four decades of Anglophone research." In: Cahiers des Sciences Humaines 31, pp. 303–328.

Lutz, Ellen (2007): "Indigenous Rights and the UN." In: Anthropology News 48/2, p. 28.

Maruyama, Junko (2010): Bushmen Living in a Changing World: Between Development Program and Indigenous Peoples' Movement, Kyoto: Sekaishisosha Publishing (in Japanese).

—— (2003): "The impacts of resettlement on livelihood and social relationships among the Central Kalahari San." In: African Study Monographs 24/4, pp. 223–245.

—— (2012): "From 'space for ruling' to 'space for living'. Indigenous people's movements among the San in Botswana." In: Japan Journal of Cultural Anthroplogy 77/2, pp. 250–272 (in Japanese).

Minde, Henry (2008): "The destination and the journey. Indigenous peoples and the United Nations from the 1960s through 1985." In: Henry Minde (ed.), Indigenous Peoples: Challenges of Indigeneity, Self-determination and Knowledge, Delft: Eburon, pp. 49–86.

Niezen, Ronald (2003): The Origins of Indigenism: Human Rights and the Politics of Identity, Los Angeles: University of California Press.

—— (2010): Public Justice and the Anthropology of Law, Cambridge et al.: Cambridge University Press.

Oldham, Paul/Frank, Miriam A. (2008): "'We the Peoples…' The United Nations Declaration on the Rights of Indigenous Peoples." In: Anthropology Today 24/2, pp. 5–9.

Pelican, Michaela (2015): Masks and Staffs. Identity Politics in the Cameroon Grassfields, Oxford/New York: Berghahn.

—— (2008): "Mbororo Claims to Regional Citizenship and Minority Status in Northwest Cameroon." In: Africa 78/4, pp. 540–560.

—— (2009): "Complexities of Indigeneity and Autochthony: an African Example." In: American Ethnologist 36/1, pp. 149–162.

—— (2010): "Umstrittene Rechte indigener Völker: das Beispiel der Mbororo in Kamerun." In: Zeitschrift für Ethnologie 135, pp. 39–60.

—— (2013): "Insights from Cameroon: Five years after the Declaration on the Rights of Indigenous Peoples." In: Anthropology Today 29/3, pp. 13–16.

—— (forthcoming): "Different Trajectories of Indigenous Rights Movements in Africa: Insights from Cameroon and Tanzania." In: Nasir Uddin/Eva Gerharz/Pradeep Chakkarath (eds.), Futures of Indigeneity: Spatiality, Identity Politics and Belonging, Oxford/New York: Berghahn.

Pelican, Michaela/Maruyama, Junko (2015): "The indigenous rights movement in Africa: Perspectives from Botswana and Cameroon." In: African Studies Monographs 36/1, pp. 49–74.

Saugestad, Sidsel (2011): "Impact of international mechanisms on indigenous rights in Botswana." In: The International Journal of Human Rights 15/1, pp. 37–61.

Suzman, James (2002): "Kalahari Conundrums: Relocation, Resistance and International Support in the Central Kalahari Botswana." In: Before Farming 4/12, pp. 1–10.

Tchoumba, Belmond (2006): "Indigenous and Tribal Peoples and Poverty Reduction Strategies in Cameroon. Project to Promote ILO Policy on

Indigenous and Tribal Peoples (PRO 169)", Publication of the International Labor Organization, May 5, 2014 (http://www.ilo.org/wcmsp5/groups/public/---ed_norm/---normes/documents/publication/wcms_100518.pdf).

Uddin, Nasir/Gerharz, Eva/Chakkarath, Pradeep (eds.) (forthcoming): Futures of Indigeneity: Spatiality, Identity Politics and Belonging, Oxford/New York: Berghahn.

Yatsuka Haruna (2015): "Reconsidering the 'indigenous peoples' in the African context from the perspective of current livelihood and its historical changes: the case of the Sandawe and the Hadza in Tanzania." In: African Studies Monographs 36/1, pp. 27–48.

Ethnicity or nationality?
Minority policy and ethnic conflict in contemporary China

LI XI YUAN

INTRODUCTION

When translating the Chinese word *minzu* into English, translators are always faced with a choice between two alternative terms: 'ethnicity' or 'nation'. Most Chinese government departments and public sectors have used 'nationalities' in English translations of the term *minzu* when it appears as part of their official names. Recently, influenced by the nation-state discourse of the Western world, the English translations of the names of some institutions which formerly included variants of the terms 'nation', 'national', or 'nationality' have begun adopting the terms 'ethnic' or 'ethnicity' instead. For example, the former State Commission of Nationalities has changed its official name in English to the 'State Ethnic Affairs Commission'. However, the former Nationalities University of China has changed its English name to 'Minzu University of China', retaining the transliterated Chinese term, while other provincial colleges have continued to use the terms 'national' or 'nationalities' as part of their names. In 2012 Chinese economist Ho Angang (2012) published an article discussing "the second generation of minority policy". He raised the argument that equality of individual rights, rather than minority policy – that is, understanding groups as ethnicities rather than nations – is the right way to reduce the differences and conflict between majority and minority. His view aroused a big debate in the Chinese academic and mass media. The most powerful opposition came from minority elites, who claimed that minority policy has provided necessary protection for minorities since 1950 (Chang 2013). The argument reflects the fact that ethnicity in China is actually a political question more than a cultural one. In this paper I use the example of Uyghur migrants in

Guangzhou to discuss different articulations of ethnicity in the rural home areas and urban destination areas of migration, and relate it to the complexities of the political construction of ethnicity in China.

ETHNICITY AND ETHNIC POLITICS

Ethnicity is often understood as a form of cultural identity. That is, culture provides the content and meaning of ethnicity, such as a shared history, ideology, shared symbols, and system of meaning. At the same time, ethnicity is also understood as a political identity that, in some cases, may be coupled with ethnic nationalism or conflict.

After World War II, many countries constituted by multiple ethnic groups had implemented minority policy in order to prevent their societies from falling into ethnic conflict. These minority policies were basically developed on the basis of two assumptions. Firstly, following the notion of the 'melting pot' in America, was that ethnic distinctions could be eliminated because of the inevitability of assimilation (McDonald 2007: 50). Secondly, following the framework of the countries that formed the alliance of Eastern Europe after World War II, was that ethnic conflict could be controlled by a powerful overarching political union of its various nations or ethnicities, even though those ethnic distinctions might continue to exist.

Two theoretical approaches have developed in social science in parallel with state politics. Some scholars, like Giddens (1985), have argued that the legitimacy of modern states must be based on the political and civil rights of autonomous individual subjects. According to this view, the state should not focus on ethnicity, but rather enforce political and legal equality of all individuals. Others, like Will Kymlicka (1995), argue that the notion of an autonomous individual is itself a cultural construct. According to this view, the state must recognize ethnic identity, and let all ethnic groups express their own identities.

However, the resurgence of ethnic nationalism around the world demonstrates that the relationship between ethnicity and nationalism is complicated and changeable (Calhoun 1993: 235). Social scientists have found that ethnicity had been socially constructed in the sense that ethnic boundaries, character, and identities are continuously negotiated, defined, and produced through social interaction both inside and outside ethnic communities (Negal 1994: 152; Eriksen 2001). State policies have great power to shape patterns of ethnic identification when controlled resources are distributed along ethnic lines.

Some researchers in America indicate that ethnicity is a rational choice in resource competition among social groups. For example, Hechter's research (1983) showed that the construction of ethnic boundaries could be seen as a strategy to gain economic advantage. Banton (1987) observed that ethnic boundaries are defined and redefined according to strategic calculations of interest.

In this paper I wish to discuss the constructed character of ethnicity in China by focusing on the complex interplay of Chinese minority politics and population movement. As I will argue, in contemporary China, minority politics has an enormous power to shape ethnic boundaries and identifications, as well as the relationship between majority and minority populations. While the central government's minority policy, which binds a minority to its territory, was originally designed with the intention of unifying the country, it no longer matches the current ethnic diversity of China's urban centers that has resulted from the past twenty years of economic opening-up coupled with internal and international migration.

CHINA'S MINORITY POLICY SINCE 1950

The Constitution of the People's Republic of China (the National Congress had passed in 1954) declared that China is a unified country with multiple *minzu*. In the definition of the country, *minzu* are those ethnic groups that live in China, classified by the country and confirmed in the Constitution. Between 1950 and 1980, fifty-six *minzu*, including Han, were defined. The state classified *minzu* according to four kinds of criteria: common territory, common language, common economy, and common psychological nature, as manifested in common culture (mainly in terms of religion and living habits), which were partly outlined by Stalin and revised in the context of Chinese conditions. (Fei 1980: 148) In this political framework of the country, national identity prevails over any ethnic identity, and every ethnicity must accept its political position and economic condition as determined by the country. The general economic advantage enjoyed by Han Chinese – who are also the majority *minzu* – has been carefully hidden behind the political discourse of 'ethnic equality' and 'solidarity'. As each *minzu* and its territory has been legally and politically established, their classification has actually made different economic resources available for each ethnic group, since different regions and lands have differing economic values. For example, Han occupy most of the regions with high economic value. In Xinjiang, Kazak and Han occupy the rich land of Zhungeer Basin and South of Tianshan Mountain, while most Uyghur live on relatively barren land north of Tianshan Mountain. As an attempt to redress the balance between the Han advantage, as majority *minzu,* and other minority *minzu*, the minority policy was implemented in the 1950s, which, writes Stevan Harrell, "in practice means developmental aid from higher level government agencies to minority districts, representation of minorities in political bodies, more lenient application of the stringent population control program, affirmative action in education at several levels, and other important benefits" (1990: 517).

According to the Constitution, this minority policy can only implemented within the confirmed *minzu* autonomous districts. It means that an ethnic people can only enjoy the benefits of the minority policy in the places where they have registered formally as members of a *minzu* and as definite residents of the *minzu* autonomous district. Once such an individual has left his home town he or she can no longer take advantage of the policy. Therefore, the minority policy is territory-bounded. The character of this policy is similar to that of other population and social welfare policies put in place by the local government for domestic inhabitants, in that the rights granted are all linked to the idea of *huji* (户籍) – migrating people (whether members of the majority or minority *minzu*) are not supposed to enjoy the same rights as the domestic people in any locality. In China *Huji* has been used by every executive region government as an exclusive policy for some purposes. Thus, while members of a *minzu* cannot be discriminated against directly on the basis of their ethnicity (as stipulated by the constitution), they nevertheless may be discriminated against on the basis of their status as migrants (*huji* exclusion). Even members of the Han majority could find themselves disadvantaged by this exclusive rule. For example, in the city Urumqi, in Xinjiang region, the population of Han was greater than that of Uyghur, but Han people in the region refer to themselves as 'border supporters' (*zhibianzhe,* 支边者) and 'constructors' (*jianshezhe,* 建设者), who contribute to nation-building in an "ethnic region" (*minzu diqu,* 民族地区) (Cliff 2012: 82). These names mean that Han in the region are guest inhabitants, living in Xinjiang for some work-related reason. Even though some Han individuals have lived there all their lives, they still retain this 'guest' identity.

XIAOBEI: A MULTICULTURAL/MULTIETHNIC IMMIGRANT QUARTER

Let me begin by introducing one of China's ethnically most heterogeneous locations, the Xiaobei community of Guangzhou. Guangzhou is a megacity in the Southeast of China that looks back on a long history of international connections, including the historical emigration of Chinese workers and entrepreneurs to the Americas (Zhou 1992) as well as the contemporary immigration of African traders and Arab businesspeople (Li/Du 2012). While today, Xiaobei is well known for its African immigrant community, it is actually a multiethnic quarter where members of different nationalities and ethnicities live together, including Africans, Arabs, and Sala Huizu (a branch of Muslims in China), as well as Uyghur, Han, and other *minzu*. Africans and Uyghurs are the two biggest immigrant communities in this quarter. Both are treated in roughly the same way by the locals, who see them first and foremost as immigrants, not differentiating between national/domestic and international migrants. For the purpose of this article, all immigrant groups (irrespective of whether they are national or ethnic units) are here considered as ethnic immigrant communities.

Similarly to migrant communities elsewhere, the different ethnic immigrant groups in Xiaobei tend to occupy separate economic niches. Africans are primarily international traders who buy from China and sell in their home countries in Africa; many members of Turkish and Arab communities run restaurants or commercial firms; many Uyghur work as Muslim intra-community food suppliers, cooks, butchers, or mobile snack-sellers; and a large number of Han work as wholesalers and service providers. Ethnic immigrants from different regions or countries have developed a self-sufficient environment.

According to the record of the local immigrant registration office,[1] the Uyghur population is the most numerous, followed by Sala-huizu. Most Uyghur migrants are male; no female has been registered officially as a contemporary resident. In fact, Uyghur women are seldom seen on the streets. Many Uyghur men say that a married Uyghur woman should stay at home to take care of the family, and that married Uyghur men here leave their wives at home. In contrast, most Sala-huizu migrants are female. They come to Xiaobei following their families, or following the neighbors or friends of hometown, as housewives or maids, some married to Uyghur. Both of these migrant groups are predominantly Muslim. They worship at home or have religious gathering in friends' homes, seldom going to the mosque like Guangzhou's domestic Muslims.

---

1 In the population administrative regulations, when a migrant wants to rent a room for accommodation in a city, he or she must go to the office of the community to register as a contemporary resident and obtain an official resident's permit. Without such a permit he or she would be kicked out of the district immediately once he was found by the police.

ETHNIC CONFLICTS IN AN IMMIGRANT SETTING

Most of the ethnic immigrants in Xiaobei quarter arrived after 2009. An informant who works in immigrant registration said that before 2009, Uyghur and African laborers had gathered in the area at daytime for employment but dispersed again at night. The Xiaobei community was recognized by the outside world because of this multi-ethnic labor flow, until two significant ethnic conflicts occurred in 2009, which changed the human ecology of Xiaobei community.

Conflict between Uyghur and Han

On June 26, 2009, a collective conflict between Uyghur and Han workers occurred in one factory (Xu Ri Toys Manufacture), located in Shaoguan, a north city of Guangzhou[2]. The factory had employed about 700 Uyghur workers and a similar amount of Han workers. According to the official reports, hundreds of workers fought with each other because some fake messages about violence between two ethnic groups had been passed among workers and aroused anger. Though the conflict was soon interrupted by police and the managers of the factory, it still resulted in 120 workers being injured (31 Han and 89 Uyghur) and two Uyghur workers being killed. Within two weeks of the conflict, the factory stopped producing. Managers from both local governments of Shaoguan city and the home towns of the Uyghur workers (all were from a same county of Xinjiang) helped to deal with the conflict. Some persons, both Han and Uyghur, had been arrested, charged with having written the fake messages and of being the instigators of the fight. Some Uyghur workers were taken back to their home areas.

Many different news stories about why and how the conflict happened, with differing and confusing details, appeared on the internet and in newspapers. According to the two most detailed official reports,[3] the situation in Shaoguan

---

2 "'Workers' fight caused two deaths in a toy factory (Wnaju gongchang gongren douou 2ren siwang)". Guangzhou Daily June 27, 2009 (http://gzdaily.dayoo.com/html/2009-06/27/content_615478.htm); Series reports in the Xinxi Shibao: June 28, 2009. A8; GuangZhou Daily (Guangzhou Ribao) July 9, 2009. A2 and July 10, 2009. A4.

3 Two reports are: a) the television talk about incidents of '6.26' and '7.5' given by the chairman of Xinjiang Ughur Autonomy in June 6, 2009 (egov.xinjiang.gov.cn/xxgk/zwdt/2009/56200.htm; b) the news report in Hainan Daily about the judgment of Court to the suspects and the case of '6.25', October 11, 2009 (http://ngdsb.hinews.cn/html/2009-10/11/content_163889.htm).

can be roughly reconstructed. Between June 16 and June 25, 2009, allegations about Han females being raped by Uyghur men were uploaded to a Shaoguan public website. These messages were forwarded by workers in the factory, and aroused panic among the female workers. At the night of June 25 one female worker, who was a newcomer and did not know the plan of the factory, walked into the male Uyghur workers' dormitory by mistake. The Uyghur workers made fun of her. The woman's scream alerted the guard nearby, and the woman escaped while the guard came to check what was happening. The woman ran back to her dormitory and complained to other Han workers. Some Han workers, both male and female, then went to the Uyghur men and asked them to apologize. The two groups of workers then argued and fought with each other in the early morning of June 26. In the statement of the court of October 10, 2009, according to the police record there were no rape cases reported between June 16 and 25, so the messages had been fake. The person who had uploaded the messages had recently been fired by the factory and wanted to arouse chaos as an act of revenge.

Unfortunately, the '6.26 Incident' was just the beginning of a series of ethnic conflicts between Uyghur and Han. On July 5, 2009, hundreds Uyghur gathered in Urumqi city, demanding an investigation into the death of two workers in the Shaoguan conflict. More political demands, including sovereignty claims, as well as violent attacks, soon followed. Two days of chaos resulted in over 1,700 persons being injured, most of them Han.

Conflict between African immigrants and Guangzhou police

While the influence of the '6.26 Incident' was still being felt, another conflict emerged in Guangzhou city. On July 15, 2009, hundreds of African immigrants gathered outside the police station in Xiaobei area to protest about police officers causing the death of a Nigerian. According to the news report, at midday, a Nigerian man had jumped out of a high window and died while he was attempting to escape from a passport check by the policemen. Since an entry visa to China cost a lot of money at that time, many immigrants from central Africa were overstaying. As they said, the one thing they hated the most was a passport check by the Chinese police. The death of the young Nigerian aroused the sympathy of other Africa immigrants, and the protest made the city government and police very nervous. Soon armed police surrounded the crowd and declared the protest was illegal, stating that those protesters who did not disperse would be expelled from the country. Most participants left from the place within two hours, with some representatives remaining in order to negotiate with the police and the immigration department of the province.[4]

Ramifications after the conflicts

As I will show in the following, the Uyghur-Han conflict has impacted significantly on the living and working conditions of Uyghur migrants in Guangzhou, and has caused a shift in their self-identification, from stressing their identity as an ethnic minority to emphasizing their identity as part of the wider Muslim community of Xiaobei.

In the minds of Han people, Uyghur were previously associated with an ethnic image of vigor, humor and kindness, since all movies stories and novels had portrayed Uyghur in this way. Unfortunately, this has changed toward a stereotype of fierceness, anger, and violence since 2009.[5] After the conflict, Uyghur people were no longer welcomed in Guangzhou, or in other cities of Han majority. Moreover, ethnic labor employment (as a previously favorable ethnic policy before) has been stopped by the city's manufactures. It is difficult for Uyghur to get hired, to rent houses, or to earn their food on streets – "once they saw my ID they refused to hire me"; "they saw my face, then immediately refused to let me stay"; many informants of Uyghur complained that they were in the same terrible situation. Many migrating laborers have had to leave the city. The Uyghur people who remained in Guangzhou gradually moved to the Xiaobei area, where most African immigrants also live.

Since most immigrants in Xiaobei are Muslim, it is easier for Uyghur to earn money by selling food to other Muslims, and to rent houses from African leaseholders, and they feel less hostility from their Muslim neighbors than from local Han people. In this multi-ethnic community, Uyghur tend to emphasize their religious identity as Muslims to a much greater extent than they express

---

4   "Embassy to aid investigation into Nigerian trader's death", June 21, 2012 (www.chinadaily.com.cn/hqgj/jryw/2012-06-21): The Nigerian embassy in Beijing has sent officials to Guangzhou to cope with the investigation of a Nigerian's death in police custody. "We have sent officials to Guangzhou to observe the investigation and calm the Nigerians in the Nigerian residential areas," Ademola Oladele, official for public communications at the Nigerian embassy in Beijing, said on Wednesday. Elebechi Celestine, 28, the man who died, comes from a town in southeast Nigeria, he said. Celestine is said to have argued with a motorbike taxi driver on Monday.

5   Here I refer to the notion of 'others' as described in terms of difference from 'us' – where 'us' – the 'we-group', are Han in this case. Cp. the critical dissertation by Gladney, 1994.

their ethnic identity as Chinese. For example, ethnic restaurants in the community hang many Islamic signs and scriptures on their walls, and place Arab items on tables, compared with ethnic restaurants in other place of city, which are decorated with many pictures of Xinjiang landscapes and ethnic symbols. Uyghur wear more Arabian-style dress in the community, in contrast to Uyghur in Xinjiang. Some Uyghur have even learned to write Arabic, and to speak English and French to communicate with their neighbors and customers. The meat suppliers develop a Xinjiang-Guangdong cross-provincial market network to ensure that the meat is sourced from the genuine Muslim butchers. Restaurants and meat stores in the community put up pictures of Mosques as posters.

While the Uyghur-Han conflict impacted the social and economic situation of Uyghur migrants in Guangzhou, the conflict between African immigrants and the local administration caused a shift in the city's treatment of African migrants. Subsequent to the conflict, in 2009 the Exit and Entry and Administration Department of Guangdong province modified the entry rules for the immigration of Africans in order to decrease the numbers of overstaying immigrants (Li/Du 2012). Governments of the city and district tried to renovate the commercial buildings and the public environment in Xiaobei, which led to a rise in real estate prices in the area. Two kinds of ethnic immigrants have gradually become established there, and most of them have settled down, as businesspeople rather than as mobile laborers. According to an informant from the immigrant registration office of Xiaobei area Africans and Uyghur have developed a co-existence relationship

The two conflicts in Xiaobei raise some very interesting questions about ethnicity: Why did the '6.26 Incident' cause greater ethnic conflict in the distant city of Urumqi than in the nearby city of Guangzhou? Why did Uyghur have to claim their right and privilege as a minzu in Xinjiang? In Guangzhou, under what circumstance do Uyghur join in with the multi-ethnic community, rather than with the domestic society? In order to answer these questions, we need to take a closer look at the minority and ethnic politics of the Chinese central government.

MINORITY POLITICS AND THE POLITICAL CONSTRUCTION OF ETHNICITY IN CHINA

As I have outlined at the first part of this paper, the origin of China's contemporary minority and ethnic politics dates back to the 1950s to the Mao era, when the country defined itself as a state composed of 'unified multiple *minzu*'. In the 1980s, the country underwent economic reforms and instituted new policies that promoted regional development by encouraging rural workers to migrate to urban production centers. These policies are ongoing, but as they are managed on the local level, different regions pursue different strategies. These three factors are relevant in understanding the outcomes of the described ethnic conflicts.

Post-Mao era: Regional development and ethnic gap

Between 1950 and 1980 the minority policy fixed ethnic population in their own territories. Income inequality between regions and nationalities was unclear. The patron-client relationship between the majority and the minority constructed by minority policy seemed roughly stable, though several small conflicts had erupted in Xinjiang and Tibet.

After 1980 economic growth made Han cities much richer than the minority autonomous districts, and many ethnic people moved to the eastern cities from minority regions seeking jobs and opportunities. They saw the difference in development between central Han cities and marginal nationality districts and the income gap among nationalities, and discovered how hard it was for a person with poor education, like most Han laborers, to find a good job (Gustafsson/Li, 2003). According to reports in newspapers, many teenagers from south Xinjiang went to eastern cities to pursue their dreams of city life, but ended up becoming homeless or resorting to crime.[6] Now they have realized that the minority policy will not bring them the kind of modern life that the city people have. The Patron-client relationship between majority and minority has changed.

The central government started the 'Western Development Plan' in 2000. The plan has brought billions of dollars of investment funding to Xinjiang and developed new industries, mainly in resource exploitation, agro-industry, and tourism. The design of the plan was intended to reduce the income gap between regions and nationalities by increasing ethnic labor employment and developing industry; it is a kind of 'affirmative action' to promote minority peoples. The Western Development Plan includes other forms of economic aid, like financial aid, trade, employment, etc., and the eastern developed cities must carry the

---

6 "Homeless Children in a mainland city is not only a problem for the image of Xinjiang, but a problem for people living in Xinjiang" (Liulang ertong bujin shi xingxiang wenti, gengshi minsheng wenti. 流浪儿童不仅形象问题，更是民生问题) Reported by Ye Weimin. In South Weekend (Nanfang zhoumo 《南方周末》), June 27, 2011.

burden of implementing these 'political tasks'. This is why manufacturers in Shaoguan city hire hundreds of workers from the county of Xinjiang at one time. The factory would have been impossible to run without support by the governments of Xinjiang and Guangdong provinces. The plan has pushed the rapid economic growth in Xinjiang. Similar to the situation in other nationality districts, the gap between provincial GDP of minority regions and non-minority regions has narrowed, according to an econometric analysis by academics (Ho/Ho 2012).

However, the employment of Uyghur did not increase rapidly even though as a domestic nationality they enjoy privileges with regard to employment. The employers from Han cities found that many Uyghur laborers could not fulfil the requirements of most positions in terms of skill and qualifications. Similar issues also arose in the tourism industry. The big agencies were run by investors from mainland cities, which make most of their profit from the industry. The domestic nationalities can only take advantage of their *minzu* status by selling their ethnic products – fruits, foods, and arts. In this development pattern, it is no surprise that the domestic nationalities, especially Ugyhur, as the majority population in the district, would conceive of the development plan as a kind of invasion by Han – who take advantagers of the local resources but do not share the profits.

As the Western Development Plan has been carried out in Xinjiang, new problems have arisen from the fast economic growth.

a) The economic growth has been pushed by urbanization and industrialization rather than by the development of agriculture. Meanwhile, most Uyghur living in south Xinjiang, are considered as being of relatively low value for the economy, and are weak in terms of competition in the labor market. The new growth has widened the development gap between city and countryside, as well as the income gap between Uyghur, Han, Kazak and other minorities within a given region or district (Hannum/Xie 1998: 327).

b) The elites of minorities now live in cities far from their hometowns. Though in official documents the numbers of ethnic representatives continue to increase in the state congress, they are mostly administrators of government and members of the Party. These elites may call themselves ethnic representatives, but they have actually been distanced from the grassroots society for a long time. Most Uyghur administrators, as the important agents of the state-nationality connection, remained silent about the '7.5 Incident' and the series of subsequent violent events, because they might not know what and why exactly happened in south Xinjiang, and also because as members of a *minzu* they cannnot betray their own ethnic community.

New problems diversify the society of Xinjiang. The inner social stratification prompts members of each *minzu* to focus primarily on the interests and welfare of their own ethnic community. In other words, the Western Development Plan leads interested competition to localize in Xinjiang, while at the same time the connection between *minzu* and country has become less reliable. The '6.26 Incident' was one reason for this, but was not the only one that led to the '7.5 Incident' and series of violent events following it.

Different Regions, Different Strategies

However, for the mainland majority, especially for city governments, keeping the nationwide inter-ethnic relationship stable is not a major concern. They mainly focus on domestic economic growth and peaceful politics. From the point of view of city governments and domestic society, Uyghur are just one kind of migrant, like the migrants from other Han regions. The domestic newspapers and public media of Guangzhou and Shaoguan reported the '6.26 Incident' as just a workers' fight; ethnicity and nationality were not mentioned in the media coverage.

In the '6.26 Incident', Uyghur workers and Han workers alike were viewed as migrant laborers and chaos-makers by the domestic government and society of Shaoguan. Those found responsible were dismissed by the factory after the '6.26 Incident', even though some of them were hired again few days later. The administrator, who came from the Uyghur workers' hometown, had to send some of those people who were fired back to their home towns. Under such circumstances workers, whether Uyghur or Han, had no chance to declare their opinions or to protest if they felt unfairly treated. But Uyghur can claim their rights in Xinjiang Uyghur Autonomous district. As the '7.5 Incident' showed, in their own territories minorities can use their nationality as a political resource. Less than two months later, on September 3, following reports of Uyghur assailants using infected hypodermic needles to attack Han women, children, and the elderly, crowds of Han people gathered outside the offices of the Xinjiang government to request effective protection for Han people, but the government made no public promises (Cliff 2012).

Since the '7.5 Incident' and the ensuing violence, the government of Guangzhou, as well as the governments of other majority cities, began to consider that Ugyhur migrants might bring about serious conflicts, and they have since increased controls over the Ugyhur staying in their jurisdictions. Following advice or suggestions from the local government, most hotels and rental houses now refuse to accept Ugyhur; the same is true of many factories and firms.

Xiaobei is an exception in the Guangzhou. As members of the first community that opened up to other *minzu*, the local residents tend to neglect the administrator's advice and to accept the Uyghur as renting residents, especially because fewer and fewer Han migrants want to rent the houses in this area since it has become a multi-ethnic community.

The Uyghur migrants have their own strategies for solving the problem of accommodation, but avoid attracting the government's attention. For example, one person might register as a contemporary resident and rent a big room in order to offer place for other acquaintances. Thus, the number of people living in one house is often higher than the number shown in official records. This approach definitely goes against the local regulations. Now the Uyghur migrants dislike ID checks by the police with the same intensity that some African immigrants do.

Ethnicity as a political resource in China

In China, ethnicity may be used as a powerful political resource, but only when it is represented in its own territory. Immediately prior to the '6.26 Incident' in Shaoguan, seven hundred Uyghur and eight hundred Han workers lived together. The dialogue between two groups increased their mutual levels of ethnic awareness. Some benefit competition among individuals inside the working system could therefore be more easily transformed into a discourse about ethnic inequality. Sexual tension between young male and female workers could become conflated with ethnic stereotypes. The factory management evidently had not paid attention to the emerging tension between these two ethnic groups. As Donald Donham (2011) had claimed in his book, some conflicts between workers would turn into or be read as ethnic conflict. Since ethnic conflict is always a sensitive political subject in China, it is easy for some people to use it as a way to gain power or as an excuse to escape their responsibilities. After the '6.26 Incident' the governments of provinces and cities did not expect the Uyghur migrants to gather together, so they advised domestic society to push the Uyghur migrants away. The Uyghur migrants gathering in Xiaobei went contrary to the government's expectations and purpose. However, the Uyghur people didn't present their collective nature as a *minzu*, but rather present themselves in religious terms, as Muslims. By employing the strategy of using their religious community as a shield, the Uyghur have found a way to survive in a multi-ethnic community in an unfriendly majority city. Apart from their territory in south Xinjiang and the ethnic group to which they belong, Ughur immigrants in Xiaobei are a minority *minzu* distinct from Han Chinese; they are immigrants distinguished from other local residents, and are also one a Chinese nationality distinct from African immigrants. Separated from the majority by different policies of the country – minority policy, *huji* policy, and religious policy – the identities of Uyghur migrants have to be redefined flexibly and situationally. In other words, ethnicity is manipulated for political and economic purposes (Brubaker 2002).

If one investigates the behaviour and presentation of Uyghur people in Shaoguan factory, Xiaobei community and Xinjiang city, one can see the character of their ethnicity shift. This demonstrates clearly how an ethnicity may be politically constructed by the state. The political alliance built on the minority policy, which has specific nationality-territories at its core, could once maintain a balance between the majority and the minority in the relatively homogeneous society that existed before, but it cannot continue to play that role in today's increasingly diversified circumstances. China has never had as many foreign immigrants as it has today. Some academics have begun to argue for the depoliticization of nationality – for ethnicity to be recognized without being associated with territorially bounded privileges, and for equality and individual right instead (Ho/Ho 2012). Furthermore, prior to international immigration, Chinese people saw ethnicity mostly in terms of their own ethnic minorities, as a question of different political treatment within the Chinese nation state because these groups were classified and named as *minzu* in the country's minority policy. Although Chinese people were aware of cultural differences, they were hidden to some extent behind political discourse, and religion was formerly thought to be unrelated to ethnicity because even individual Han had different religious beliefs and practices. With the arrival of African immigrants, the Chinese have begun to understand ethnicity purely in terms of cultural difference, without additional political treatment.

Conclusion

China's original notion of 'unified multiple nationalities', created in 1950, did not definitely follow the idea of multicultural citizenship, because the concepts of 'citizenship' and 'individual civil rights' do not constitute the basis of China's national political framework. In China, rather, rights are formulated on on the basis of a common sense of the political and economic differences between majority and minority, and have allowed minority peoples to continue to live according to ethnic cultural mores on their own land through the introduction of the minority policy (for example, in ethnic regions the regional mother tongue can be used in school lessons instead of Mandarin) (Attané/Youssef 2000). In this way ethnicity has more or less become a part of multicultural 'citizenship'. However, in China political discussion and conflict over ethnicity have never ceased (Dreyer 1977; Karmel 1996). The Xiaobei case demonstrates that the people continue to use ethnicity as a political resource, but that the frontier has now moved from marginal ethnic regions to central city areas (Zhang 2003).

Ethnicity is not only a cultural but also a political construct. According to this view, it should be possible to reshape ethnic distinctions by political demand, even though assimilation among ethnicity is inevitable. The relationship between ethnicity and nationalism is dynamic, and both can be evoked by the same factors. Thus, ethnic conflict certainly will not disappear, no matter what efforts are made to address issues of individual equality or ethnic demands.

Since ethnic identifications and the relationships between 'ethnicity', 'nationality', and 'personal identity' are being continually renegotiated, a dynamic concept of 'ethnic community' can help to explain why and how ethnic conflict occurs. China's case shows that the kinds of strategy (whether conflict or negotiation) an ethnicity might choose is at least partly determined by individuals' knowledge about control of territory, about their own group's historical and contemporary relationship with other groups, and about the possibilities that exist for reforming their communities. Ethnicity can therefore be understood as a political resource which leads and supports the idea that the relationships between ethnic groups must continually form and reform, in term of 'ethnicifying'. By keeping these points in mind we may be able to better understand why and how ethnic conflicts begin or are resolved by comparing different cases in the world.

REFERENCES

Attané, Isabelle/Courbage, Youssef (2000): "Transitional Stages and Identity Boundaries: The Case of Ethnic Minorities in China." In: Population and Environment 21/3, pp. 257–280.
Banton, Michael (1983): Ethnic and Racial Competition, Cambridge: Cambridge University Press.
Brubaker, Roger (2002): "Ethnicity without groups." In: European Journal of Sociology 43/2, pp 163–189.
Calhoun, Craig. (1993): "Nationalism and Ethnicity." In: Annual Review of Sociology 19, pp. 211–239.

Chang, Bao (2013): "Review to China's Minority Policy and Mizu Theory (shehui zhuanxing yu fansi zhongde zhongguo minzu zhengce yu minzu lilun)." In: Journal of Minzu University of China (zhongyang minzu daxue xuebao) 40/3, Beijing: Minzu University Press.

Cliff, Thomas (2012): "The Partnership of Stability in Xinjiang: State–Society Interactions Following the July 2009 Unrest." In: The China Journal 68, pp. 79–105.

Dreyer Teufel, June (1977): "Ethnic Relations in China." In: Annals of the American Academy of Political and Social Science 433, pp. 100–111.

Donham, Donald (2011): Violence in a Time of Liberation: Murder and Ethnicity at a South African Gold Mine 1994, Durham: Duke University Press.

Eriksen, T.H. (2001): "Ethnic identity, national identity and intergroup conflict: The significance of personal experiences." In: Ashmore/Jussim/Wilder (eds.): Social identity, intergroup conflict, and conflict reduction, Oxford: Oxford University Press, pp. 42–70.

Fei, Xiao Tong (1980): "Questions of Ethnicities Distinguish in China." In: China Social Science 1, pp. 147–162.

Giddens, Anthony (1985): A Contemporary Critique of Historical Materialism The Nation-state and Violence, Vol.2, Cambrige: Polity Press.

Gladney, Dru C. (1994): "Representing Nationality in China: Refiguring Majority/ Minority Identities." In: The Journal of Asian Studies, 53/1, pp. 92–123.

Gustafsson, Björn/Li, Shi (2003): "The Ethnic Minority-Majority Income Gap in Rural China during Transition." In: Economic Development and Cultural Change 51/4, pp. 805–822.

Harrell, Stevan (1990): "Ethnicity, Local Interests, and the State: Yi Communities in Southwest China." In: Comparative Studies in Society and History 32/3, pp. 515–548.

Hannum, Emily/Yu, Xie (1998): "Ethnic Stratification in Northwest China: Occupational Differences between Han Chinese and National Minorities in Xinjiang, 1982-1990." In: Demography 35/3, pp. 323–333.

Hechter, Michael (1987): Principles of Group Solidarity, Berkeley: University of California Press.

Ho, Angang/Ho, Lianhe (2011): "The Second Generation minority Policy: To facilitate the assimilation and common Prosperity of all Nationalities." (Dierdai minzu zhengce: cujin minzu jiaorong he fanrong yiti 第二代民族政策：促进民族交融一体和繁荣一体) In: Journal of Xinjiang Normal University (Social Sciences) 32/5.

Karmel, Solomon M. (1995): "Ethnic Tension and the Struggle for Order: China's Policies in Tibet." In: Pacific Affairs 68/4, pp. 485–508.

Kymlicka, Will (1995): Multicultural Citizenship: A Liberal Theory of Minority Rights, Oxford: Oxford University Press.

Li, Zhigang/Du, Fan (2012): "A Study on Foreign Ethnic Community in China: A case of "chocolate city" of Guangzhou (zhongguo de waiguo "zuyi jingjiqu" yanjiu-guangzhou "qiaokeli cheng" de shizheng yanjiu)." In: Human Geography (renwen dili), 6.

McDonald, Jason J. (2007): American Ethnic History: Themes and Perspectives, Edinburgh: Edinburgh University Press.

Zhang, Xiaowei (2003): "Ethnic Difference in Neighboring Behavior in Urban China." In: Sociological Focus 36/3, pp. 197–218.

Zhou, Min (1992): Chinatown: The Socioeconomic Potential of an Urban Enclave, Philadelphia: Temple University Press.

Ethnicity as a political resource
across different historical periods

Introduction: Ethnicity as a political resource across different historical periods

SARAH ALBIEZ-WIECK

UNIVERSAL OR HISTORICALLY SPECIFIC?

Is ethnicity a universal social categorization that has existed since the beginning of humankind or is it historically contingent, with its beginnings in a specific historical period? Scholars from various disciplines have answered this question quite differently, as do the contributors to this volume. Generally speaking, we can distinguish three groups of arguments: those in the first group assume that ethnicity is a human universal which has always existed (e.g. Antweiler 2009; also this volume; Gat/Yakobson 2013) or at least has done so in a couple of pre-modern societies; those in the second group associate the emergence of ethnicity and/or race with European colonialism (e.g. Quijano 2000; Thomson 2007); while the third group of arguments state that ethnicity is entirely modern (e.g. Hannaford 1996), or at least did not exist before the formation of nation states (e.g. Klinger 2008; Müller/Zifonun 2010). Of course, there also exist intermediate positions, like that of Wimmer (2010: 120), who is convinced that pre-modern territorial states were also interested in ethnic boundaries, but that this interest became much stronger with the formation of the nation states; or that of Takezawa (2005; also this volume) who distinguishes between several dimensions to which she assigns different historical starting points – although she speaks of race rather than of ethnicity. Dealing with colonial authorities and with the state in general is often mentioned as fostering ethnogenesis (e.g. Stark and Chance 2008), and the importance of European overseas expansion and the colonial encounter(s) are often mentioned as an important turning point in the history of ethnicity. The first guiding question for this chapter, therefore, is whether we can conceive of ethnicity without reference to the European expansion. The second question is twofold and more specific, and concerns the general topic of this volume: Has ethnicity been employed as a political resource in other, especially pre-modern, historical periods? If so, when and where did this apply?

The time period covered by the contributions in this chapter ranges from early medieval times (Pohl) to the present (Sáez-Arance) and includes both specific case studies – which may address rather short- (Manke) or medium-range periods (O'Toole) or span several centuries (Sáez-Arance, Pohl) – and more theoretically oriented texts (Gabbert).

As seems natural, most answers in this chapter are offered by historians, but there is also one contribution from an anthropologist (Gabbert), who is nevertheless quite concerned with historical periods reaching far back into time. Also, there is a strong predominance of scholars working on Latin America. On the one hand, this has to do with the Forum's internal structure and the unpredictable changes the elaboration of an edited volume often suffers. On the other hand, Latin America seems to be an especially fertile ground in which to seek answers to the guiding questions of this chapter. The whole region was subject to European – mainly Iberian – colonialism from the sixteenth to the 19th century, in the process encompassing different steps in the modernization of the Western world and the emergence of the idea of the nation state. Furthermore, we can talk about colonialism in some parts of the subcontinent even in pre-Hispanic times, as carried out by the Inca, Mexica and Tarascans, among others. The reference to pre-Hispanic times as well as to the colonial experience is an important topic in the discourse of many indigenous movements and NGOs today, which use the colonial oppression as a central argument in their struggle for political rights. They argue that the Europeans in the 16th century encountered 'native inhabitants', the indigenous people, whose ethnic identity has persisted in its original form to this day (cp. e.g. CONAIE 2011; *Pueblos y Organizaciones Indígenas del Continente de Abya Yala* 2005). In this they are supported by many scholars, generally implicitly. Many others argue that the Europeans brought the idea of ethnicity, which they more often call race, to the Americas, but also point to the continuous transformation of ethnic identities. It therefore seems especially interesting to look into European conceptions of ethnicity or similar categorizations before the European expansion took place, as Pohl does in this chapter. He also mentions the fact that in European historiography the concept of ethnicity has been linked to (proto-) national narratives since the late 18th century.

Although not addressed by a specific contribution in this chapter, experiences from other parts of the world should also be taken into account when delving into the history of ethnicity. Two types of comparison seem particularly enlightening: On the one hand the one with the European colonial expansion into Africa which was mainly considerably later than in the American case, and may be referred to as the 'classic' period of imperialism which lasted from the 1880s to the First World War (Osterhammel/Jansen [1995] 2012: 26–28). Parallels may be found in the colonialism that took place in parts of Asia and Australia, which, like that in Africa, was mainly carried out by the non-Iberian states. As to Africa, according to many scholars, European colonialism there was instrumental in the creation of ethnic groups and boundaries which did not exist previously (cp. e.g.Ranger 1981; Lentz 2001), although some acknowledge the existence of ethnic markers before this period, as does Marx (2003) for the centralized kingdoms in the Transvaal region of South Africa in the beginning of the 19th century. Contributions on the African perspective in this volume are offered by Feyissa, Pelican, and Widlok. On the other hand, the comparison with non-Western forms of colonization in Asia, such as the case of imperial Japan, as studied by Takezawa in this volume, can offer interesting insights, as can the contributions on post-colonial states in Asia (Holst on Malaysia, Büschges on Nepal among others) or on those who were never (fully) colonialized and/or colonialized others (Li Xi Yuan on China).

So, can the concept of ethnicity primarily be traced back to European colonial expansion, or might we also envisage it against the background of other empires in history or other cycles of global development? And since when has ethnicity been employed as a political resource?

DEFINITIONS SHAPE ANSWERS AND TERMINOLOGIES

Surprisingly, the answers in this and other chapters of this book (e.g. Holst, Antweiler) as well as in other works do not seem to depend so much on the period or region studied as on the respective definition of ethnicity. Or, to put it more provocatively: It seems possible to find arguments for one's own position in nearly every region and period, and thereby to interpret the available evidence in favour of one's reasoning. The definitions used by the scholars are generally closely intertwined with their respective academic backgrounds, as is the terminology employed, the usage of which is to be distinguished as being either emic or etic. The authors are aware of the importance of their definitions and the terminology employed. The most visible and discussed difference in terminology concerns the opposition between *ethnicity* and *race*. The positions in this chapter reflect the most common viewpoints in the academic and socio-political world.

The German (and Austrian) scholars in this section (Gabbert, Pohl, Manke) employ only the term 'ethnicity', which reflects to some degree the experience of the Holocaust, after which the term 'race' has for the most part been banned from the German public and scientific discourse and, if used at all, is generally placed in quotation marks. This tendency has been strongly supported by the several statements on race by the UN starting in 1950, which favour the employment of the term 'ethnicity' instead (Unesco 1969). Scholars from the US, like O'Toole, however, don't have such reservations about using the term 'race', which in their country is still used widely in census data and plays an important (historical) role in political struggles. But even regarding each of these terms separately, definitions and answers to the guiding questions may still be quite different in different cases.

Wolfgang Gabbert, whose text has a rather theoretical focus and spans an especially long period of time and a broad variety of regions, defines ethnicity as "a phenomenon of social differentiation in which actors use cultural or phenotypical markers or symbols to distinguish themselves from others. It is a method of classifying people into categories which include individuals of both sexes and all age groups using (socially constructed) origin as its primary reference." He uses 'ethnicity' as a strictly etic term and highlights that ethnic groups are "imagined communities" not congruent with cultures, kin, or residential groups. He would not speak of ethnic groups existing in pre-Hispanic Mesoamerica, and comes to the conclusion that ethnic groups are not universal forms of social categorization. He believes, however, that ethnicity as a form of social categorization existed before the European expansion and outside of Europe, but that it was much boosted by European colonialism and the rise of the nation state.

Pohl's temporal focus on the 'migration period' after the fall of the Roman Empire lies mainly prior to Gabbert's, but in contrast to the latter, Pohl prefers the employment of the term 'ethnicity'. He is in favor of historicizing the term and is against cultural definitions, but his definition is wider and more operational, and encompasses both emic and etic conceptions. He sees ethnicity as "a principle of distinction between social groupings that can be more or less salient or relevant according to the context", taking into account external as well as internal ascriptions, and also denotes biological frames of reference in the historical terms. In his opinion, it makes sense to apply the concept of ethnicity to many, but not to all pre-modern societies. Interestingly, he finds important parallels between the politics of the Roman Empire toward alleged ethnic groups and the politics employed by later European colonial empires.

One of these European empires, that of Spain, or more specifically of the Peruvian Viceroyalty, is discussed by O'Toole. According to her, this fully fledged colonial system employed racial discourse which developed out of Iberian ideas of 'blood purity' linked to religion and social categorizations. These racial categorizations were employed by colonial authorities as well as by their subjects. She prefers to use 'race' rather than 'ethnicity' because in her point of view the former term draws attention to "the ways that situations became fixed and [to] their material implications", which she calls "the work of race". But she is of the opinion that ethnicity was also an identity present in colonial Latin America, which mainly differentiated the different racial groups internally through cultural characteristics. Cultural characteristics were also part of the racial ascriptions, which furthermore included concerns with descent, blood and physical characteristics – which, however, were not fixed as they are in modern definitions of race. Though not directly answering the first guiding questions, she hints at the intensification of racial categorizations by the Spanish colonialism and combines emic and etic usages of the term 'race'. When comparing her work to those of other scholars on colonial Latin America, it seems striking that those working on Afrodescendants seem to favour the term 'race' over 'ethnicity'.

Sáez-Arance points in his contribution to the fact that the European colonial enterprises can be seen as a continuation of domestic state-building processes. They, as well as the later Latin American national historiographies, emphasized a presumed evolutionary gap between 'highly developed civilizations' and 'primitive peoples', and alluded to 'pre-conceptions' of ethnicity as deeply rooted in European culture, thereby connecting to ideas about European medieval categorizations such as 'Germans', 'Visigoths' and 'Romans', as studied by Pohl, which were sometimes transferred to Latin America. As Sáez-Arance shows how in current national Chilean historiography and also in the wider society as reflected in some newspapers, assumptions of superiority about the Mapuche still linger.

Cuba was one of the last colonies to gain independence from Spain, only to be subsequently heavily dominated by the US – a domination which ended with the Cuban revolution of 1959. Manke's article addresses this period, particularly focusing on the ethnically marked mobilization of Chinese Cubans in the context of a situation in which the revolutionary discourse tended towards a de-emphasizing of ethnic boundaries.

Another point which distinguishes the different contributions is the importance given to historical and local or emic terminology,[1] as well as to their interdependence with other types of social categorizations.

While Gabbert argues strongly for the historical contingency of terms and for taking into account other types of social categorizations, especially when it comes to premodern periods; Pohl thinks that emic medieval terms such as *ethnē, gentes,* or *nationes* can correctly be described as referring to ethnic groups. O'Toole, though having favoured the colonial term *casta* in her earlier work, now argues strongly for the employment of 'race' instead; she also highlights important intersectionalities with gender and class/labour issues. Similarly to Gabbert, Sáez-Arance makes a strong case for emphasizing the concrete temporal and regional contexts of every term, and for deconstructing myths of homogenous identity and criticizing organic and biological metaphors. As Manke studies the history of the 20th century, he has the advantage of being able to access emic categorisations directly via interviews.

ETHNICITY AS A POLITICAL RESOURCE

Another dimension along which to compare the contributions in this section is to ask what relevance they attribute to the employment of ethnicity as a political resource, and how this is realized in the cases studied by them. Answering this question may involve two or even three aspects: On the one hand it is possible to look at how the actors in each case historically used social categorizations to achieve political means. On the other hand, it is also possible to to ask how discourses about history are exploited in political debates much later, even today. Lastly, we can also examine the positioning of the scholar.

The first line of enquiry is especially clear in the case study offered by Manke, which researches the agency of the Chinese Cubans defending the revolution and asks whether they employed their ethnic identity as a political resource, researching this aspect on several interacting levels. The article by Pohl aims in a similar direction. Dependent on the sources available, imperial politics are the easiest to analyze, but the agency of elite groups and some ethnic minorities can also be addressed. According to Pohl, the actions such actors take aim at different ends: the reinforcement of ethnic cleavages; the improvements

---

[1] Examples of this can be found in the other chapters of this book, e.g. in Li Xi Yuan's contribution, which elaborates on the Chinese term *minzu*, sometimes translated as 'nationality' and sometimes as 'ethnic group'.

of some groups' status and prerogatives; or the legitimization for ruling – in all such cases there is a definite preeminence on ethnic politics from above. Pohl also addresses the second strand mentioned above, noting that the Early Middle Ages have been regarded as the period of origin of most European nations – but he points out that this process was not as linear and clearly defined as is often presented, and that it included many mythical aspects exploited for political ends. He only sees an intermittent continuity in what he calls the "model of ethnic rule". Gabbert, too, addresses this hypothesis of some ethnic groups being the 'forerunners' of modern nations, but is even harsher in his criticism towards its posterior constructedness than Pohl. As already mentioned, Sáez-Arance bridges back to conceptions of the 'Other' fostered by European overseas colonialism, which framed mutual cultural perceptions and justified the quality of the response of the colonial power. The 'evoking power' of these 'ethnic' categories, in his point of view, were inherited and amplified by the modern nations and legitimized the rule of their elites. He also argues in favor of a reflection of the positioning of the scholar *vis-à-vis* current political debates; something which Gabbert tries to stay out by restricting himself to an analysis of the scientific realm. O'Toole is the author who most clearly positions herself as a scholar by making clear that she consciously chooses the term 'race' over *casta, calidad* or 'ethnicity' to highlight the impact of slavery, colonial exclusion and discrimination, the effects of which can still be felt today.

To a certain point, this can be connected to the current debate about indigeneity which has been linked to European (settler) colonialism (De la Cadena 2007: 203), although Merlan has convincingly argued that it is mainly a product of the 'postcolony' in an "effort to move away from colonial relations" (2009:319).

In every single strand mentioned, one issue that shapes social categorizations, among them ethnicity, is more or less visibly present: power relations. They are detectable in the imperial ascriptions, and often transferred to legal categorizations, in the Roman Empire and Early Medieval kingdoms as well as in prehispanic and Hispanic colonial Latin America. They are also traceable in the relationships between settlers of Northern and Central European descent, between the Mapuche and the Chilean state, and between the Chinese militia and the leaders of the Cuban revolution. The authors of this volume describe various elites' strategies of domination, as well as those employed by the subordinated in reaction.

METHODOLOGY

Texts are the principal sources the authors in this chapter use to investigate ethnicity as a political resource. For those scholars researching periods stretching far back – mainly Gabbert and Pohl – archaeological remains would be an alternative source. However, archaeological data present a problem in that they do not tell us anything about group consciousness, and ethnic boundaries are not necessarily marked by extant remains of material culture (Albiez-Wieck 2013). Or, as Quilter (2010: 228–29) puts it, the "one-to-one correspondence of an archaeological assemblage with an ethnic or cultural group" has already been undermined by many studies. Gabbert shares my skepticism about making inferences about ethnicity on the basis of archaeological data. He is even cautious about contemporary texts about distant periods such as pre-Hispanic Mesoamerica or the European Middle Ages, since they reflect mainly elite points of view. In this regard, Pohl is less prejudiced, and seems to judge it to be possible in principle to gain insights based on the richness of the archaeological record, but is quite skeptical regarding the possibilities offered by data from the early medieval period.

All authors agree on the importance on focusing of the precise meaning and context of the terminology employed in the sources, since the historical meaning might differ from that valid today. Manke is the only author who draws on oral history for his case study, which enables him to gather subjective meanings and identifications more easily.

THE CONTRIBUTIONS

Many aspects of the contributions in this chapter have already been mentioned, but I want to very briefly sum up their content to facilitate the readers' orientation throughout the chapter.

The article by *Wolfgang Gabbert* has a rather theoretical focus, and elaborates widely on conceptualisations and dimensions of ethnicity. To support his argument that probably "ethnicity was rarely present before the 17th or 18th century AD or cannot be proven due to the lack of data", he draws on an ample variety of examples, ranging from Ancient Greece to that of present-day Tukanoans in the Northwest Amazon. He lingers a bit longer on the case study of pre-Hispanic central Mesoamerica.

Walter Pohl's argumentation is in many aspects contrary to Gabbert's. His temporal and regional focus is on Late Antiquity and the Early Middle Ages, especially the 5th and 6th centuries AD, where he detects the emergence of an ethnic rule. He argues that discourses of ethnicity and political strategies highly influenced later perceptions of identity and otherness.

Rachel Sarah O'Toole presents the strategies adopted by people of color in a 17th-century Peruvian city to maintain and improve their status, making delicate distinctions when employing colonial terminology in the legal record. These examples are used to demonstrate how race was constructed in colonial Latin America on multiple axes.

Antonio Sáez-Arance's case study is about the current and historical conflicts in southern Chile and the present-day historiographic and political debates about the role of the Mapuche activists and the violent so-called 'pacification of the *Araucanía*' in the 19th century. He points to the homogenizing and often racist lines of argument used by historians as well as journalists.

Compared to most of the other contributions, *Albert Manke's* text analyses a rather short period of time, framed by the larger scope of Chinese migration to Cuba since the early 20th century. By addressing the period of the early Cuban revolution, he relates the situation of the members of the 'Popular Chinese Militia' in this new setting. However, by drawing on oral history, among other sources, he shows the uniqueness of the ethnicization of this political conflict.

REFERENCES

Albiez-Wieck, Sarah (2013): "Social categorisations in the Tarascan State: Debates about the existence of Ethnicity in Prehispanic West Mexico." In: Daniela Célleri/Tobias Schwarz/Bea Wittger (eds.), Interdependencies of social categorizations, Ethnicity, Citizenship and Belonging in Latin America 2, Frankfurt a.M/Madrid: Vervuert/Iberoamericana, pp. 265–288.

Antweiler, Christoph (2009): Was ist den Menschen gemeinsam? Über Kultur und Kulturen, Darmstadt: Wissenschaftliche Buchgesellschaft.

CONAIE (Confederación de Nacionalidades Indígenas del Ecuador) (2011): Proyecto Político de la CONAIE: Declaración Política, December 6, 2011 (http://www.conaie.org/images/stories/pdfs/proyecto%20poltico%20de%20la%20conaie.pdf).

De la Cadena, M. (ed.) (2007): Formaciones de indianidad: Articulaciones raciales, mestizaje y nación en América Latina, Colombia: Envión.

Gat, Azar/Yakobson Alexander (2013): Nations: The long history and deep roots of political ethnicity and nationalism, Cambridge: Cambridge University Press.

Hannaford, Ivan (1996): Race: The history of an idea in the West, Washington D. C.: Woodrow Wilson Center Press/John Hopkins University Press.
Klinger, Cornelia (2008): "Überkreuzende Identitäten – Ineinandergreifende Strukturen: Plädoyer für einen Kurswechsel in der Intersektionalitätsdebatte." In: Cornelia Klinger/Gudrun Axeli Knapp (eds.), ÜberKreuzungen: Fremdheit, Ungleichheit, Differenz, Forum Frauen- und Geschlechterforschung 23, Münster: Westfälisches Dampfboot, pp. 38–67.
Lentz, Carola (2001): "Ethnizität in Afrika: Konzepte, Kontroversen, Praktiken." In: Ethnoscripts 3/1, pp. 67–82.
Marx, Christoph (2003): "Grenzfälle. Zur Geschichte und Potential des Frontierbegriffs." In: Saeculum (ed.), Jahrbuch für Universalgeschichte 54, pp. 123–43.
Merlan, Francesca (2009): "Indigeneity: Global and Local." In: Current Anthropology 50/3, pp. 303–33, November 25, 2014 (http://archanth.anu.edu.au/sites/default/files/documents/ merlan_capaper.pdf).
Müller, Marion/Zifonun Darius. (2010): "Wissenssoziologische Perspektiven auf ethnische Differenzierung und Migration: Eine Einführung." In: Marion Müller/Darius Zifonun (eds.), Ethnowissen: Soziologische Beiträge zu ethnischer Differenzierung und Migration, Wiesbaden: VS Verlag für Sozialwissenschaften (GWV), pp. 9–32.
Osterhammel, Jürgen/Jansen Jan C. (2012 [1995]): Kolonialismus: Geschichte – Formen – Folgen. 7., vollst. überarb. und aktual. Aufl., München: Beck.
Pueblos y Organizaciones Indígenas del Continente de Abya Yala (2005): "Declaración de la Cumbre Continental de Pueblos y Organizaciones Indigenas, Territorio Mapuche, Mar Del Plata, Argentina," del 02 al 04 de noviembre de 2005, December 13, 2011 (http://www.cumbrecontinental indigena.org/declaracion.php).
Quijano, Anibal (2000): "Coloniality of Power, Eurocentrism and Latin America." In: Nepantla: Views from South 1/3, pp. 533–580.
Quilter, Jeffrey (2010): "Moche: Archaeology, Ethnicity, Identity." In: Bulletin de l'Institut Français d'Etudes Andines 39/2, pp. 225–241.
Ranger, Terence (1981): "Kolonialismus in Ost- und Zentralafrika: Von der traditionellen zur traditionalen Gesellschaft – Einsprüche und Widersprüche." In: Jan-Heeren Grevemeyer (ed.), Traditionale Gesellschaften und europäischer Kolonialismus, Frankfurt a.M.: Syndikat, pp. 16–46.
Stark, Barbara L./Chance John K. (2008): "Diachronic and Multidisciplinary Perspectives on Mesoamerican Ethnicity." In: Frances F. Berdan (ed.), Ethnic identity in Nahua Mesoamerica: The view from archaeology, art

history, ethnohistory, and contemporary ethnography, Salt Lake City: University of Utah Press, pp. 1–37.

Takezawa, Yasuko I. (2005): "Transcending the Western Paradigm of the Idea of Race." In: The Japanese Journal of American Studies 16, pp. 5–30, October 6, 2014 (http://sv121.wadax.ne.jp/~jaas-gr-jp/jjas/PDF/2005/No.16-005.pdf).

Thomson, Sinclair (2007): "¿Hubo raza en Latinoamérica colonial? Percepciones indígenas de la identidad colectiva en los Andes insurgents." In: Marisol De la Cadena (ed.), Formaciones de indianidad: Articulaciones raciales, mestizaje y nación en América Latina, Colombia: Envión, pp. 55–81.

Unesco (1969): "Four statements on the race question. " Paris, November 25, 2014 (http://unesdoc.unesco.org/images/0012/001229/122962eo.pdf).

Wimmer, Andreas (2010): "Ethnische Grenzziehungen: Eine prozessorientierte Mehrebenentheorie." In: Marion Müller/Darius Zifonun (eds.), Ethnowissen: Soziologische Beiträge zu ethnischer Differenzierung und Migration,, Wiesbaden: VS Verlag für Sozialwissenschaften (GWV), pp. 99–152.

Ethnicity in history

WOLFGANG GABBERT

INTRODUCTION

Today, most people – academics and non-academics alike – accept the idea that mankind has always been differentiated into groups that share descent and culture, and are separated from other such groups by clear boundaries. These groupings have been referred to by various terms, such as 'peoples', 'tribes', 'ethnic groups/ethnies', or 'nations', and belonging to any of these collectivities has usually been referred to in terms of ethnicity. Ethnic communities are seen by many scholars as ubiquitous forms of social organization existing both in the past and the present all over the world (e.g. Jenkins 1997: 46–47, 74, 77; Eriksen 2002: 11; Gat 2013: 27–43). For example, Anthony D. Smith, one of the leading scholars of nationalism and ethnicity, suggests a strong continuity between many modern nations and premodern ethnic communities (ethnies) starting with the development of sedentary agriculturalists in the neolithic revolution in the Near East. Thus, he characterizes the ancient Egyptians and Sumerians, the classical Greeks and medieval Normans as ethnic communities ('ethnies') (Smith 1991: 28–30, 37–51; cp. also Gat 2013: 17, 19, 23, 71–110, 380). In his view, the 'ethnic revival' of the last decades is considered as "the recent phase of a long cycle of ethnic emergence and decline, which has been going on since the dawn of recorded history" (Smith 1981: 85–86; cp. also 1991: 39–43, 52; Gat 2013: 42). Consequently, ethnicity has been used as a comparative concept and employed for the analysis of past and present societies ranging from several millennia B.C. up until today. However, these views have come under attack by scholars who consider the phenomena referred to by the term 'ethnicity' as historically specific notions of difference that only emerged as a consequence of the generalization of the nation-state model since the late 18th century.[1] Richard Fardon, for example, bluntly states that "there is no universal ethnic phenomenon", and argues that the "application of a concept of universal ethnicity is historical and obfuscates the course of historical change" (1987: 175).

Since any reflection on the presence or absence of ethnicity in the past presupposes a clarification of what one is talking about, I will first discuss the concept of ethnicity and argue for the need to differentiate among its several dimensions. Then, the question of whether ethnicity is a modern phenomenon will be addressed. In the final section, the notions of difference in precolonial Central Mexico will be sketched out to illustrate some of the issues raised in the more conceptual parts of the text.

ETHNICITY – A MUDDLED CONCEPT

The discussions about ethnicity are complicated by the diversity of usages of the term and its derivatives in recent academic discourse. Many authors employ 'ethnic group' merely to describe forms of socio-cultural differentiation *within* existing states (e.g. Fenton 2003: 52). Others consider the *ethnie* or ethnic group to be a forerunner of the nation, or the nation as a special variant of the *ethnie*, with nation characterized by its ideological reference to a bygone, existing or desired state (e.g. Gellner 1983; Elwert 1989; Nash 1989; Smith 1991; Jenkins 1997; Eriksen 2002; Gat 2013). Authors like Francis (1947), Rothschild (1981) or Brass (1991) do not make a systematic distinction between *ethnie* and nation, but instead consider the terms to be largely synonymous. Francis (1947: 397, 400), for example, employs 'ethnic group' to denote a minority within a state,

---

1   Rothschild (1981: 11–13), Fardon (1987: 177–178), Nash (1989: 1, 14, 124, 127), and Brass (1991: 8) relate the emergence of ethnicity to changes in the foundations of political legitimacy in state societies. Political domination in Europe and in other parts of the world, at least up to the 17th century, was legitimized 'from above' by referring to, among other things, divine right, noble descent, inter-dynastic marriage, or conquest. Only later did the idea that legitimacy was to be derived 'from below' and emanate from the will and consent of the ruled become widespread. Beyond this, the sovereign 'people' were thought to be unique, and united by a common history and culture. As Manning Nash argues: "Those people who were not politically dominant in the nation-state and who still had significant cultural markers of difference and sufficient social cleavages from the dominant political majority were 'ethnic' groups" (1989: 2).

e.g., French Canadians in Canada, as well as to refer to the French in France or the Irish in Ireland.

The conceptual differences sketched above notwithstanding, most scholars would probably agree that the term 'ethnicity' should be employed for a subclass of the 'we/they' distinctions people make. Thus, the question arises as to what features make such distinctions 'ethnic'? The debate about ethnicity has been considerably hindered not only by the diversity of usages but also by a vague and imprecise utilization of the term. Max Weber ([1922] 1980: 235–240) stressed that there was no one-to-one relationship between cultural differences and ethnicity. This insight was popularized by Fredrik Barth (1969) several decades later. However, in the older as well as in some of the more recent scholarship, cultural differences are equated with ethnicity.[2] The problem is particularly apparent in archaeological studies that have to rely entirely on material remains to reconstruct the past. Beyond this, all kinds of social groups and categories are referred to as 'ethnic' in the literature. Two examples will illustrate the problem:

In an otherwise sound article, Patrick Geary analyses supposedly 'ethnic' identities in Europe's Early Middle Ages such as 'Franci', 'Alamanni', or 'Burgundiones'. However, as he makes clear, these terms appear in the sources mostly in relation to kings or warriors. "The *gens Francorum* was the *exercitus Francorum*, led by its king or its *duces*. [...] Membership in the *gens Francorum* or *Burgundionum* in the sense of the exercitus did not depend on shared cultural, linguistic, or legal background" (Geary 1983: 22). Anthony Smith considers certain polities in antiquity and the Middle Ages as 'ethnic states' – that is, "state[s] dominated by a ruling class drawn from a particular *ethnie* which forms the majority of the state's population". He mentions ancient Egypt "at certain points in history" and Russia "before it acquired its empire", as examples (Smith 1991: 38–39, 44–51, 54–59).[3] However, Geary as well as Smith both subsume under the rubric 'ethnic' political collectivities constituted through vassalage. As such, they are not held together by horizontal bonds among the members of the collectivity, but through their individual relationship to the king or chief. Neither cultural sameness nor common descent among leaders and followers, or elite and masses, are implied.

Employing the concept of ethnicity in such a broad way deprives us of the possibility of distinguishing among quite different bases for categorization and social cohesion. It seems more fertile to differentiate ethnicity from other

---

2   Cp., for example, McInerney (2001: 52), for the discussion on ancient Greece. Cp. Gat (2013: 21–22, 24, 30–33, 49, 382) for a recent example.
3   Gat (2013: 85) even calls ancient Egypt the first 'national state'.

principles of social organization such as cohabitation (common residence), kinship, political loyalty, dynastic ties or religious cult membership, which often go beyond or crosscut linguistic or cultural boundaries. Thus, 'ethnicity' is understood here as referring to a phenomenon of social differentiation in which actors use cultural or phenotypic markers or symbols to distinguish themselves from others. It is a method of classifying people into categories which include individuals of both sexes and all age groups using (socially constructed) origin as its primary reference (Gabbert 2006: 90). The term 'ethnic' should therefore be reserved for social groups or categories that are founded on the idea of common descent, usually based on alleged cultural or phenotypic similarities. Such collectivities should integrate several families and kin groups (to distinguish ethnicity from kinship) (cp. Elwert 1989: 33), and integrate several residential groups (to distinguish ethnicity from cohabitation). While kinship has a gradual and segmentary logic – i.e. you can have closer or more remote kin – ethnicity implies a binary logic – you are either a member of the group or you are not. In this view, ethnicity refers to a particular form of social cohesion in groups that cannot be integrated merely by direct social, economic, or kin relationships. They are therefore, like nations, "imagined communities" (Anderson 1991: 6–7) because they are larger than face-to-face groups and lack the latters' particular means of enforcing compliance with social norms among their members (Elwert 1989: 32).

DIMENSIONS OF ETHNICITY

Ethnicity can be a means of reducing social complexity and of orienting interpersonal behavior (categorization) or a basis for social cohesion (the production of loyalty and community). In addition to the excessively loose usage of the term 'ethnic', tendencies to conflate different levels of analysis (social categorization, individual identification/identity, the integration of groups) have also complicated the discussion.[4] It is, however, of fundamental importance for any consideration of the concept's pertinence for more remote historical periods in general, and for its potential as a political resource in particular, to

---

4 A differentiation between the various levels of the phenomenon is not only conspicuously absent in most of the literature on preconquest Mesoamerica (cp. for example Smith 2003; Berdan 2008) but also in the otherwise sophisticated debate on ethnicity in ancient Greece. Cp. for example Hall (1995; 2005) and the Review Feature in the Cambridge Archaeological Journal (1998).

differentiate between these dimensions. Ethnic *categories*, the *groups* or organizations based on such categories, and the *individuals* using these categories in daily interaction must be kept separate, analytically. This analytical distinction allows for the tackling of a feature of ethnicity that Ronald Cohen addresses as its "nesting quality" (1978: 387), meaning that ethnic distinctions between 'us' and 'them' can exist alternately or simultaneously on various levels, and are actualized in certain interactions depending on those involved:

"[E]thnicity is a historically derived lumping of sets of diacritics at varying distances outward from the person, so that each of these lumpings acts as a potential boundary or nameable grouping that can be identified or referred to in ethnic terms, given the proper conditions. [...] the division into an exclusive group is always done in relation to significant others whose exclusion at any particular level or scale creates the we/they dichotomy" (1978: 387).

In a similar vein Eriksen argues: "For ethnicity to come about, the groups must have a minimum of contact with each other, and they must entertain ideas of each other as being culturally different from themselves. [...] ethnicity is essentially an aspect of a relationship, not a property of a group" (2002: 12).[5] Two caveats are necessary here; first, 'group' has to be understood in the broad sense as referring to any aggregate of people; and second, the ideas all 'groups' maintain of themselves and of others do not necessarily chime with one another.

An example of the mismatch between categorization by outsiders and self-identification is provided by the situation in colonial Latin America, where the Spaniards collectively referred to the native people as Indians (*indios*). This, however, ignored linguistic and cultural differences as well as political cleavages and identifications within the native population. Beyond this, it did not establish a common identification among indigenous people. Indigenous colonial sources rarely employed the term *indio*, and more localized units, such as the city-state in Central Mexico or the community in Yucatán, remained the predominant reference for social identification beyond the family and kin (Lockhart 1993: 13; Restall 1997: 15–19; Terraciano 2001: 348; Gabbert 2004: 26–36).

---

5   However, this view disregards the fact that, in addition to categorization, certain internal social and communicative structures are necessary for community formation.

IS ETHNICITY MODERN?

That people distinguish between 'we-group' and 'they-group' (or "others-group", as Sumner ([1907] 2002: 12) put it), and that attribution of these terms is generally associated with attitudes of comradeship and hostility respectively is probably as old as mankind. However, Sumner somewhat misleadingly called "this view of things in which one's own group is the center of everything, and all others are scaled and rated with reference to it" (ibid: 13) "ethnocentrism". 'Group-centrism' would be a more adequate term, since the idea is related to any kind of collectivity, and the principles on which it is based are not specified. Ethnographic and linguistic evidence shows that even relatively small groups in history considered themselves as 'men' (in the sense of human beings) or 'real people', while others were "something else – perhaps not defined – but not real men" (ibid: 14). Ideas about the 'others-group(s)' were frequently quite general and unspecific, often lumping them into such encompassing categories as 'cannibals'. In other cases, people were referred to in relative terms. In the Philippines, for example, *Subanun* means 'upstream people', and in what is now Tanzania *Sukuma* means 'north' (Southall 1970: 36–37). In many non-stratified societies kinship is the dominant conceptual model for understanding the social world. People were either kin (by birth or adoption) or non-kin, i.e. potentially dangerous aliens. Most of these categories certainly do not meet the defining criteria for ethnic categories proposed above. Group membership depended on being a member of certain kin groups, such as clans, lineages or families (by birth or adoption). Shared culture was "neither necessary nor sufficient" (Gellner 1964: 156).

The notion of ethnicity rests on a specific combination of ideas of common descent and cultural difference. The latter is taken as an indicator for the existence of the former by actors. However, the meaning and importance of descent and cultural difference have changed dramatically in the course of time, varying with social complexity and organization. As Gellner argued, for most of human history political units were "[s]mall tribal or village units; city states; feudal segments loosely associated with each other or higher authority; dynastic empires; the loose moral communities of a shared religion" (ibid: 152; cp. also Anderson 1991: 9–22). Political and cultural units rarely coincided, and "there is nothing to indicate that men have found this divergence either inconvenient or unnatural" (Gellner 1964: 152). For a feudal system, for example, there was no need for lord and peasant to speak the same language or to share a similar culture:

> "In a highly structured society, culture is not indispensable. Where relationships are fairly well-known (because the community is small, and because the types of relationship are

small in number), shared culture is not a precondition of effective communication. In the stable repetitive relationship of lord and peasant, it matters very little whether they both speak (in the literal sense) the same language. They have long ago sized each other up: each knows what the other wants, the tricks he may get up to, the defences and countermeasures which, in the given situation, are available, and so on. [...] [In modern societies] one's relationships and encounters [...] are ephemeral, non-repetitive, and optional [...] communication, the symbols, language (in the literal or in the extended sense) that is employed become crucial. The burden of comprehension is shifted from the context, to the communication itself: when interlocutors and contexts are all unfamiliar, the message itself must become intelligible [...] and those who communicate must speak the same language." (Ibid: 154–155)

In contrast to present-day concepts, until the 18th century in Europe as well as in other world areas, stratified societies were generally based on the idea of a fundamental difference between the rulers and the ruled, from the point of view of culture and descent. Ruling dynasties were of foreign origin, or were at least considered as such.[6] African chiefs and kings frequently claimed descent from lineages of alien hunters who arrived from abroad to rule over the local agriculturalists (e.g. Mair 1962: 125–137). In Yucatán, Mexico, the aristocracy considered conqueror lineages from distant places or gods to be their forefathers prior to the Spanish conquest (Roys 1972: 33, 59, 175–176). Social communities were not constituted on the basis of cultural or phenotypical commonalities, but rested on locality, kinship, or political vassalage. Political legitimacy was not derived from a cultural or biological tie between rulers, nobles, and commoners. On the contrary, it was based on the claim to a special relationship with God, or the gods, and on the idea of noble descent. Cultural and genealogical differences between rulers and commoners were not concealed or minimized, as the modern model of ethnicity and nationalism would require, but were stressed and openly demonstrated.

Smith, however, wants to keep such situations within the conceptual realm of ethnicity by suggesting a distinction between "vertical ethnie", including both the elite and the masses, and "lateral ethnie", restricted to the elite (1991: 52–59; 2002: 713–715). This would allow the aristocracies mentioned above to be considered as ethnic communities. Such a view, however, seems to be misleading. In the European Middle Ages, for example, the elites of different polities generally did not distinguish among themselves according to cultural

---

6   Cp. for example Gellner (1964: 152–153; 1983: 1, 10–12), Rothschild (1981: 11–14), and Anderson (1991: 19–22); Brown (1973) for Brunei and Sahlins (1985: 73–103) for Polynesia.

criteria, at least if they were Christian. Cultural differences, however, played an important role within political entities:

"The medieval knight had at any rate his smattering of Latin, and stood far nearer to the 'clerk' than to the tiller of the soil who could speak only in his local tongue. During the earlier Middle Ages [...] a French knight, like a French priest, had more in common with a knight or a priest from Italy or Germany than with a French peasant." (Royal Institute of International Affairs [1939] 1966: 8-9)

Beyond this, the nobles in the different polities generally did not see themselves as belonging to an ethnic community but rather, in a segmentary fashion, as part of a network of descent lines dispersed across the Christian world. As Anderson puts it for the French nobility during the *ancien régime*:

"To the question 'Who is the Comte de X?' the normal answer would have been, not 'a member of the aristocracy', but 'the lord of X', 'the uncle of the Baronet de Y',or 'a client of the Duc de Z'." (1991: 7)

Colonial bureaucrats and most of the early anthropologists, permeated by the ideology of the nation state, both had erroneously assumed that humanity was generally organized into ('modern') nations and ('premodern') tribes. However, since the 1970s anthropologists and historians, mostly studying societies in Africa, have shown that tribes, understood as political and cultural units, were generally recent creations of colonialism and not remnants of a distant past. They have also suggested that Africans had previously been organized in terms of various social forms such as dynastic kingdoms, age grades, marriage classes, socio-occupational groups, kin groups and networks (Southall 1970: 33–44; Ranger 1981: 18–32; King 1982: 27; Fardon 1987: 179–183; Elwert 1989: 25–31). The idea of clear cultural or social boundaries itself has to be questioned in many cases. As Frake puts it for the Subanun in the Philippines in the mid-20th century:

"It is impossible to draw clearly defined linguistic or sociological boundaries between any adjacent groups. There is, rather, an overlapping network of small socio-linguistic communities, whose boundary can be defined only from the point of view of each of the minimal discrete units of which Subanun society is built [...] The maximal social group – the total society from the point of view of the individual – is non-discrete. Of Subanun social groups,only the family,the household,and the settlement are discrete." (1960:52–53)

This situation was quite typical for most non-state societies. The network of the various cultural, social and political intersecting and partly overlapping differentiations and political loyalties in which people were enmeshed was much more subtle and complicated than the simple, Eurocentric idea of clearly bounded socio-political units with their own culture – tribes or ethnic communities – would ever permit. Thus there is strong evidence to argue that ethnic groupings are not a ubiquitous form of social organization, in either non-state or stratified societies, and that European colonialism did much to generalize the concept of ethnicity around the world.

CULTURAL CATEGORIES OR HORIZONS

While I would argue that ethnic communities were rare or possibly even nonexistent before the age of nationalism, actors nevertheless recognized broad cultural categories or horizons in different times and places. Noblemen in the Middle Ages, for example, considered themselves to be part of either the Christian or the Arabic Muslim civilization. In antiquity a shared Hellenistic (elite) culture emerged in Greece. In each case a common lingua franca (Latin, Arabic, or Greek) developed. That differences in language and custom (i.e. in culture), were noted is thus obviously not a recent phenomenon. From a Greek or Roman perspective, "barbarians were all those who spoke unintelligible languages and lacked civilization, order and decency" in antiquity (Chapman/ McDonald/Tonkin 1989: 12–13).[7] As Veyne makes clear: "'Barbarian' did not designate a living species different from the Hellenes; it was a xenophobic term of opprobrium of the sort that all peoples use to speak of foreigners" (1993: 351). He aptly summarizes the situation in the Greco-Roman Empire, which was "one unit of civilization with two international languages, confronting the barbarians":

"Republican Rome had taken the culture of another people, the Greeks, as its own and had not felt that culture as foreign but as being civilization itself. Similarly, in the empire and even beyond its frontiers, Greco-Roman civilization was simply civilization: those populations were not Romanized or Hellenized as much as they were simply civilized. [...] 'Roman', 'Latin' or *peregrinus* [a foreigner from the provinces without Roman citizenship] designed a status, not an ethnic origin, and the Romans made no difference whatsoever between Roman citizens of Italian origin and those of provincial origin. Ethnic

---

7   Cp. Hall (2005) for a reconstruction of the complex history of 'Hellenism' and the concept of the 'barbarian' in Greek antiquity.

differences counted for so little that in late antiquity Romans showed no repugnance toward recruiting their generals from among the Germans." (Ibid: 365, 367, emphasis in the original)

Therefore, neither the Christian nor the Arabic or Hellenic civilizations should be regarded as ethnic communities, but rather as religious or cultural categories.

CONCEPTS OF DIFFERENCE
IN PRECOLONIAL CENTRAL MEXICO

A similar juxtaposition of civilization and barbarity can also be detected in precolonial Central Mexico, where a common cultural horizon encompassing numerous deities, Nahuatl as a kind of *lingua franca*, and many other aspects of elite culture and world view emerged in the centuries after 900 AC. About 50 city-states (sing. *altepetl* = *atl*-water, *tepetl*-hill), each comprising an urban center and its more or less extended rural hinterland, were the basic political units in the region. Neighboring *altepetl* were linked by war, trade, political alliance, interdynastic marriage, and common participation in rituals (Smith 2003: 38–39, 148–149, 151–155). The city-state rulers (sing. *tlatoani*) were elected by a council from the male relatives of the deceased sovereign. Rulership was legitimized by the elite's claim to genealogical connections with the Toltec dynasty of the semi-mythical city of Tollan or Tulan (Tula) in central Mexico, who were renowned for being particularly cultured (Carmack 1981: 3, 43–44, 62–63, 68, 149; León-Portilla 1992: 50–53; Stark/Chance 2008: 33–34). As Berdan puts it: "The separation of nobles and commoners was quite marked: nobles and commoners were judged in separate courts, and behavior expectations were different depending on one's social station. Nobles and commoners also spoke the language differently" (2008: 128).

A distinction was drawn between the local sedentary agricultural societies, comprising several million people – sometimes referred to as "Aztecs" or "Nahuas" by researchers, though they lacked an encompassing term for self-identification – and groups of nomadic hunters and gatherers to the north, collectively addressed as "chichimeca" or "teochichimeca" (Sahagún 1982: 595–602; Alva Ixtlilxóchitl 1985: 289–291, 417; Lockhart 1992: 1; Smith 2003: 3–4, 36, 38; Berdan 2008: 114).[8] Beyond this the Aztecs used broad linguistic or

---

8 Chichimeca did not refer to a specific group but in most instances denoted a nomadic hunting and gathering way of life. 'Aztec' ruling lineages claimed that their ancestors

cultural categories to refer to larger, generally not self-defined populations, such as *Otomí* or *Huastec* (Sahagún 1982: 602–610; Stark/Chance 2008: 29). Languages other than Nahuatl were considered 'barbarous tongues' (Sahagún 1982: 608; Berdan 2008: 117). Such groups were ascribed certain cultural practices, such as clothing, hairstyles etc., and physical or character traits (cp. the list in Berdan 2008: 118–120). Terms such as *Totonac, Tlahuica* or *Otomí* were also used to indicate that someone was incompetent, stupid or coarse (Sahagún 1982: 603, 608).

Most terms referring to people were related to place. "From the names of provinces, cities, and settlements are derived the nouns signifying the natives and inhabitants of the said provinces, cities, and settlements" (Carochi [1645] 2001: 219 cited in Berdan 2008: 108). Groups were also named after their leaders (Berdan 2008: 109). As Sahagún put it for the Otomí: "The term *otómitl*, which is the name of the *otomies*, was taken from their leader whose name was *Oton*, and his children and descendants, as well as the vassals he was in charge of, all were called otomites" (Sahagún 1982: 602, transl. W.G.). The fact that vassals are included into the category suggests that here a hierarchical and political relationship is indicated, and not an ethnic one of shared origin or substance.[9]

The altepetl itself was not a culturally homogenous entity. Most city-states were inhabited by members of different language groups (e.g. Otomi, Matlatzinca or Mixtec) as well as by Nahuatl-speakers claiming descent from different ancestors who had moved into central Mexico between the 12th and the 14th century AC (e.g. Mexica, Alcolhua, Chalca, Tlahuica) (Lockhart 1992: 25–26; Smith 2003: 148; Berdan 2008: 109, 116). Nahuatl sources show that the city-state was the main focus of identification even after the conquest by the Spanish. As Lockhart pointed out:

"'We' and 'they' divides along altepetl lines, not between New Worlders and Old Worlders". [...] In most contexts, 'we' are the individual altepetl group and 'they' are all other humans, imagined as other altepetl groups. The Spaniards coming on the scene are viewed as one more such group. Their altepetl is Caxtillan and they are Caxtilteca (or

---

had migrated into central Mexico from the north. In some native accounts these immigrants are described as barbaric Chichimecs who became civilized in central Mexico, adopting 'Toltec' traits (Smith 2003: 35–37; Prem 2008: 29). Cp. Smith (1984) for a critical discussion of the Aztec migrations and possible meanings of the term *Chichimec*.

9   Some of the preconquest provinces in Yucatán were named after their ruling lineages (Roys 1972: 11).

other names meaning the same), just as there is an altepetl Tepoztlan, land of the Tepozteca. In other words, the Spaniards did not have the effect of creating a polarization between the indigenous inhabitants and the intruders. The Nahuas continued to see the world as they had before, divided between the altepetl group and all outsiders, be they indigenous or Spaniards." (1993: 14-15, 21)

Berdan did not find evidence that the Aztec empire made particular ethnic considerations in their choices or treatment of adversaries. "No special pattern, based on ethnicity, appears in a survey of tributary versus client subjects" (2008: 111). The same is true when considering marriages between the elites of different city-states (ibid: 128).

Stark and Chance (2008: 3–4) recently proposed the differentiation of a "soft" form of ethnicity, related to place and common history, from ethnicity in the "hard" sense, including ideas of shared descent. Consequently, they find evidence for the first in preconquest Mexico. This, however, runs the risk of fostering the already too common tendency to conflate different forms of categorization and group formation instead of providing analytical tools to differentiate among them.[10]

CONCLUSION

There is strong evidence that the nation concept and the idea of nationalism emerged in Western Europe no earlier than the 17th or 18th centuries A.D. As the idea that homogenous units of language, culture, and people were the natural form of social organization became generalized in Europe, it also became dominant in other parts of the world in the course of Western colonialism. Thus, people lacking their own state, and cultural minorities within existing states, were considered as ethnic communities. The trend to see peoples (tribes, ethnies, or nations) as the main actors both throughout history and in the present present has more recently been further strengthened by legal-political ideas such as the 'peoples' right to self-determination'.

To provide an example from Latin America: Tukanoans, as the indigenous riverine inhabitants of the central Northwest Amazon along the Brazilian-Columbian border are generally known, lived in patrilocal longhouses until

---

10   It also seems confusing to consider the male citizens of ancient democratic Athens an 'ethnic group', as Cohen (2001: 240–243) suggests in an attempt to come to terms with the fact that women were excluded from citizenship.

recently, when they began to settle in nucleated villages. Each community belongs to one of 16 different named language groups composed of anything from six to more than 30 patrilineal clans. To the astonishment of the Western observer accustomed to the 'unholy trinity' of one language = one culture = one people, Tukano individuals are obliged to marry someone from a different community and with a different primary language. Thus, multilingualism is generalized (Sorensen 1967; Jackson 1995). However, confronted with the need to be recognized as an indigenous people and adapt their discourse to Western understandings in order to obtain benefits from the government, NGOs or international development agencies, Tukano organizations have begun to present their 'traditional' language groups as 'ethnic communities', with their own culture and forms of social, political and religious organization (Jackson 1995: 12–15). Thus, as in the case of the African tribes, an ethnic form of organization may result as a consequence of Western influence.

However, although the European expansion and the rise of the nation-state did much to spread ethnicity as an ideology and a form of social organization, cultural or ethnic distinctions were possibly made in former times and outside of Europe, albeit far less than earlier accounts have suggested. In general however, these were merely categories employed by outsiders that rarely crystallized into self-conscious ethnic communities. Under particular conditions, gross categorical distinctions, such as those between 'civilized' and 'barbarian' peoples, were employed for political or other reasons. Thus, classical Greek authors tried to forge a military coalition among city-states (*poleis*) of Greek-speaking populations when confronted with an invasion by the Persian Achaemenid empire in the 5th century BC summoning a common Hellenicity against the 'barbarian' invaders (Hall 2005: 173–189). Nothing comparable happened in Mesoamerica. As has been shown above, Nahuatl-Speakers did not build an alliance against the intruders, even when confronted with the Spaniards, but the lines of conflict followed city-state or factional lines. However, even in the Greek case, Hall states that "Hellenic identity arose in the élite environment of the Olympic games during the course of the 6th century and that it served both to cement alliances between the ruling families of various regions and to promote the hegemonic claims of the Thessalians over their neighbours in central Greece" (2005: 227). The idea of Hellenicity was based on a genealogical model and referred to the supposed descendants of the mythical ancestor Hellen (grandson of Prometheus). This indicates, *pace* Hall (ibid: 7), not an ethnic identification but rather corresponds to a kinship model placing elite families and lineages into a segmented and hierarchical order, thus "validating high status through descent" (Renfrew in Review Feature 1998: 277). Later the concept was defined in cultural and relativistic terms: Hellenes and barbarians did not constitute mutually exclusive categories in 5th-century Greece. Barbarians were viewed "as being situated at the other end of a linear continuum which did in fact permit category-crossing. [...] a barbarian could 'become' Greek by adopting Hellenic practices, customs and language" (Hall 2005: 8). Hellenicity thus became a term indicating participation in a particular civilization, but not an ethnicity.

To conclude, the study of ethnicity in history is facing immense methodological problems since we have to reconstruct the subjective meanings people attached to categories of thought and discourse as well as actions. These problems are especially acute when material remains are our sole source of information and when we lack any type of written records which could help in elucidating the meaning of artifacts. In contrast to scholars such as Jones (2002), I share Hall's (2005: 22–24) skepticism about the possibility of inferring ethnicity solely on the basis of archaeological data. As has already been mentioned above, there is no direct relationship between ethnicity and shared cultural traits such as costume or hairstyle. The significance of certain cultural traits for the construction of ethnic communities is not inherent, but depends on a complex process of interpretation and evaluation by the actors which is very difficult to reconstruct merely from material remains. The cohesion of ethnic communities does not rest on any objective likeness but, as Siegfried Nadel stated several decades ago, "hinges on a *theory* of cultural identity, which ignores or dismisses as immaterial existing variations, and ignores or disregards uniformities beyond its self-chosen boundaries". The ethnic community exists "not in virtue of any objective unity or likeness, but in virtue of [...] a likeness accepted as a dogma" (1947: 13).

Even in cases where contemporary texts are available, as, for example, with the ancient Maya in Mesoamerica or the European Middle Ages, these only reflect the views of the elite in most cases and provide little insight into how social categories were used in daily interaction. However, even if the debate might end up with the conclusion that ethnicity was never, or very rarely, present before the 17th or 18th centuries A.D., or else that this cannot be proven due to the lack of data, the concept is useful for historical studies. It can be employed as an ideal type with which to scrutinize the historical materials carving out the particular methods of classification, political integration and community-building in the past.

References

Alva Ixtlilxóchitl, Fernando de (1985): Obras Históricas [1600–1640]. II vol., México, D.F.: UNAM.
Anderson, Benedict (1991): Imagined Communities. Reflections on the Origin and Spread of Nationalism. Revised edition, London/New York: Verso.
Barth, Fredrik (1969): "Introduction." In: Fredrik Barth (ed.), Ethnic Groups and Boundaries, Bergen: Universitetsforlaget, pp. 9–38.
Berdan, Frances (2008): "Concepts of Ethnicity and Class in Aztec-Period Mexico." In: Frances Berdan/John K. Chance/Alan R. Sandstrom/Barbara L. Stark/James M. Taggart/Umberger (eds.), Ethnic Identity in Nahua Mesoamerica: The View from Archaeology, Art History, Ethnohistory, and Contemporary Ethnography, Salt Lake City: University of Utah Press, pp. 105–132.
Brass, Paul R. (1991): Ethnicity and Nationalism, New Delhi/Newbury/London: Sage.
Brown, Donald E. (1973): "Hereditary Rank and Ethnic History: An Analysis of Brunei Historiography." In: Journal of Anthropological Research 29/2, pp. 113–122.
Carmack, Robert M. (1981): The Quiché Mayas of Utatlán. The Evolution of a Highland Guatemala Kingdom, Norman: University of Oklahoma Press.
Chapman, Malcolm/McDonald, Maryon/Tonkin, Elizabeth (1989): "Introduction." In: Elizabeth Tonkin/Maryon McDonald/Malcolm Chapman (eds.), History and Ethnicity, London: Routledge, pp. 1–21.
Cohen, Beth (2001): "Ethnic Identity in Democratic Athens and the Visual Vocabulary of Male Costume." In: Irad Malkin (ed.), Ancient Perceptions of Greek Ethnicity, Cambridge, MA: Harvard University Press, pp. 235–74.
Cohen, Ronald (1978): "Ethnicity: Problem and Focus in Anthropology." In: Annual Review of Anthropology 7, pp. 379–403.
Elwert, Georg (1989): "Nationalismus, Ethnizität und Nativismus – über Wir-Gruppenprozesse." In: Peter Waldmann/Georg Elwert (eds.), Ethnizität im Wandel, Saarbrücken: Breitenbach, pp. 21–60.
Eriksen, Thomas Hylland (2002): Ethnicity and Nationalism. Anthropological Perspectives. 2nd ed., London: Pluto Press.
Fardon, Richard (1987): "'African Ethnogenesis': Limits to the Comparability of Ethnic Phenomena." In: Ladislav Holy (ed.), Comparative Anthropology, Oxford: Blackwell, pp. 168–88.
Fenton, Steve (2003): Ethnicity, Cambridge: Pluto Press.

Frake, Charles O. (1960): "The Eastern Subanun of Mindanao." In: George P. Murdock (ed.), Social Structure in Southeast Asia, New York: Wenner-Gren Foundation for Anthropological Research, pp. 51–64.
Francis, E.K. (1947): "The Nature of the Ethnic Group." In: American Journal of Sociology 52/3, pp. 393–400.
Gabbert, Wolfgang (2004): Becoming Maya. Ethnicity and Social Inequality in Yucatán since 1500, Tucson, AZ: University of Arizona Press.
—— (2006): "Concepts of Ethnicity." In: Latin American and Caribbean Ethnic Studies 1/1, pp. 85–103.
Gat, Azar (2013): Nations - the Long History and Deep Roots of Political Ethnicity and Nationalism, Cambridge, MA: Cambridge University Press.
Geary, Patrick J. (1983): "Ethnic Identity as a Situational Construct in the Early Middle Ages." In: Mitteilungen der anthropologischen Gesellschaft in Wien 113, pp. 15–26.
Gellner, Ernest (1964): Thought and Change, London: Weidenfeld and Nicholson.
—— (1983): Nations and Nationalism, Oxford: Basil Blackwell.
Hall, Jonathan M. (1995): Ethnic Identity in Greek Antiquity, Cambridge: Cambridge University Press.
—— (2005): Hellenicity. Between Ethnicity and Culture, Chicago, Ill.: University of Chicago Press.
Jackson, Jean E. (1995): "Culture, Genuine and Spurious: The Politics of Indianness in the Vaupés, Colombia." In: American Ethnologist 22/1, pp. 3–27.
Jenkins, Richard (1997): Rethinking Etnicity. Arguments and Explorations, Thousand Oaks/New Delhi: Sage.
Jones, Sian (2002): The Archaeology of Ethnicity. Constructing Identities in the Past and Present, London: Routledge.
King, Victor T. (1982): "Ethnicity in Borneo: An Anthropological Problem." In: Southeast Asian Journal of Social Science 10/1, pp. 23–43.
León-Portilla, Miguel (1992): "Imágenes de los otros en Mesoamérica antes del encuentro." In: Miguel León-Portilla/Manuel Gutiérrez Estévez/Gary Gossen (eds.), De palabra y obra en el Nuevo Mundo. Vol. 1. Imágenes interétnicas, Madrid: Siglo XXI, pp. 35–56.
Lockhart, James (1992): The Nahuas After the Conquest. A Social and Cultural History of the Indians of Central Mexico, Sixteenth to Eighteenth Centuries, Stanford: Stanford University Press.
—— (1993): We People Here: Nahuatl Accounts of the Conquest of Mexico, Berkeley, CA: University of California Press.
Mair, Lucy (1962): Primitive Government, Harmondsworth: Penguin.

McInerney, Jeremy (2001): "Ethnos and Ethnicity in Early Greece". In: Irad Malkin (ed.), Ancient Perceptions of Greek Ethnicity, Cambridge, MA: Harvard University Press, pp. 51-73.
Nadel, Siegfried F. (1947): The Nuba, London: Oxford University Press.
Nash, Manning (1989): The Cauldron of Ethnicity in the Modern World, Chicago: University of Chicago Press.
Prem, Hanns J. (2008): Geschichte Altamerikas. 2nd revised ed., München: Oldenbourg Verlag.
Ranger, Terence (1981): "Kolonialismus in Ost- und Zentralafrika. Von der traditionellen zur traditionalen Gesellschaft - Einsprüche und Widersprüche." In: Jan-Heeren Grevemeyer (ed.), Traditionale Gesellschaften und europäischer Kolonialismus, Frankfurt a.M.: Syndikat, pp. 16-46.
Restall, Matthew (1997): The Maya World, Stanford: Stanford University Press.
Review Feature (1998): "Ethnic Identity in Greek Antiquity." In: Cambridge Archaeological Journal 8/2, pp. 265-83.
Rothschild, Joseph (1981): Ethnopolitics. A Conceptual Framework, New York: Columbia University Press.
Royal Institute of International Affairs (1966 [1939]): Nationalism. A Report by a Study Group of Members of the Royal Institute of International Affairs, New York: Kelley.
Roys, Ralph (1972 [1943]): The Indian Background of Colonial Yucatan, Norman: University of Oklahoma Press.
Sahagún, Fray Bernadino de (1982): Historia general de las cosas de Nueva España [1575-77], México, D.F.: Porrúa.
Sahlins, Marshall (1985): Islands of History, Chicago, Ill.: University of Chicago Press.
Smith, Anthony D. (1981): The Ethnic Revival, New York: Cambridge University Press.
―― (1991): National Identity, London: Penguin.
Smith, Michael E. (1984): "The Aztlan Migrations of the Nahuatl Chronicles: Myth or History?" In: Ethnohistory 31/3, pp. 153-86.
―― (2003): The Aztecs. Second edition, Oxford: Blackwell.
Sorensen, Arthur P. (1967): "Multilingualism in the Amazon." In: American Anthropologist 69/6, pp. 670-84.
Southall, Aidan W. (1970): "The Illusion of Tribe." In: Journal of Asian and African Studies 5/1-2, pp. 28-50.
Stark, Barbara L/Chance, John K. (2008): "Diachronic and Multudisciplinary Perspectives on Mesoamerican Ethnicity." In: Frances Berdan/John K. Chance/Alan R. Sandstrom/Barbara L. Stark/James M. Taggart/Umberger (eds.), Ethnic Identity in Nahua Mesoamerica: The View from Archaeology,

Art History, Ethnohistory, and Contemporary Ethnography, Salt Lake City: University of Utah Press, pp. 1–37.
Sumner, William Graham (2002 [1907]): Folkways. A Study of Mores, Manners, Customs and Morals, Mineola, NY: Dover.
Terraciano, Kevin (2001): The Mixtec of Colonial Oaxaca.Ñudzahui History, Sixteenth through Eighteenth Centuries, Stanford: Stanford University Press.
Veyne, Paul (1993): "Humanitas: Romans and Non-Romans." In: Andrea Giardina (ed.), The Romans, Chicago, Ill.: University of Chicago Press, pp. 342–369.
Weber, Max (1980 [1922]): Wirtschaft und Gesellschaft, Tübingen: Mohr.

Political uses of ethnicity in early medieval Europe

WALTER POHL

ETHNICITY AND ROMAN EXPANSION

I would like to start this contribution by making a general point: the so-called 'migration period' in Europe at the end of Antiquity is crucial for our understanding of ethnicity in several respects.[1] First, it can help to explain how the emerging modern European nations built on resources of the past that had been accumulated in Late Antiquity and the Early Middle Ages, and what that may have implied for their development. Second, attitudes towards ethnic and political communities and discourses of ethnicity that took shape in this period influenced much later perceptions of identity and otherness. For instance, ethnic perceptions of African peoples in the 19th century were not least promoted by European missionaries, who were familiar with biblical and classical concepts of ethnicity that had been synthesized in the period between the 4th and the 9th century (Geary 2001: 157–74). Third, although the European Early Middle Ages are still regarded as 'Dark Ages', we do in fact have a considerable number and variety of sources from this period at our disposal (including rich archaeological material). This evidence allows a long-term overview of ethnic processes that can serve as test-cases for theories of ethnicity. It shows many facets of the importance and the limits of ethnicity as a cognitive model and as a political resource. Unfortunately, in most debates about ethnicity this fascinating

---

[1] This article sums up research published in Pohl (2002; 2008; 2013a; 2013b, among others). The research leading to these results received funding from the European Research Council in the Seventh Framework Programme (FP7/2007–13) under the ERC grant agreement No. 269591.

evidence is still being ignored. Admittedly, the appropriations of ethnic identities by nationalist ideologies in the 19th and 20th centuries make the contemporary research on the topic somewhat uncomfortable.[2] But these appropriations do not make it any less interesting, since they become subject to analysis themselves.

One thing that studying the Early Middle Ages can teach us is that some current grand narratives and general theories of ethnicity are too simple to be profitably applicable to the whole range of historical cases. The debate over whether ethnicity and/or the nation are primordial or modern phenomena does not link neatly with the evidence about the early medieval situation (Smith 2000). There is broad agreement that ethnicity is socially constructed, but that does not mean that it is a mere invention, or any less real for that.[3] If ethnicity was only created by European colonial expansion, which research term should we use for earlier periods? The ancient and medieval *ethnē*, *gentes* or *nationes* may not always coincide with modern scholarly concepts of ethnicity, but they were quite consistently used to describe related phenomena, which should by no means be excluded from interdisciplinary research on ethnicity.

The fact that European colonial powers established ethnic divides as a cognitive and repressive tool does not imply that this is the only way in which ethnicity can become meaningful in history. In fact, the relations between the Roman Empire and the "ethnic" groups in its periphery provide a very instructive case for comparison, which displays both striking parallels with and differences from the uses of ethnicity by European colonial empires. The Romans divided their 'barbarian' periphery according to *gentes*, while they distinguished Romans by their cities of origin, and regarded them as a *populus*, a 'people by constitution' defined by common polity and law. The implication was that the barbarians lived in a natural world, where social groups were formed by procreation, whereas Romans lived in a cultured universe where communities were established by law and politics. The ethnic ascriptions used for the barbarian 'Other' were partly fictive; that applied first of all to ethnographic umbrella categories, such as *Germani* or Scythians, which hardly corresponded to any established self-ascription. Ethnic designations of smaller groups were aimed at controlling the periphery of the empire. These groups could then be integrated into the empire under specific conditions depending on political

---

2   For instance, German nationalists appropriated the ancient and migration-age Germans, and the French the Gauls and Franks, which led to widely discordant views of the end of the Roman Empire (cp. Geary 2001; Pohl 2002).

3   The term "imagined communities", coined by Anderson (1991: 6), is often understood that way, in spite of his assertion that all communities larger than face-to-face groups are imagined, in the sense not of falsification but of creation.

circumstances, and were granted varying degrees of autonomy. Alternatively, Rome also constructed alliances with its barbarian neighbours, playing them off against each other, or identifying them as enemies who had to be subjected to a wide range of repressive measures.

This is, in fact, what many empires have done in history – first in the course of their expansion, and then once they had consolidated their positions, by establishing asymmetrical relations with their peripheries. But that does not necessarily mean that the system of ethnic distinctions applied to the 'barbarians' outside the empire was constructed from scratch; several observations contradict such a conclusion. Our evidence rarely allows us to track the previous identities of populations before they had come under the sway of the Roman Empire. However, we can make a number of useful observations. No one would doubt that the Jews already had a very strong identity long before they were subdued by the Romans; and although scholars have tried to minimize the ethnic element in Jewish identity, it is certainly very present in the Old Testament.

The evidence for the barbarians in the Northern parts of Europe is more indirect. Greek and Roman ethnography since Herodotus had collected considerable informations about them (Müller 1997). This material may not have been wholly adequate and was coloured by stereotypes, but the distinctions between different groups had to be reliable enough to deal with them on a political level. Greeks and Romans did not have the military or political means to impose ethnic identifications on 'barbarian' populations outside their realms. Thus, they simply could not afford to apply a cognitive model to these barbarians that had nothing to do with real groupings and feelings of solidarity among the latter. We know of a number of cases in which relatively slight mistakes in diplomatic dealings with barbarian groups beyond the frontier led to serious military trouble for the Roman Empire. Roman propaganda could certainly fantasize about 'barbarians' in triumphal inscriptions and panegyric poems, and give them antiquated or imaginary names; some of which might also appear in works of ethnography or historiography. But we have enough evidence to see that in their diplomatic and military contacts with foreign *gentes*, the Romans relied on excellent intelligence. On the whole, their perception of ethnic groups around them was adequate and allowed them some form of control over their 'barbarian' periphery for many centuries. We cannot not always trust the details. However, the ways in which the Romans distinguished the populations beyond the frontiers using ethnonyms surely corresponded broadly to the latters' internal organisation and self-perceptions.

Ethnicity in the Political Landscape of Post-Roman Europe

From the beginning of the 5th century CE, Roman rule in the West slowly eroded. Large bands of soldiers of 'barbarian' origin, most of them with families and followers, settled on Roman territory under their own commanders, often at least nominally in the service of the empire. Although their composition was initially more or less heterogeneous and volatile, they were consistently distinguished by ethnic names. Increasingly, instances of self-identification come to be attested. As these groups became more familiar with their late-Roman environment, they built up their own power bases. In the course of the 5th and 6th century CE, Roman provinces were thus transformed into kingdoms named after ruling ethnic groups – Vandals, Goths, Franks, Angles or Saxons – which constituted small minorities. The new political units were not distinguished by their long-standing regional names – Africa, Hispania, Gaul or Britain – but by these ethnic designations, which became proud self-designations.

Generations of historians who thought in terms of national histories considered it natural that it should have happened that way – invading Germanic peoples established their states in conquered regions and stamped their names on them. But that was not natural at all. We know now that the composition of the invading groups changed considerably in the course of their migration and integration into the Roman World (Wolfram 1997; Pohl 2002). Furthermore, things developed very differently in the East when Muslim armies conquered Syria, Egypt and other Roman provinces. They established the rule of Islam, of dynasties, or of sectarian groups, but not of tribes or peoples (although tribal distinctions played a great role in Arab society) (Pohl/Gantner/Payne 2012). Thus, the process by which ethnicity became a political resource in the early medieval West is much less linear and teleological, and much more contingent, than has been assumed. For a long time, the Early Middle Ages were regarded as the period of origin of most European nations. But these ethnic and national histories were much more fragmented and contradictory than the old master narratives assumed. It was not nations that emerged in the Middle Ages, but a model of ethnic rule that continued to be used, intermittently but repeatedly, in European history. Ultimately, this precedent could serve as an ideological device for building European nations on myths of distant origins.

Accordingly, there is a lot more to explain about the rise of ethnic kingdoms in early medieval Europe than traditional historiography has assumed. But whichever explanation we choose, it would hardly work without using the category of ethnicity. Scholars may of course decide that 'ethnicity' is not very useful for their topic of study, but in this particular field we would miss an important element of the political process if we abandoned it. Ethnic designations not only served as distinctions among polities and their elites: agency was ascribed to the ethnic groups, and not to their states. The Franks, and not their kingdom, waged war or raised a king. Soon, ethnic representations of rulership became current: 'king of the Franks' (*rex Francorum*), 'king of the people of the Longobards' (*rex gentis Langobardorum*) and suchlike.

Initially, the armed ethnic groups that dominated the new kingdoms constituted small minorities. In a process that took centuries, the Latin-speaking majority population took on the ruling identity, while the ethnic elites largely adopted the language and culture of the majority. Thus, the kingdom of the Germanic Franks, the most successful of the new units, gradually turned into Romance-speaking France. This integration was possible because the distinctive feature of common blood and kinship among the ruling elite could be bypassed quite comfortably. The Franks even came to believe that they had originated from the Trojans, which made them relatives of the Romans.

Still, Latin terminology implied a biological frame of reference: *gens*, *genus* and *natio* were all derived from verbs denoting birth. And, perhaps surprisingly, the ethnic framing for the new kingdoms was supported by Christianity. The Old Testament offered a rich repertoire of ideas to support an ethnic view of the political world: a people chosen by God over all the others, constituted by tribal units and competing with other peoples, whom God sometimes employed as instruments of his wrath. The Jewish people periodically ruled their own state, which sometimes was split in two, or destroyed by enemies, so that the Jewish people would be forced to live under foreign rule or be dispersed in exile. In a set of very impressive stories, the Old Testament explained the origin of peoples (from Noah's sons after the flood) and of languages (the Tower of Babel), and recounted a model migration (in Exodus). These stories became basic in Western culture. In the New Testament, the message of Christ was to be taken to all peoples, and the Jews thus assumed a role in the history of salvation. However universal a doctrine Christianity presented itself as, its holy books reserved an important role for ethnicity.

I would argue that the early medieval evidence, sketched here very briefly, supports the use of ethnicity as a category to describe how the post-Roman kingdoms operated. Without it, we would miss an important indicator with which to distinguish the changes that took place in the Latin West from different transformations of the Roman World in other regions. Therefore, we have to employ a definition of ethnicity that is adequate to the material that we are studying. There are of course several definitions available; objective or subjective, by common cultural features or by the belief in common origins (which I find more helpful). A cultural definition would fail to grasp the continuity of Frankish identity and its political role, while the Franks successively adopted the religion, language, costume and many other cultural traits of the majority in their kingdom. The definition that we choose must then be put in perspective with contemporary definitions and perceptions of the phenomena that we want to describe as 'ethnic'. That would allow us to historicize the term, and to take on board 'native' knowledge about its application. This is of course an open, hermeneutic process aimed at arriving at an operational definition that might not fit the strict requirements of a definition in some sectors of the social sciences. But it is adequate to the needs of historical research, an activity which risks being limited by overly narrow definitions while studying phenomena that were in constant transformation.

An approach that has proved productive in early medieval studies is to see ethnicity as a principle of distinction between social groupings that may be more or less salient or relevant according to the context. The significance of ethnic distinctions and identifications is well attested in the period (as in many premodern contexts), but they were by no means equally important everywhere. Ethnicity does not only exist due to outside or imperial ascription, but external perceptions nevertheless play an integral part in the process of identification that establishes ethnic identities. They are rarely exclusively emic or etic; they only acquire some stability if individual identifications with a group, collective or symbolic self-identification of a group as such are engaged in a relatively continuous process of communication with external identifications. Ethnicity has no teleological development, but undergoes irregular periods of relative inactivity. Its politicization can take very different forms: reinforcing ethnic cleavages; aiming for a better status as an ethnic minority; or, as in the cases that I have sketched, legitimizing privileges for an elite, or its right to rule. Ethnicity is socially constructed and built on myths, but has an impact in the social world, and can have real significance for peoples' identities.

In fact, the question of whether a social group is ethnic or not is often wrongly put. For instance, it is not very productive to debate whether the Jews were an ethnic or a religious community; they were both, and to different degrees in different contexts. We rarely encounter ethnicity in its 'pure' form – it often overlaps to a large extent with political, religious, territorial, military or other types of identifications. The same social group can be more or less ethnic at different times, and even appear more or less ethnic to different individuals at the same time (Pohl 2013a). Ultimately, the claim that ethnicity makes is that it defines groups that people are born into. Therefore, the solidarity associated with an ethnic group is not accidental or episodic, but is seen as an expression of an intrinsic nature, bound by kinship and common origin. Of course, we know that this essentialist claim is highly ideological. It can also go along with much more pragmatic attitudes that allow for changes of ethnic identity, at least over time. Likewise, the promise of ethnic solidarity is never entirely reliable. But we also know that ethnic groups have often proven surprisingly stable, not least in the face of adversity.

This tension between strong concepts and weak practices of ethnicity creates conceptual problems; some scholars insist that we should only speak of ethnicity when we can prove that a strong concept is actually exemplified by a specific case (Gruen 2013). However, such an approach would be unnecessarily limited. Ethnicity is a relational system of distinctions which allows orientation to all actors involved, regardless of the intensity of ethnic identifications on the ground. Ethnic distinctions only require a basic consensus about their broad significance and applicability. In the period between the 5th and 8th centuries, ethnonyms were consistently used to identify collective political actors, who were described as *gentes*, and sometimes also as *nationes* or *genera*. The etymologies of these words already suggested notions of common origin. The Old Testament provided strong models of providential ethnic history. Furthermore, in some texts we find theoretical reflections about the meaning of contemporary ethnic names and terminology, as in Isidore of Seville's 7th-century *Etymologies*, which give access to an underlying discourse. In this matrix, the rather fragmented histories of the peoples that emerged during the dissolution of the Roman Empire in the 5th and 6th centuries CE could be understood. In research, it would be hard to grasp the dynamics of these histories without tapping into the rich (if controversial) theoretical toolbox provided by research on ethnicity. In turn, these remote histories offer test-cases that can be very valuable for the study of ethnicity in very different times and places.

REFERENCES

Anderson, Benedict (1991): Imagined Communities. Reflections on the Origin and Spread of Nationalism. Revised edition, London/New York: Verso.
Geary, Patrick J. (2001): The Myth of Nations. The Medieval Origins of Europe, Princeton/Oxford: Princeton University Press.
Gruen, Erich (2013): "Did Ancient Identity Depend on Ethnicity? A Preliminary Probe." In: Phoenix 67, 1/2, pp. 1–22.

Müller, Klaus E. (1997): Geschichte der antiken Ethnologie, Reinbek: rororo.
Pohl, Walter (2002): Die Völkerwanderung. Eroberung und Integration, Stuttgart/Berlin/Cologne: Kohlhammer.
—— (2008): "Rome and the Barbarians in the Fifth Century." In: Antiquité Tardive 16, pp. 93–101.
—— (2013a): "Introduction: Strategies of identification. A methodological profile." In: Walter Pohl/Gerda Heydemann (eds.), Strategies of Identification. Ethnicity and Religion in Early Medieval Europe, Turnhout: Brepols, pp. 1–64.
—— (2013b): "Christian and barbarian identities in the early medieval West: introduction." In: Walter Pohl/Gerda Heydemann (eds.), Post-Roman Transitions: Christian and Barbarian Identities in the Early Medieval West, Turnhout: Brepols, pp. 1–46.
Pohl, Walter/Gantner, Clemens/Payne, Richard (eds.) (2012): Visions of Community in the Post-Roman World. The West, Byzantium and the Islamic World, 300-1100, Farnham and Burlington: Ashgate.
Smith, Anthony D. (2000): The Nation in History. Historiographical Debates about Ethnicity and Nationalism, Hanover, NH: University Press of New England.
Wolfram, Herwig (1997): The Roman Empire and Its Germanic Peoples, Berkeley/Los Angeles: University of California Press.

The work of race in colonial Peru[1]

RACHEL SARAH O'TOOLE

Is 'race' an appropriate term to describe the affinities and enmities, or the identities and affiliations in colonial Spanish America, a center of the early modern Iberian realms? In the 1970s and 1980s Patricia Seed (1983), Robert McCaa (1979), John Chance and William Taylor (1979), and other U.S. historians of Latin America quantified data, for example, collected from 17th- and 18th-century parish records to ascertain whether colonial Latin Americans distinguished themselves according to class, honor, sex, occupation, or caste – or a mixture of these categories. Race, for these scholars, constituted any of the multiple categories employed by Spanish colonizers and the colonized, to mark themselves and others as *mestizo* or *mulato*.[2] Subsequently, historians suggested race was both a social construction and a biological fact and agreed regarding its imposition by colonizers (Cope 1994: 15, 23; Fisher/O'Hara 2009: 6). Since then, historians have questioned whether 'race' was a suitable term to describe the ways that colonizers, enslaved men and women, and indigenous inhabitants claimed their identities and marked their differences in the 16th, 17th, and 18th centuries (Fisher/ O'Hara 2009: 8; Tavárez 2009: 82). For instance, colonizers

---

[1] I thank the participants in the conference *Conceptualizing Ethnicity as a Political Resource* (April 2014) for their questions and commentary, in particular Wolfgang Gabbert, Karoline Noack, and Lok Siu.

[2] In colonial Latin America, *mestizo* or *mestiza* could mean a person who was of mixed indigenous and Spanish descent, but also referred to an indigenous person who took on colonial or Spanish cultural characteristics. In contrast, *mulato* or *mulata* indicated a person of African and Spanish descent, and also indicated a person who spoke Spanish, dressed like a free person, and lived among Spaniards, indigenous people, and other people of mixed cultural characteristics.

and colonized did not employ only fixed, physical characteristics, critical to a modern definition of race, to describe themselves or others. Colonial terminology, in addition, emerged from the religious context of medieval and early modern Spain where Muslims, Jews, and Catholics were associated with a particular lineage or *casta*. Following this historiographical tendency to maintain fidelity to the historical specificity marked by the term, in my Ph.D. dissertation I claimed that the term *casta* was a more appropriate way to label colonial terminologies such as *negro*[3] and 'Indian' that circulated throughout the Spanish Americas (O'Toole 2001: 4). In addition to referencing origin or descent, assumed class, or cultural affect (previous definitions of *casta*), I examined how everyday people employed the names they were called, or their castas. Recognizing the malleability of *casta*– or what I theorized was a performance of identity – I argued that people who inhabited colonial Spanish America noticed speech, language abilities, and clothing as much as, if not more than, physical characteristics. Simplistic notions of race, it would seem, could not be applied to a multi-faceted colonial reality that included slavery, violent labor impositions on indigenous communities, and resource extraction to global markets including tribute collection.

To describe the colonial Latin American past by employing the term 'race', however, illuminates a key colonial logic. Reversing the position I took in my dissertation, following the publication of my monograph I find that 'race' is the most appropriate to describe how people of the colonial Spanish Americas articulated colonial categories of difference. Defined by Sebastián de Covarrubias y Horozco in his 1611 Castilian dictionary, *casta* referred to 'lineage' as well as 'offspring' (Covarrubias [1611] 1994: 316). Thus, according to María Elena Martínez, racial discourse emerged from Iberian ideas of blood purity that began with the policing of religious distinctions in Iberia and was transferred to the Americas as gendered concerns with ancestry and descent. In other words, while Muslims and Jews (identified or hidden) made Catholic rulers and their proxies anxious in the Iberian kingdoms, by the 16th and 17th centuries, a discourse of feminized Indians and masculinized blacks circulated in the Americas (Martínez 2008: 61, 158-159, 169). In a colonial setting, the work of race therefore signifies radical economic, political, and economic changes constituted by institutions such as slavery and those that policed indigenous communities. The construction of colonial Latin American race, took place along multiple axes, with cultural expectations informing how Spanish colonial officials imagined, and eventually attempted to fix, the legal and cultural

---

3   In colonial Latin America, *negro* or *negra* meant an African or an African-descent person as well as a person associated with slavery.

locations (for instance) of Africans, indigenous people of the Americas, and their descendants. As Laura Lewis (2003: 69), Martínez (2008: 221), and I (O'Toole 2012: 86, 150) have found (among many scholars), colonial legislation favored indigenous people partly because Iberian religious state ideology came to conceive of sedentary native groups as naïfs who could conform to Catholicism and therefore deserved land rights and protection as native vassals. Additionally, Martínez describes a colonial construction of blackness that criminalized men of African descent (2008: 158), and in my recent work I point to a legal exclusion of Africans and their descendants (O'Toole 2012: 36, 123). Martínez deftly illustrates that medieval and early modern elite concerns with descent and blood transformed into the marking of racial otherness in the colonial context through assumed cultural characteristics and physical manifestations. While fictional and performative, colonial race was fixed and fixing in ways that discriminated against indigenous and African peoples in the Americas.

In recent historical studies, the term 'race' also performs analytical work to remind us of how authorities, colonizers, intermediaries, and other participants constructed colonial institutions. Slavery, tribute collection, distribution of land, and membership of guilds (as well as other powerful systems) exploited categories of people based on cultural conjecture regarding their perceived differences. Why not employ the historically specific term *casta*, the one found in the historical documents composed by the colonizer and the colonized in the 17th century, in these instances? Undoubtedly, whether they were referred to according to *casta* or race, or whether they were understood as *mestizo* or 'Indian', *morena* or *negra*, had material, political, and legal consequences for the majority of colonial Latin American inhabitants. The term 'race', in my estimation, draws our attention to the ways in which situations became fixed in legal language that – even given the plurality of the law in the 17th century (Benton 2002: 6, 11) – illustrates how the Crown and colonizers attempted to impose order and exact labor. It appears that the choice to engage the analytical, historically fraught, and culturally specific term of race appears to be made according to whether scholars wish to engage with the political consequences of categorization. In other words, not only does the term race indicate a forceful fixity of a colonial reality that included slavery, as well as early modern global economies that relied on indigenous labor, but race also signals an imbalance of power that was located within the multiple structures of Spanish rule. Spanish colonial rule under the Hapsburgs, therefore, was not merely a form of paternalistic neglect, but one of the world's most dynamic empires, which infused the world with silver currency based on industrialized, paid indigenous labor while also jump-starting the transatlantic slave trade. Is it then possible to theorize how *casta* in colonial Latin America did the work of race as we would understand it in the modern Americas?

Lastly, why not employ the notion of ethnicity to describe these markings and exclusions? Ethnicity was a critical criterion of identity in colonial Latin America, since, for example, indigenous communities developed (or continued) clothing styles to suggest rank and occupation, just as the African Diaspora articulated their *naciones* or ethnicities through religious practices and kinship formation, all critical characteristics of ethnicity (Graubart 2015: 194, 196). Indeed, further elaborating a definition of ethnicity, the term can point to how cultural characteristics including language, residency, and foodways both bound and separated colonial communities (ibid: 192, 195). More pointedly, modern discrimination based on ethnic distinctions in the Americas has denied communities their rights as citizens, targeted groups for genocide, and led to a host of economic and institutional exclusions. To choose between the terms 'race' and 'ethnicity,' or *casta, calidad*, or any of the other terms invoked by colonial Latin American historians, however, is to call upon particular intellectual histories. Most especially in the Andes and in Mexico, academic use of the term 'ethnicity' or 'ethnic' has served to elide discussions of slavery's impact, colonial exclusion of land distribution, and state-sponsored discrimination. In Peru, nationalism based on Inca identity, and in Mexico the post-revolutionary hegemonization of regional indigeneities, have served to erase the differences between native populations as well as the complicated national histories of Africans and their descendants. In addition, race has operated in the Andes as a negative descriptor. As is astutely explained by Marisol de la Cadena, because Peruvians, from early 20th-century intellectuals to present-day academics, have subsumed physical markers beneath cultural distinctions, racism becomes a cultural impossibility in the Andes (De la Cadena 2000: 3, 5). Likewise, Mary Weismantel's keen analysis of how Andean 'racism' becomes wrapped up in a rejection of 'race' exposes why both lenses are so profoundly discarded (Weismantel 2001: 92). These and other scholars indicate precisely why other Andeanists, including myself, actually silenced the work of race by delving into the history of casta or other terminologies deemed more historically accurate. Indeed, my choice to employ race, as a historian of colonial Latin America, is, in some ways, an election to engage in a historical accounting that is as much about the present as it is about the past. In the case of my own research and writing, the term 'race' helps to name the distinctions between Africans and Andeans that were not solely ethnic, or about cultural differentiations, however violent, but about imposed legal, religious, and ideological distinctions that, in turn, became useful to both the enslaved and colonized.

THE WORK OF RACE

In the mid-colonial period, or the 17th century, indigenous people who served *mita*, people of African descent who were enslaved, or many people who sold their labor were marked according to a racial categorization. For example, though capable of recognizing broad distinctions, Catholic clerics and Spanish authorities infused the juridical category of 'Indian' with expectations of service. Indigenous communities who converted, settled, and agreed to pay tribute (in labor or in kind) were 'awarded' royal protection as native vassals, or members of the Republic of Indians. As I argued, from their racial location – a constructed and powerful legal category of difference – indigenous people were therefore able to take advantage of limited powers when they correctly 'acted' as Indians or in accord with colonial expectations of docile and child-like subjects (O'Toole 2012: 65, 76). Africans and their descendants were not afforded a similar judicial location; there was not a 'Republic of the Blacks' in colonial Spanish America, and enslaved and free Africans and their descendants were not afforded the status of native vassals. Their *casta* of black often functioned as shorthand for 'slave'. Judicially active and astute in the marketplace though, Africans and their descendants appealed for some limited form of protection against extreme abuse, and requested for some guarantee from ecclesiastical courts to guard against the separation of wedded spouses. Imposed by colonial authorities, slaveholders, and local officials, racial categories perpetuated how Andeans, Africans, and their descendants would experience their exploitation within a colonial society that depended on slavery.

Race also marked and created the means of obtaining freedom. In my current project regarding the meaning of freedom in colonial Spanish America, I find that in notarized manumission agreements that relied on individual negotiations, enslaved and freed people rearranged their racial identities within the web of paternalistic relationships with slaveholders. Often, in their attempt to secure legal freedom, the person attempting to gain individual manumission, or for a member of their family, would document exchanges of funds or agreements of debts and payments that were separate from the official 'letter of freedom'. The contrast between the two documents, the manumission agreement and the debt agreement, could allow enslaved people to identify their relationship with slaveholders and ex-owners as more financial than familiar. Racial categories were crucial to these distinctions. For example, in the official manumission agreement, a slaveholder referred to one Catalina del Risco as "my *negra* [black woman], my slave" (ADL. Cortijo Quero. Leg. 124 (1714), f. 168v). In the debt agreement that followed in the bound notary book, Catalina del Risco named herself not only as free, but also as a *morena*, or a 'brown woman' (ADL. Cortijo Quero. Leg. 124 (1714), f. 170v). Though Risco agreed to pay 470 *pesos* and remain in the provincial city of Trujillo on the northern Peruvian coast until her debt was paid, she had transacted a change in her race.

In this context, the deliberate use of specific racial categories shifted a person from their status as slave to a status as free person. Her claim was not about culture or clothing. Risco employed a term to affect an institutional change. The transition, however, was difficult. It could take years for enslaved people such as Risco to save the necessary funds to pay for their freedom and that of their family members, and their strategies included borrowing money from multiple parties. Rather than wait until they had collected the complete amount, however, enslaved people would also seize upon an opportune moment such as the death of an owner. One such example is Catalina de Ayala, who promised to pay her deceased owner's testator 401 *pesos* within three and an half years as part of her manumission payment (ADL. Salinas. Leg. 232 (1673), f. 563). Debt agreements around manumission arrangements bound legally free people into new obligations, but also allowed women and men to participate as subjects who would pay, rather than objects who would garner payment. Clara de Carbajal entered into a debt agreement for 410 *pesos* to pay for her manumission from the Santa Clara convent, which totaled 600 *pesos*. She agreed to repay the large sum within a year, but also shifted the language in her official manumission papers (ADL. Ximeno Bohórquez. Leg. 82, Escrituras 15 (1662), f. 137). At the beginning of the document, the notary referred to Carabajal as a *negra criolla*, or a black woman from the Americas, but when discussing the payment in full, switched to identifying her as *morena* (ADL. Ximeno Bohórquez. Leg. 82, Escrituras 15(1662), f. 135v). In this case, a change in her racial self-description worked to secure Carabajal's position as she labored to purchase her freedom. Ethnic or cultural changes may also have occurred during this transaction, in that Carabajal may have moved to another neighborhood or altered her manner of speaking. The notary evidence, however, provides evidence that most pointedly she, and others, used the change in racial category to distance themselves from slavery.

The racial terms *morena* and *moreno* ('brown woman' and 'brown man' respectively) could also work as a way to maintain people's association with the status of free individuals, even when they felt the pull back to a status more similar to bondage. As can be imagined, those who had gained their legal freedom often defaulted on their debt agreements and found themselves making unfavorable arrangements to pay the price of their freedom. Ana María de Santa Cruz explained that she owed *don* Diego Rodriguez de Gusman one hundred *pesos*, and in compensation for the loan she also agreed to serve him, along with her young son (ADL. Cortijo Quero. Leg. 104 (1688), f. 383). Like Ana María de Santa Cruz, in apprenticing her son to a hatmaker, Ana María retained her self-identification as free *morena*, but called her child a *negrito*, or 'little black one'. Though Ana María had gained and maintained her own freedom, her son was entering into another form of servitude, which she marked by using this distinct category. These transitional spaces were dangerous and could provoke free women and men of color to grasp onto the terms *morena* and *moreno* in order to maintain their legal status while they entered into a gray area of contracted servitude. Juan Delgado's notarized agreement read like a standard indigenous laborer's contract, while Feliciana de Ozerin agreed in 1666 to serve as a cook, laundress, and "all the rest that is ordered" on a ship – surely a difficult job for the only woman on board – in exchange for ten *pesos* a month and fifty in advance (ADL. Suárez del Corral. Leg. 242 (1661), ff. 550 – 550v; ADL. Ortiz de Peralta. Leg. 190 (1666), f. 588v). In the shaky terrain where they had gained a legal free status but were still working through a number of economic arrangements to secure their status, freed people of color employed racial categories to stake out what could be rather unstable positions.

Most critically, claiming to be a *morena* or a *moreno* meant a clear separation from the racial categorization of 'black' as slave. As Michele Reid-Vazquez has explained in the context of the way in which Cuban men of color employed colonial militias to mark themselves apart from civilian populations (Reid-Vazquez 2011: 129), free people of color in Trujillo employed racial terms to distinguish themselves from slaves. When selling their own slaves in notarized agreements, free men and women referred to themselves as *morenas* and *morenos*, in contrast to their slaves, who they referred to in the notarized documents as *negras* and *negros*. Illuminating the importance of this distinction among free people of color, when *doña* Escolástica de Toledo Pancorbo and the Royal Treasurer, Cristobal de Egurca, identified Antonia de Toledo in an agreement where they had agreed to exchange slaves, they called her a *negra criolla*. When it became her turn to voice her part of the agreement, she subtly but critically corrected the elite couple. She identified herself as "I, the said Antonia de Toledo *morena*" to clearly distinguish herself from her *negra* (her slave) as well as what the Spanish-descent slaveholders had called her (ADL. Ortiz de Peralta. Leg. 196 (1672), f. 205). There were certainly material distinctions that Toledo wished to mark between the free *negra* she had been labeled as and the free *morena* she took herself to be. In the transaction between this woman, who was free but could claim no other titles, and one of Trujillo's most powerful couples, the racial term *morena* worked to secure her position – certainly not as an equal, but at least as worthy to engage in the market transaction.

Indicating how free people of color employed the power of a term like *morena*, other free women of color could be relegated to the category of *negra*. Antonia de Toledo was especially vulnerable around Trujillo's most elite. In another exchange of a slave, *Capitan don* Juan de Zevallos, a legally recognized gentleman and city resident who represented *doña* Escolástica de Toledo Pancorbo, demoted Toledo by referring to her as a free *criolla negra*. Still, when the notary turned to Toledo for confirmation regarding the money that would be exchanged, she used the moment to identify herself as a *morena* (ADL. Ortiz de Peralta. Leg. 196 (1672), f. 203). As Michele Reid-Vazquez and Kimberly Hanger have suggested, free women of color negotiated honor in their public displays and employment (Hanger 1997: 98; Reid-Vazquez 2011: 40). If Toledo, like other *morenas* in Trujillo, earned her living from her slaves' daily wages, petty merchandising, and debt management, then her reputation was exceptionally critical to her financial wellbeing. More than merely a cultural marker, their status as *morena* allowed free women of African descent to guarantee that they could engage in the market according to their own volition, and therefore be able to engage in the debt-credit economy that predominated in the colonial Andes.

In addition to distinguishing free people of color from the enslaved, peers were more likely to correctly employ the terms *moreno* and *morena* than Trujillo's elite. In my extensive study of Trujillo's notary records, a scribe's widow, a temporary resident, and a *ladino* indigenous man, immediately named the partners in their transactions *morena* or *moreno*. In these cases, the terms *morena* and *moreno* worked as an adequate nomenclature not only of the people but also of the relationship. Free people of color, like others of modest but adequate means, could work to make a store profit, or pay the rent on a house, as did Agustina de Bracamonte and Catalina de Jesús y San Joan (ADL. Cortijo Quero. Leg. 101 (1681), f. 179; ADL. Cortijo Quero. Leg. 106 (1692), f. 219v). In some cases, *morena* or *moreno* was easily employed in the notarial document – for example, when free people of color like Juana Sanbrossia lent money to a merchant who did not employ the honorific don (ADL. Álvarez. Leg. 83 (1653), f. 328v). Though the official documents were written by a notary, in their use of *moreno* and *morena* these middling urban landlords and petty merchants who were not identified as free people of color indicated that they recognized *morenas* and *morenos* as independent, responsible, and worthy of engagement in financial transactions. In this way, those who were not free people of color undertook the task of communicating the value of racial categories to themselves and to others.

CONCLUSIONS

Moreno and *morena* marked a thin line that was carefully policed between those who were free and respectable, and those closer to slavery. Free people of color employed these and other terms to maintain their distance from the enslaved. Since the time between slavery and freedom could extend indefinitely, in the seventeenth and early 18th centuries, when those who had secured a legally free status often continued to pay their debts, multiple markers were necessary. Surely there were ethnic distinctions. Free people of color tried to change their residency, their clothing, and other cultural markings, which were also significant ways to change their status. At the same time, there were clearly material consequences of either the invocation or the dismissal of the terms *moreno* or *morena*. Those who referred to themselves using these racial categories worked to assure their positions as free people, a status that meant they, unlike slaves, were capable of being responsible for debts, keeping their own households, and serving in the local militia. The categories of *moreno* and *morena*, therefore, carried the financial possibilities of freedom when employed by a free person of color or their peer. It would remain to be seen how these economic and military positions would translate into dominant political positions in the later 18th century.

Indicating the discriminatory uses of race, Trujillo's elites could deny free people of color their claim to the status of *moreno* and *morena*. With the exception of one or two wealthy free people of color, most *morenos* and *morenas* inhabited this status tentatively. By labelling them with another racial category such as *negra* (through a public performance or a legal exchange), a slaveholder or wealthy patron demoted a free person of color and reduced their abilities to maintain their freedom by associating them with the category employed for slaves. These terms, therefore, performed racial work in that the labels themselves affixed, people to material positions, though they could also unfix. Hardly an example of class in the modern sense, race work in the 17th century included the cultural manipulations of casta terminology. Legally, free people of color had gained their manumission papers, but economically as well as in day-to-day relations they continued to struggle to maintain their positions.

These activities could be cultural, legal, and economic, or a combination thereof. In this case, the work of race marked the distinctions between those allowed into credit networks and those who were excluded based on complicated formulations of performances of loyalty, Catholic sensibilities of debt, and the intimate labor of social bondage. Hardly modern and codified, but likewise, though changeable, not simply fluid, the status of free people of color depended on how they could gain access to these multiple valences of the work of race. Regardless, when a person named someone a *moreno* or a *morena*, or named themselves thus, they engaged in a construction of race particular to the mid- to late 17th-century Trujillo, and one that was both useful to and binding of free people of color, and one that worked.

REFERENCES

Archivo Departamental de La Libertad (ADL). Protocols.
- Álvarez
- Cortijo Quero
- Ortiz de Peralta
- Salinas
- Suárez del Corral
- Ximeno Bohórquez

Benton, Lauren (2002): Law and Colonial Cultures: Legal Regimes in World History, 1400 – 1900, Cambridge: Cambridge University Press.
Chance, John/William Taylor (1979): "Estate *and* Class: A Reply." In: Comparative Studies in Society and History 21/3, pp. 434–442.
Cope, R. Douglas (1994): The Limits of Racial Domination: Plebeian Society in Colonial Mexico City, 1660-1720, Madison: University of Wisconsin Press.
Covarrubias, Sebastián (1994 [1611]): Tesoro de la lengua castellana o española, Madrid: Nueva Biblioteca de Erudición y Crítica.
De la Cadena, Marisol (2000): Indigenous Mestizos: The Politics of Race and Culture in Cuzco, Peru, 1919-1991, Durham: Duke University Press.
Fisher, Andrew/Matthew O'Hara (2009): "Introduction: Racial Identities and Their Interpreters in Colonial Latin America." In: Andrew Fisher/Matthew O'Hara (eds.), Imperial Subjects: Race and Identity in Colonial Latin America, Durham: Duke University Press, pp. 1–38.
Graubart, Karen (2015): "Ethnicity." In: Joseph Miller (ed.), The Princeton Companion to Atlantic History, Princeton: Princeton University Press, pp.192–196.

Hanger, Kimberly (1997): Bounded Lives, Bounded Places: Free Black Society in Colonial New Orleans, 1769-1803, Durham: Duke University Press.

Lewis, Laura (2003): Hall of Mirrors: Power, Witchcraft, and Caste in Colonial Mexico, Durham: Duke University Press.

Martínez, María Elena (2008): Genealogical Fictions: Limpieza de Sangre, Religion, and Gender in Colonial Mexico, Stanford: Stanford University Press.

McCaa, Robert/Stuart Schwartz/Arturo Grubessich (1979): "Race and Class in Colonial Latin America: A Critique." In: Comparative Studies in Society and History 21/3, pp. 421-433.

O'Toole, Rachel Sarah (2001): "Inventing Difference: Africans, Indians and the Antecedents of Race in Colonial Peru (1580s-1720s)." Ph.D. Dissertation, University of North Carolina at Chapel Hill.

—— (2012): Bound Lives: Africans, Indians, and the Making of Race in Colonial Peru, Pittsburgh: University of Pittsburgh Press.

Reid-Vazquez, Michele (2011): The Year of the Lash: Free People of Color in Cuba and the Nineteenth-Century Atlantic World, Athens: University of Georgia Press.

Seed, Patricia/Philip Rust (1983): "Estate and Class in Colonial Oaxaca Revisited." In: Comparative Studies in Society and History 25/4, pp. 703-710.

Tavárez, David (2009): "Legally Indian: Inquisitorial Readings of Indigenous Identity in New Spain." In: Andrew Fisher/Matthew O'Hara (eds.), Imperial Subjects: Race and Identity in Colonial Latin America, Durham: Duke University Press, pp. 81-100.

Weismantel, Mary (2001): Cholas and Pishtacos: Stories of Race and Sex in the Andes, Chicago: University of Chicago Press.

Araucanos or 'Mapuches'?
Prejudice vs. recognition in the Chilean media and academia

ANTONIO SÁEZ-ARANCE

In dealing with the question of whether ethnicity is an atemporal, universal categorization or a contingent, historically specific one, the historian often has to confront the phenomenon of naturalization of social and cultural norms. Regardless of the plausibility of the assumption that ethnicity is a human universal, the practices of coexistence in complex societies show to which extent socially constructed differences and boundaries can successfully be adopted as a 'natural' consequence of an enforced otherness.[1] Thus, 'naturalized' prejudice and stereotypes become the dangerous core of everyday racism (cp. Essed 1990; 1991) or of radical nationalism,[2] and they complicate the implementation of integrative and human rights-based policies. Fortunately, the development of social and historical sciences, at least since the end of the Second World War, has provided us with a host of arguments, instruments, methods and strategies with which to critique and deconstruct such beliefs. Nevertheless, the distance between openly discriminating popular attitudes and official, even scholarly discourses may sometimes be smaller than we think or wish.

Let me take an apparently banal example from *El Mercurio*, the leading Chilean conservative newspaper. In a long, typically 'human touch'-style report about adoption, published in 2002, a woman journalist described the reality of

---

1 Cp. "We reach here the very principle of myth: it transforms history into nature" (Barthes 1972: 129). I would like to thank Corinna Di Stefano (Konstanz) and Katharina Motzkau (Cologne/Tucumán) for their very helpful comments and suggestions.

2 Cp. the historical reflection on the German experience of radical nationalism as a xenophobic integration ideology (Wehler 1995).

Chilean childless couples waiting to adopt a baby (Aguilar 2002). Showing obvious empathy with the affected families, the author outlined the legal and institutional mechanism of adoption, delivered some relevant figures, and discussed the fears and hopes of the expectant parents. Central aspects of the report were the possibility of 'choosing one's own child' and the criteria used in order to guarantee the welfare of the new families. Talking with one of the waiting wives, the journalist quoted her main priorities: her baby "should be healthy and not belong to the ethnic group (*etnia*) of the Mapuche". The reason: "here in Temuco we live all together with them, and they truly have a difficult character" (*Acá en Temuco uno convive mucho con ellos, y la verdad es que tienen un carácter difícil*). The woman journalist presented this statement without comment, notwithstanding its obvious racism as well as the fact that the husband, "of Japanese descent", had added other very significant 'hard' criteria ("that the boy or the girl is not conceived by rape or by incest"). *En pedir no hay engaño* ("You can't blame [them] for asking") – the woman journalist continued, in a further display of ignorance and unconscious banalization of the discriminatory attitude of her interviewees. The thoughtless act of effectively putting illness, disability, and Mapuche ethnicity on the same level not only indicates the depth of the interviewees' personal mistrust toward the Mapuche people but also expresses a collective reluctance to come to terms with the other. One could argue that in this case it is a matter of ignorance, or maybe a relic of a situation which, since 2002, has hopefully been overcome. The fact is, however, that the diction of the article is still quite characteristic of the approach of *El Mercurio*, especially with regard to the Mapuche reality, and to issues of ethnic diversity in general.[3] Continuing a tradition from the days of Salvador Allende's *Unidad Popular*, when the newspaper often included reports of marauding Mapuche 'gangs' in the southern provinces, one of its favorite motifs since the 1990s is the reporting of Mapuche 'terrorists' installing panic and fear among the Chilean farmers and putting all economic activities at risk. This asymmetry in the media coverage of the growing social conflicts in Southern Chile and the frequent eruptions of violence between Mapuche activists and agents of the Chilean State reached a peak in the first weeks of 2013 with the occasion of the murder of the Luchsinger-Mackays, a couple who were members of an old colonist family of Swiss descent. On January 4, 2013, Werner Luchsinger's residence in Vilcún, in the *Araucanía* Region, was attacked and burned down by a group of hooded persons. An hour after the act, the Police found Mapuche Celestino Córdova with a gunshot wound on a field near the crime scene. He had been injured by the victim, who had tried to defend his own and his wife's life

---

3   The same accounts for *El Diario Austral*, its regional subsidiary in Temuco.

by firing a gun at his aggressor. The two lifeless bodies had been found asphyxiated and burned on the floor of their house (Human Rights Watch 2004). From the very beginning of the investigation, security forces, local politicians and government officials, as well as the majority of the mass media in Santiago proceeded on the assumption that this was an act of Mapuche 'terrorism'. In Chile, such an accusation implies significant consequences, since the Anti-Terrorist Law allows an extraordinarily severe treatment of suspects – widely criticized by human rights organizations, including Human Rights Watch and the UN Human Rights Council (2013). The Anti-Terrorist Law dates from the Pinochet regime (1984) and abrogates due process rights for the accused, including a longer wait before arraignment and access to a lawyer once charged. The law also authorizes the imposition of penalties up to three times higher than those established in the Chilean Criminal Code, and considers that acts perpetrated with the aim of 'causing fear in the population' or 'imposing demands upon authorities' have a 'terrorist intent'.[4] In the case of the Luchsinger-Mackay couple, the insistence of both regional and national *pressure* groups as well as mass media on considering the crime as an act of 'terrorism' negatively affected both the normal course of the trial and the associated public discussion, and prompted a number of discriminatory – if not openly racist – comments about the Mapuche people. No attack on the Mapuche or their houses had ever attracted such intense attention from the media and authorities; neither had the perpetrators of those attacks ever been brought to justice.[5] Almost no attention had been paid to the fact that the pamphlets scattered at the Luchsinger ranch during the arson attack referred to the fifth anniversary of Matías Catrileo's death. Catrileo, a 26-year-old Mapuche activist, had been shot in the back by police during a land rights protest on the property of Jorge Luchsinger, son of the Luchsinger-Mackay couple, on January 3, 2008. But only a few publications went to all the bother of reconstructing the complex background of a neighborhood dispute with historical roots back in the last decades of the 19th century (Bengoa 2014: 103-125).[6] The majority of the print comments in *El*

---

4 *Ley 18.314, que determina conductas terroristas y fija su penalidad*, (translation: that determines terrorist acts and defines penalties) enacted by the Junta Militar on April 16, 1984 (http://bcn.cl/1m3cx).

5 One year later, Córdova, the only suspect, was found guilty, while the other participants in the arson attack could not be arrested. Celestino Córdova is the *machi* (a kind of spiritual healer) within the Mapuche community in the region.

6 Only alternative newspapers (*El Ciudadano, The Clinic*) and the radio station of the Universidad de Chile have reported on the long-standing work of the historian Martín Correa Cabrera, a researcher of the *Observatorio Ciudadano* (the former *Observatorio*

Mercurio and (to a lesser extent) *La Tercera* continued to reproduce the negative stereotypes regarding the 'violence' of Mapuche activism, thus contributing to the further criminalization of ethnic belonging. The editorial line of these newspapers has been clear and consistent until nowadays: exaggerated reporting of acts of violence, denial of ethnic diversity in the Chilean nation-state, and concentration on the defense of values of 'order' and 'security' – those values supposedly threatened by the 'violent' Mapuche (Foerster/Vergara 2000: 29–33; Crow 2013: 148–49, 167–68; Pairican 2014: 28).

The mainstream media also serve as a platform for the diffusion of a more sophisticated, academic version of the dominant discourse of exclusion. An illustrative case was the controversy that kept both political and scholarly circles in Chile busy throughout March 2014. A new policy regarding indigenous peoples, announced by the just-elected left-wing government of President Michelle Bachelet, included novel approaches to political participation, legal and constitutional recognition, and a reconsideration of the use of the Anti-Terrorist Law against Mapuche activists. Additionally, Bachelet appointed a Mapuche politician, the Christian-democrat Francisco Huenchumilla, as the new governor (*intendente*) of the territory of the *Araucanía* (*IX Región*), with the explicit aim of helping to implement the governmental reforms. These announcements provoked a furious reaction from several conservative Chilean historians and publicists, who rejected the whole project of the new administration. Again making intensive use of the traditional conservative platform of *El Mercurio*, they openly questioned the existence of distinct 'native' or 'indigenous' groups in the Chilean society by categorically denying the validity of collective 'historical' rights, especially in the case of the Chilean Mapuche people. Above all, Sergio Villalobos, professor at the Universidad de Chile and 'grand old man' of Chilean national historiography, insisted in several print and TV interviews on avoiding the use of the term 'Mapuche' at all, which is, in his opinion, purely and simply an 'invention' of leftist intellectuals (Villalobos 2014; Huenchumilla 2014; Antileo/Pairican 2014). Instead, he refers to 'Araucanians', adopting Spanish colonial terminology. Similarly to the 19th-century elites, Villalobos, interviewed in 2014, seems to deal with the reality of ethnic diversity by imagining the pre-conquest past rather than conveying in any sense an indigenous vision. Regarding the current conflict, Villalobos sides with the colonists of Northern and Central European descent (German, Swiss, French, British) in denouncing the 'political violence' the Mapuche organizations have

---

de Derechos de los Pueblos Indígenas), who has described meticulously the economic activities of the Luchsingers since their arrival in Chile (Soto 2013; cp. also Correa Cabrera 2008).

employed. He justifies the repressive aspects of state policy and explains the social underdevelopment of the *Araucanía* by referring to *defectos ancestrales* of Mapuche people, namely to their traditionally supposed disposition toward alcoholism, or their purportedly inadequate aptitude for productive working. According to the opinion of Villalobos, the so-called 'Pacification', i.e. the forced expropriation of Mapuche lands at the end of the 19th century, was the 'necessary' result of progress and the precondition of national modernization. Villalobos' statement of 2014 was consistent with his earlier political comments. He reproduced the same arguments he had already used in May 2000 when criticizing the work of the *Comisión de Verdad Histórica y Nuevo Trato* (CVHNT, Commission for Historical Truth and New Treatment of Indigenous Peoples) (Villalobos 2011: 46-66). The final report of this commission, convoked by President Ricardo Lagos Escobar, had concluded that the occupation of the *Araucanía* by the Chilean state was made possible only "through violent means", and described the fifteen years between 1869 and 1883 as "a period of great violence" (Crow 2013: 187-194). This statement, notwithstanding the lack of real political effects, was contrary to the nationalist-assimilationist consensus, and right-wing historians and publicists did not receive it favorably.[7]

Even if Villalobos' language obviously contains harsh racist elements, the consequences of his political and historiographical positions certainly go beyond a simple matter of political correctness (cp. Pavez 2012; Pairican 2014: 208). His argumentation, supposedly founded on historical evidence, serves the political purpose of invisibilizing ethnic differences (cp. Miller 2003: 197-200, for the link between invisibilization and nonrecognition in Chile). Furthermore, his standpoint consistently supports the idea of a homogeneous and monocultural Chilean society, implicitly contrasting it to the much lesser stable and compact societies of the South American neighborhood (and especially in the Andean region). By using systematically the label 'ancestral', as Villalobos does, the suggestion is that the so-called '*Araucanía* Conflict' is an artificial one. The most effective instrument of its invisibilization is the biased 'historicizing' of its historical causes by dating it in the most recondite past and retrojecting its origins not to the Chilean process of state-building in the 19th century, but to an

---

7 Paradoxically, the publication of the CVHNT's report activated at the same time the rising of a kind of 'radical' Mapuche historiography 'from below', condemning not only the 'distorted history' contained in the report, but also the 'postcolonial epistemology' behind of the dominant political and scientific approach to the Mapuche issues. The criticism included by the way the most progressive historians and anthropologists (cp. Caniuqueo/Levil/Marimán/Millalén 2006).

indeterminate 'colonial' (i.e. 'Spanish') pre-historical time. So it is not unusual to hear Chilean politicians relativizing current demands of the Mapuche people by referring to a '500-year-old question'. But national historians also play a problematic role when they suggest a (positively connoted) continuity between the Spanish conquest of Chile in the 16th century and the Chilean conquest of the *Araucanía* at the end of the 19th century.[8] As the anthropologist José Bengoa, one of the greatest specialists in Mapuche history, has pointed out, the Chilean public's systematic refusal to accept the 'modernity' of the conflict has both a scientific and a political dimension (Bengoa 2014: 294). A realistic historical explanation of the occupation of the *Araucanía* since the end of the 19th century would include accounts not only of the violence perpetrated against the Mapuche, but also of their dispossession of their own land, the fragmentation of their traditional power structures, their increasing exposure to external socioeconomic and political threats, and, last but not least, their exclusion from the Chilean national project. All these elements would make the 'Mapuche issue' a Chilean national one, because they all contrast with a well-established national consensus on the successful 'Chilean way' and reveal the limits and contradictions of the national modernization process.

The reconstruction of the origins of Villalobos' nationalist-apologetic narrative, besides its relevance for the History of Chilean Historiography, also provides an insight into the ways in which the public role of historians in Chile has been shaped and defined through the 200 years of independent life. Villalobos represents a national tradition of dealing with ethnic diversity, a specifically *wingka*[9] perspective *vis à vis* the Mapuche reality, which also radiates out beyond the historical discipline. Since the end of the 19th century, the conquest of the *Araucanía* has always been presented as an inevitable, quite unproblematic and uncomplicated element of the Chilean nation-building process, fitting perfectly into the self-satisfied discourse of Chilean exceptionalism (Jocelyn-Holt 2005). The occupation of the vast territories southern of the Bío Bío River, whose inhabitants had resisted the Spanish colonial power for almost three centuries, received very little attention in the great historical works of renowned Chilean historians of the *fin de siècle* or the

---

8   Or suggesting continuity, by declaring that "the task assumed by the Spanish" more than three hundred years before was "thus" finally concluded in the 1880s (Villalobos 2008: 152).

9   The Mapuzugun word '*wingka*' (in Spanish *huinca*), which originally refers to the Inca (*ingka*) and Spanish (*ui-ingka*, i.e., 'new Inca') invaders of Mapuche territory, but also means 'thief' or 'bandit', is a stereotype the Mapuche use, often in a derogatory way, for describing practices or habits conceived as non-Mapuche.

first half of the 20th century (Diego Barros Arana, Francisco Encina, Luis Galdames etc.). The consequence of the dominance of 'minimalist narratives' in the historiography was the diffusion of a biased interpretation in school curricula and in the Chilean State Museums (Crow 2013: 24-25). Even under Pinochet's dictatorship, and although the regime was not known for its rhetorical carefulness, the official interpretation of the occupation was that it had been an example of 'peaceful resolution of border conflicts'. Curiously, the military campaigns against the Mapuche have also been sidelined in the most influential Anglophone studies of Chilean History, especially in those adopting almost enthusiastically the common interpretation of national order and political stability.[10] A cruel war as well as a bloody military occupation regime would seriously put into question this self-satisfied picture of Chilean history. For instance, the professionalism and modernity of the Chilean army belong to the "myths of Chilean democracy" (Portales 2004: 81–98, 263–273), while the inglorious participation of Chilean soldiers in the occupation of the *Araucania* tends to be overlooked or at least relativized. Chilean forces killed, raped and set fire to the *rukas* (houses) of the Mapuche. The profusion of primary sources confirming the existence of gruesome war crimes on both sides, and the numerous testimonies of the brutality of the post-war occupation contrast with the idyllic discourse of mainstream Chilean historiography until at least the 1980s.

An additional crucial aspect of the historical invisibilization of the Mapuche is the strategy of avoiding a colonial framing of the issue. The acquisition of the *Araucania* coincided with the annexation of large tracts of Bolivian and Peruvian territory during the War of the Pacific (1879-1883), and was followed shortly thereafter by the appropriation of Rapa Nui/Easter Island (1888). Another specifically colonial trait of the mainstream narrative is the fact that it is a history without Mapuche protagonists. Mapuche people are usually presented as a homogenous and defeated mass. In fact, mainstream Chilean historiography still insists that relations between the Mapuche and Spanish were relatively peaceful and that commercial relations and *mestizaje* proceeded rapidly at the end of the Spanish colonial age. While Villalobos and his followers are absolutely right in emphasizing the long history of frontier relations and the impact of transculturation processes and the mutually beneficial economic relations between the Mapuche and Spanish (with the concomitant decline in

---

10 A paradigmatic case is the 'classic' handbook of Simon Collier and William Sater (2004), with only 1½ pages dedicated to war and occupation. Cp. the criticism of Jocelyn-Holt (2014: 295–308); for the general historiographical context cp. Sáez Arance (2015).

military aggression), their conclusion in terms of suggesting a 'pacific integration' of the *Araucanía* into Chile and a more or less 'automatic' conversion of 'Mapuche' into 'Araucanian Chilean' is misleading and apologetic (cp. among others Jara 1971; Villalobos 1992: 265–410 and 1995; Blancpain 1996; Bengoa 2003; Rinke 2003). The picture is much more complicated than this, especially if indigenous sources are taken into account. In the exceptionally valuable collection of *Cartas Mapuches*, edited by the historian and anthropologist Jorge Pavez, we find several examples of the ambivalence of the relation between the Mapuche and the Chilean state before, during, and after the 'Pacification' of the *Araucanía* (Pavez Ojeda 2008; cp. also Navarro 2014). In fact, there were Mapuche leaders who supported the Chilean military forces. Continuing a tradition of the colonial time, the so-called *indios amigos* received regular payments from the Chilean government for providing information or for helping to keep peace in their communities. On the other side, the testimonies of the deported Mapuche collected by the German ethnographer Robert Lehmann-Nitsch in the *Museo de Ciencias Naturales* in La Plata (Argentina) reveal the extent of the long-term damages done to the indigenous people (Canio/Pozo 2013). The social and political reality of indigenous people in Chile of the last 125 years certainly looks quite different from the harmonious picture painted by the Chilean national historiography. The main problems they are faced with are indubitably poverty and marginalization. But in addition, for the Mapuche activists, the question is also a matter of (cultural) rights and collective identity seeking expression in a pluralist society. Regarding the trends with respect to the recognition of ethnicity in Latin America, Chile is the most extreme case of legal underdevelopment (Clavero 2008b: 30–33).[11] For instance, Chile's current constitution, which was written by Pinochet and his advisers in 1980, is the only one in the entire South American continent which does not recognize indigenous peoples. Notwithstanding the fact that the number of indigenous people is clearly lower in some other regions than in Chile, neighboring states such as Argentina included such recognition in their constitutions back in 1994. In several Latin American nation states such as Ecuador, Colombia, and Venezuela, new constitutions designate seats in the national congress specifically for indigenous representatives. Other countries such as Bolivia go even further, declaring the plurinational and multicultural character of the state (Bengoa 2007; Clavero 2008a).[12]

---

11 Clavero makes explicitly the link between the academic 'ignorance' and the legal nonrecognition of the Mapuche reality.

12 Cp. Bengoa (2007: 93-147) on the social and political background of this indigenous 'emergence'.

How did this special path taken by Chile come about? The described dominant discourse on the Mapuche conflict reunites exemplarily almost all elements of the evolution of the ethnicity discussion in the independent Latin American republics, but it also contains specifically national elements (Crow 2014). Firstly, it is necessary to consider the (historiographical and political) decision to use the term 'Araucanian' or 'Mapuche'. Notwithstanding the relatively recent use of 'ethnicity' as both a technical term and a field of scientific study, historians of ancient, medieval and early modern history have been mostly aware of the centrality of ethnic cleavages in processes of social, political and cultural transformation across the centuries. However, their traditional emphasis on state-building, especially considering the genuine legitimating function of history as a discipline, resulted in a relative neglect of all those dimensions of 'ethnicity' that challenged the conceptual dominance of the State in historical discourse. The rise of state structures in Europe's early modern overseas empires can generally be interpreted as a continuation of domestic state-building processes (e.g. in the case of the Spanish and Portuguese colonies). Hence, the dominant master narratives of the European colonial period tended to emphasize a presumed evolutionary gap between 'highly developed' state-like *civilizations* on the one hand and 'primitive' *peoples, nations* or *tribes* on the other. Emergent national historiographies in the young Latin American republics perpetuated this dichotomous approach, in accordance with European and North American social conventions. In the Chilean case, the national historiography received strong European influences from the beginning, and very early on it adopted a methodologically and ideologically conservative matrix, focusing on the 'order' as the central social category and favoring the political exclusion of all those individuals as well as all those social and ethnic groups which potentially could put this 'order' in question (Stuven 2000; Sáez Arance 2014).[13] The presumptive lack, or simply the otherness, of the structures of socio-political organization among the Mapuche became much more than a purely historical argument – to this day it still serves to legitimate the absence of – or at least the weak disposition of Chilean authorities to open – a political dialogue with indigenous activists.

By making the choice for the elder Spanish denomination, the Chilean national(ist) historians also demonstrate their constancy in the defense of the vision of creole elites throughout Spanish America since the wars of independence in the early 19th century. In fact, Spanish American 'patriots' made an extensive use of the pre-conquest Amerindian past for the construction

---

13 Stuven (2000) makes a systematic treatment of the importance of 'order' categories in all cultural and political debates of this era.

of meaningful national myths and histories *vis à vis* their royalist enemies. Generally speaking, both in humanist-oriented Spanish *crónicas* of the Renaissance and in the republican historiography of the 19th century, heavily influenced by romanticism, authors alluded to conceptions (we should rather say: to *pre*conceptions) of 'ethnicity' as an element deeply rooted in European culture. The existence of 'Romans' and 'Germans', of 'Iberians', 'Lusitans' and 'Visigoths' in Antiquity and the early Middle Ages became a relevant fact for the interpretation and explanation of ongoing ethnic conflicts in the New World. There was not even a lack of bizarre transfers of stereotypes in one way or another (cultural similarities between 'Basques' and '*Araucanos*', '*Flandes indiano*' as a characterization for the not-pacified Southern Chile, in analogy to the Spanish Netherlands, etc.) (Sáez Arance 2010: 137–139). It is obvious that the concerned peoples had little or nothing to do with such heroic clichés, but the evocative power of these bequeathed 'ethnic' terms and categories, combined with additional criteria of social and religious distinction, significantly framed the mutual cultural perception.[14] Sometimes they were even used to justify the quality of the response of the colonial power. After 1820, these traditional narratives, as well as the associated new national symbols, compensated for the lack (or at least for the deficits) of a strong, clear and distinct collective identity among the mostly 'white', Catholic, wealthy and Spanish-speaking actors of the independence in the different regions of the dismembered empire. The British historian Rebecca Earle has underlined the similarities in the development and social implementation of this 'elite nationalism' across Spanish America (2007: 9–15). The Chilean case is outstanding because of the persistence of its identitarian leitmotifs and its extremely contradictory foundations. On the one side, Chilean 'ethno-patriotism' of 1820 was fed through the exaltation of Mapuche (i.e. 'Araucanian') heroism by the Spaniards in literature, especially in Alonso de Ercilla's *La Araucana* (Ercilla 1993 [1569–89]). This epic poem, written in the 16th century by a Basque soldier in Madrid, who had spent no more than a couple of years in the most distant place of the Spanish Monarchy, for a very long time (to some extent, even to the present day!) enjoyed the curious status of being the 'first history book' about Chile (Álvarez Vilela 1986). The Mapuche, or the 'Araucanians', as Ercilla called them, became a people renowned in Spanish America for the ferocity with which they resisted Spanish ambitions of conquest. The success of Mapuche resistance was symbolized by the fact that the Spaniards were never able to establish a permanent foothold in the *Araucanía* south of the river Bío Bío, and of course in the 1820s and 1830s this was a very god reason to be proud to be a 'Chilean'. On the other side, this

---

14 On the Mapuche 'ethnogenesis' in the context of colonial frontier cp. Boccara 1999.

rhetorical sympathy for the indigenous had no positive consequences for the tense situation at the border of the new state. The Araucanian image began to vary substantially: from 1845 onwards the Mapuche were much less frequently described as hardy and brave ancestors of the Chileans, and much more often as "barbarous savages" instead (Pinto 2003: 151–160). The institutional consolidation of the Republic and the launch of an ambitious settlement program for Central European immigrants in the south of the country brought along a fundamental revision of the official statements with regard to the indigenous. Liberal politicians and positivist-influenced writers started to talk about 'Araucanians' in a similarly disparaging way to Sergio Villalobos nowadays (sometimes their statements were even published by the same newspapers – such as *El Mercurio*). This discursive change became the prelude for the so-called *Pacificación de la Araucanía* (1861–1883) – in other words, for the invasion and the military occupation of the territories south of the Bío Bío (Pinto 2003: 185–208). The justification was the assumption of a civilizing mission towards the indigenous inhabitants by raising their material standard of living as well as "their spirit to the moral and religious truths".[15] The invasion of the *Araucanía* sparked a violent war which caused the death and the displacement of numerous Mapuche, destroyed the communitarian structures, and opened the way for German and Swiss settlers, who were often influenced by modernist racist ideas, and in any case were scarcely sensitive to the historical merits of good old Araucanian warriors.

From this date, the relations between the Mapuche and the Chilean nation state became practically reduced to an economic-assistential dimension on the one hand and, on the other, to an issue of security policy. Seen from a social perspective, the state was (legally) entitled to force an assimilation of living conditions, as the Mapuche should now be perceived as equal citizens of the Chilean nation. This was manifested in a political practice of coercion and repression beyond party-political boundaries, mostly in favor of the big landowners of European descent, and later on in the 20th century, in favor of forestry companies, both local and from abroad (Mallon 1999; Kaltmeier 2004: 93–96, 151–153, 182–185; Pairican 2014: 33–65). The 'Mapuche issue' therefore became a military 'Mapuche conflict'. Nevertheless, the Chilean occupation did not entail the complete elimination of Mapuche cultural practices. Notwithstanding the limits of the reservation system, it allowed the Mapuche a framework within which to continue their communitarian traditions. Long – term local studies such as Florencia Mallon's book on the community of Nicolas Ailio

---

15 Cp. Pinto (2003: 118–119, 167–170, and 171–179) on the specific role of historians, Bengoa (2014: 51–54) and Bottinelli (2009: 109–113).

show the changing dynamics of social interaction, political tension and cultural appropriation characteristic of the relations between Mapuche and the Chilean state in the 20th century (Mallon 2005). On the other side, the most positive developments in the interethnic dialogue grew out of the initiative of Mapuche intellectuals to occupy their own place in the Chilean public sphere, for instance by creating new indigenous media or simply by participating much more actively in the great 'national' debates.[16] Despite the obsessive concentration of the public discourse on security issues, the mostly pacific activism of today's Mapuche organisations contributes to clarifying the historically grown, real nature of the 'Mapuche problem' by placing emphasis on the question of identity and the recognition of this identity.[17] This recognition is surely compatible with a modern, inclusive and pluralist redefinition of the Chilean state.[18] Furthermore, it would be a real contribution to sociocultural change, for the benefit of all inhabitants of "that *ruka* called Chile".[19] From the perspective of critical historians, an important aim should be to help public opinion to focus on the real problems of the present, instead of helping the political elites to functionally relegate the so-called Mapuche-conflict to the past. It is not the 'ancestral defects' of the Mapuche that are at fault, but rather the structural defects of a colonialist state, which turned out to be unable to manage social and ethnic diversity.

---

16 This is the case of the quite influential Mapuche publicist Pedro Cayuqueo, who launched the Mapuche newspaper *Azkintuwe* in October 2003 (cp. Cayuqueo 2012b), and became in the following years a prolific political columnist in *The Clinic* and even sometimes in mainstream media as *La Tercera* (Cayuqueo 2012a, 2014).

17 One of the first (and unfortunately quite isolated) scholarly inputs in this sense was the programmatic contribution of the anthropologists Rolf Foerster and Iván Vergara (2000). They proposed an analysis of the Mapuche conflict from the perspective of the "struggle for recognition", i.e. as a dispute over the sense and the character of the relationship between the Mapuches and the Chilean society. The authors connect their analysis with the international philosophical and sociological research on recognition (Jürgen Habermas, Charles Taylor and Axel Honneth) and compare it critically with the typically Schmittian 'friend/foe' reductionism of the Chilean mainstream media.

18 A central aspect of this redefinition should be an anyhow necessary process of decentralization and political devolution. For the development of own political concepts among the Mapuche cp. Marimán (2013).

19 I am adopting the programmatic formulation of Pedro Cayuqueo (2014), arguing in the pursuit of a "national dialogue" in Chile. For an earlier reflection on the perspectives of a Chilean 'multiculturalism', which overcomes the traditional reduction of Mapuche to a problematic 'minority', cp. also Foerster and Vergara (2002).

References

Aguilar, Marcela (2002): "Adopción en Chile: Elija a su hijo." In: El Mercurio, April 12.

Antileo, Enrique/Pairican, Fernando (2014): "Carta abierta a Sergio Villalobos: Cuando la historia se convierte en instrumento racial y colonial." The Clinic, March 25.

Álvarez Vilela, Ángel (1986): "Histoire et fiction dans *La Araucana*: les personnages indiens et l'épreuve du tronc." In: Etudes de lettres 2, Université de Lausanne, Faculté des Lettres, pp. 39–67.

Barthes, Roland (1972): Mythologies, translated by Annette Lavers, New York: Hill and Wang.

Bengoa, José (2003): Historia de los antiguos mapuches del sur: Desde antes de la llegada de los españoles hasta las paces de Quilín, Santiago de Chile: Catalonia.

—— (2007[2000]): La emergencia indígena en América Latina, Mexico DF: Fondo de Cultura Económica.

—— (2014): Mapuche, colonos y el Estado nacional, Santiago de Chile: Catalonia.

Blancpain, Jean-Pierre (1996): Les Araucans et le Chili Des origines au XIXe siècle, Paris: L'Harmattan.

Boccara, Guillaume (1999): Guerre et ethnogenèse mapuche dans le Chili colonial. L'invention du soi, Paris: L'Harmattan.

Bottinelli Wolleter, Alejandra (2009): "'El oro y la sangre que vamos a prodigar'. Benjamín Vicuña Mackenna, la ocupación de la Araucanía y la inscripción del imperativo civilizador en el discurso público chileno." In: Rafael Gaune Corradi/Martín Lara Ortega (eds.), Historias de racismo y discriminación en Chile, Santiago de Chile: uqbar editores, pp. 105–122.

Canio Llanquinao, Margarita/Pozo Menares, Gabriel (eds.) (2013): Historia y conocimiento oral mapuche: sobrevivientes de la "Campaña del Desierto" y "Ocupación de la Araucanía" (1899-1926), Santiago de Chile: LOM Ediciones.

Caniuqueo, Sergio/Levil, Rodrigo/Marimán, Pablo/Millalén, José (2006): ¡...Escucha, winka...! Cuatro ensayos de Historia Nacional Mapuche y un epílogo sobre el futuro, Santiago de Chile: LOM Ediciones.

Cayuqueo, Pedro (2012a): Sólo por ser indios y otras crónicas mapuches, Santiago de Chile: Catalonia.

—— (2012b): La voz de los lonkos. Selección de reportajes del periódico Azkintuwe, Santiago de Chile: Catalonia.

—— (2014): Esa ruca llamada Chile y otras crónicas mapuches, Santiago de Chile: Catalonia.

Clavero, Bartolomé (2008a): Geografía Jurídica de América Latina. Pueblos Indígenas entre Constituciones Mestizas, México DF: Siglo XXI.

—— (2008b): "Reconocimiento mapuche de Chile: Tratado ante Constitución, historia frente a derecho." In: Revista de la Universidad de Chile, Derecho y Humanidades 13, pp. 13–40.

Collier, Simon/Sater, William (2004): A History of Chile 1808–2002, Cambridge: University Press.

Correa Cabrera, Martín (2008): "El fundo Santa Margarita, su origen, historia y su relación con las comunidades mapuches vecinas y colindantes", March 11, 2008 (http://mapuexpress.net).

Crow, Joanna (2013): The Mapuche in Modern Chile: A Cultural History, Gainesville: University Press of Florida.

—— (2014): "From Araucanian warriors to Mapuche terrorists: contesting discourses of gender, race and nation in modern Chile (1810–2010)." In: Journal of Iberian and Latin American Studies 20, pp. 75–101.

Earle, Rebecca (2007): The Return of the Native: Indians and Myth-Making in Spanish America, 1810–1930, Durham: Duke University Press.

Ercilla, Alonso de (1993 [1569–1589]): La Araucana. Edition by Isaías Lerner, Madrid: Ediciones Cátedra.

Essed, Philomena (1990): Everyday Racism: *Reports From Women of Two Cultures, Claremont:* Hunter House.

—— (1991): Understanding Everyday Racism. An interdisciplinary Theory, Newbury Park/London/New Delhi: Sage Publications.

Foerster G., Rolf/ Vergara, Jorge Iván (2000): "Etnia y nación en la lucha por el reconocimiento. Los mapuches en la sociedad chilena." In: Estudios Atacameños 19, pp. 11–42.

Foerster G., Rolf/Vergara, Jorge Iván (2002): "Permanencia y transformación del conflicto mapuche." In: Mapocho, Revista de Humanidades 51, pp. 235–240.

Human Rights Watch (2004): "Undue Process: Terrorism Trials, Military Courts, and the Mapuche in Southern Chile," HRW Report 16/5(B), (http://www.hrw.org/en/node/11920/section/1).

Huenchumilla, Francisco (2014): "Respuesta a Sergio Villalobos." In: El Mercurio, March 20.

Jara, Álvaro (1971): Guerra y Sociedad en Chile. La transformación de la guerra de Arauco y la esclavitud de los indios, Santiago de Chile: Editorial Universitaria.

Jocelyn-Holt, Alfredo (2005): "¿Un proyecto nacional exitoso? La supuesta excepcionalidad chilena." In: Colom González, Francisco (ed.), Relatos de la nación. La construcción de las identidades nacionales en el mundo hispánico, Madrid: Vervuert, pp. 417–438.

—— (2014): El peso de la noche. Nuestra frágil fortaleza histórica, Santiago de Chile: Random House/De bolsillo.

Kaltmeier, Olaf (2004): *Marichiweu! Zehnmal werden wir siegen! Eine Rekonstruktion der Mapuche-Bewegung in Chile aus der Dialektik von Herrschaft und Widerstand seit der Conquista*, Münster: Westfälisches Dampfboot.

Mallon, Florencia (1999): "Cuando la amnesia se impone con sangre, el abuso se hace costumbre: El pueblo Mapuche y el estado chileno, 1883-1998." In: Paul Drake/Iván Jaksic (eds.), El modelo chileno: Democracia y desarrollo en los noventa, Santiago de Chile: LOM Editores, pp. 435–464.

—— (2005): *Courage Tastes of Blood: The Mapuche Community of Nicolas Ailio and the Chilean State, 1906-2001*, Durham: Duke University Press.

Marimán, José A. (2013): Autodeterminación. Ideas políticas mapuche en el albor del siglo XXI, Santiago de Chile: LOM Editores.

Miller, Bruce G. (2003): *Invisible Indigenes: The Politics of Nonrecognition*, Lincoln: University of Nebraska Press.

Navarro R., Leandro (2014): Crónica militar de la conquista y pacificación de la Araucanía, Santiago de Chile: Pehuén.

Pairican, Fernando (2014): Malon. La rebelión del movimiento mapuche 1990-2013, Santiago de Chile: Pehuén.

Pavez Ojeda, Jorge (ed.) (2008): Cartas mapuche, siglo XIX, Santiago de Chile: CoLibris & Ocholibros.

—— (2012): "Colonialismo republicano, censura fronteriza y ortogramas reaccionarios. Respuesta a Sergio Villalobos Rivera." In: Cuadernos de Historia 36, pp. 119–136.

Pinto, Jorge (2003[2000]): La formación del Estado, la nación y el pueblo mapuche. De la inclusión a la exclusión, Santiago de Chile: Dibam/Centro de Investigaciones Diego Barros Arana (original edition published by the Instituto de Estudios Avanzados de la Universidad de Santiago de Chile).

Portales, Felipe (2004): Los mitos de la democracia chilena. Desde los orígenes a 1925, Santiago de Chile: Catalonia.

Rinke, Stefan (2003): "'Grenze' als Urerfahrung in Lateinamerika: Mapuche in Chile zwischen Mythos und Verleugnung." In: Stefan Rinke et al. (eds.), Abgrenzen oder Entgrenzen: Zur Produktivität von Grenzen, Frankfurt: IKO-Verlag, pp. 111–130.

Sáez Arance, Antonio (2010): "El rebelde flamenco, ¿'enemigo de España'? Sobre la persistencia de un estereotipo dudoso." In: Xosé M. Núñez Seixas/ Francisco Sevillano Calero (eds.), Los enemigos de España: Imagen del otro, conflictos bélicos y disputas nacionales (siglos XVI-XX), Madrid: Centro de Estudios Constitucionales, pp. 119–139.

—— (2014): "Constitución disciplinaria e identidad nacional en los inicios de la historiografía chilena." In: Sandra Carreras/Katja Carrillo Zeiter (eds.), Las ciencias en la formación de las naciones americanas, Frankfurt/Madrid: Iberoamericana/Vervuert, pp. 91–110.

—— (forthcoming): "Historias de la chilenidad: académicos e indoctrinadores." In: Vanessa Höse/Katharina Motzkau/Antonio Sáez Arance (eds.), Identidades nacionales en América Latina: discursos, saberes, representaciones, Frankfurt/Madrid: Iberoamericana/Vervuert.

Soto, Loreto (2013): "La historia de la familia Luchsinger en La Araucanía", (http://radio.uchile.cl/2013/01/04/la-historia-de-la-familia-luchsinger-en-la-araucania).

Stuven, Ana María (2000): La seducción de un orden. Las élites y la construcción de Chile en las polémicas culturales y políticas del siglo XIX, Santiago de Chile: Editorial Universidad Católica de Chile.

UN Human Rights Council (2003): "Statement by the UN Special Rapporteur on the promotion and protection of human rights and fundamental freedoms while countering terrorism", (http://www.ohchr.org/EN/NewsEvents/Pages/DisplayNews.aspx?NewsID=13598&LangID=E).

Villalobos Rivera, Sergio (1989): Los Pehuenches en la vida fronteriza, Santiago de Chile: Ediciones Universidad Católica de Chile.

—— (1992): La vida fronteriza en Chile, Madrid: Mapfre.

—— (1995): Vida fronteriza en la Araucanía: el mito de la Guerra de Arauco, Santiago de Chile: Andrés Bello.

—— (2008): Breve historia de Chile, Santiago de Chile: Universitaria.

—— (2011): La historia por la historia. Crítica de la historiografía actual, Santiago de Chile: Universidad Andrés Bello.

—— (2014): "Intendencia de La Araucanía." In: El Mercurio, March 19.

Wehler, Hans-Ulrich (1995): "Nationalismus und Fremdenhass." In: Hans-Ulrich Wehler, Die Gegenwart der Geschichte. Essays, Munich: C.H. Beck, pp. 144–158.

Chinese in the Cuban revolution
An ethnically marked political mobilization?

ALBERT MANKE

While the history of Chinese immigrants in Cuba since 1847 has been investigated by a number of studies that have focused primarily on the coolie trade and on the immigration wave of the 1920s,[1] the history of Chinese immigrants, and also that of their descendants, in revolutionary Cuba after 1959 still remains a field of study worthy of exploration.[2] In particular, their participation in the Cuban revolution of 1959 seems quite significant, though, like the history of Overseas Chinese in other regions of the world during the Cold War, this has also not been studied in detail (Ho/Madokoro/Peterson 2014: 131). Scholars have pointed to the turn away from Cuba and the revolution, mostly for economic reasons, of a large part of the Chinese Cuban community due to economic problems that hit them with the revolution, especially after the expropriations of small and medium-sized business in 1968 (Herrera/Castillo 2003: 166).

But there were also groups and individuals of Chinese descent that actively supported the Cuban revolutionary government, some of them for decades.[3] In

---

1 On coolies, cp. Álvarez Ríos (1995); Yun (2008); García/Eng (2009); for a more general approach the already classic study Meagher (2008, on Cuba in particular pp. 201-221). For studies that partly include the 20th century, cp. Chong Martínez (1986); Baltar Rodríguez (1997a). Kathleen López (2004; 2013) has written the first comprehensive overview of Chinese in Cuba from 1847 to the late 20th century.

2 Exceptions include the above cited López (2013), Herrera/Castillo (2003), García/Eng (2009), García Triana (2003), and to some extent Waters (2005).

3 Like three Chinese Cuban revolutionaries who fought in the guerrilla war alongside Fidel Castro and were appointed generals some years after the triumph of the Cuban revolution (cp. García Triana 2003; Waters 2005; my interviews with Pedro Eng

the first years, the revolution of 1959 was defended by a significant part of the Cuban population, who enrolled in popular militias (Vellinga 1976; Manke 2014a; 2014b). Significant numbers of Chinese immigrants and descendants of Chinese immigrants in Cuba also joined what can be referred to as a mass movement to defend the revolution (Eng/García 2003: 39–49), forming a 'Chinese Popular Militia'. In the course of the research underlying the present article, new evidence on Chinese Cubans involved in the revolution of 1959 emerged, especially through interviews with Pedro Eng and Guillermo Chiu, two veterans of that militia.

The aim of this article is not only to focus on the foundation and development of that militia and the agency of its members against the background of other leftist Chinese that became organized in Cuba. In reporting the first results of ongoing research, this article will elucidate whether and how ethnic identity was used as a political resource, and describes the different ways in which ethnic self-attribution on a personal level and constructions of identity on a national level entangled and interacted in this dynamic setting. This is of special interest, as the demands of national unity under the flag of a new revolutionary identity do not necessarily seem compatible with the self-attributions of individuals that also stressed their personal identity, as did many Chinese Cubans. In this respect, a key question is whether this process can be interpreted as an ethnically marked mobilization during the political conflict that characterized the early years of the revolution. The main findings will show that this is indeed possible to some extent.

CHINESE IN CUBA BEFORE AND AFTER THE CHINESE REVOLUTION: A DIVIDING COMMUNITY

When Siu-Song Chiu was born in 1933 in a village in Guangdong province, Southern China, his father, Hao-Wo Chiu, was already living in Havana.[4] At the age of around 18, Siu-Song followed his father's call to come to Cuba to work with him in a *bodega* (grocery store) in Havana, adopting the name Guillermo Chiu. He arrived in Cuba in the immediate aftermath of the establishment of the People's Republic of China (PRC) in 1949. Nevertheless, in an interview he did not point to political reasons for his relocation to Cuba. We can assume that

---

Herrera (half-Chinese, half-Cuban/Spanish) and Guillermo Chiu (born in China, both parents Chinese).

4 Cp. Interview with Guillermo Chiu, August 1, 2014, Havana, also for the following.

familial and economic reasons were important, but the turbulent Chinese political situation probably also contributed to this decision, as thousands of 'nationalist' Chinese left mainland China in those years, approximately 3,000 of them going to Cuba.[5] This had an impact not only on the quality, but also on the size of the Chinese community in Cuba, which numbered 28,829 persons in 1948 – at that time the second-largest group of 'foreigners' (i.e. persons without Cuban citizenship) in the country after the Spaniards.[6]

With the victory of Mao Zedong's troops in 1949, leftist-oriented Chinese in Cuba and their organizations were initially strengthened, among them those active in the *Alianza Nacional de Apoyo a la Democracia China* (National Alliance to Protect Chinese Democracy) (López 2013: 222), which would play a key role in Cuba's 1959 revolution. The *Alianza* had been founded in 1927 by José Wong (Wong Tao-Bai)[7] in Havana as the leftist *Alianza Revolucionaria Protectora de Obreros y Campesinos de Cuba* (Chinese Cuban Revolutionary Alliance Protecting Workers and Peasants). Arrested by the secret police of Cuban dictator Gerardo Machado, Wong suffered extralegal execution in 1930; later he became Cuba's best-known revolutionary martyr of Chinese descent. After an initial growth sponsored by the Nationalist Party,[8] the *Alianza* also faced severe persecution under Machado and went underground in Santiago de Cuba. In 1938, during a moment of national unity against Japan's invasion of China during the Second Sino-Japanese War, it was re-established as *Alianza en Defensa de la Cultura China* (Alliance for the Defense of the Chinese Culture) by leftist members of Havana's Chinatown. During China's Civil War in the 1940s, it aligned with the Chinese Communist Party, registering under its new name *Alianza Nacional de Apoyo a la Democracia China* (National Alliance for the Support of Chinese Democracy) in 1946 (López 2013: 199, 207, 222).

After World War II, Cuba became an even closer ally of the United States in its struggle against communism, including at the level of internal politics. When the PRC was founded in 1949, Cuba's position was clear; as López put it: "[…]

---

5 Though there were also a considerable number of returnees to China after 1949 (Ford 2014: 239). For Chinese migration to Cuba in the 1950s, cp. López (2013: 222).

6 The authors stress that this is only true if we do not count the Haitians, whose numbers temporarily reached to 70,629 during the sugar harvest. The Spanish population in Cuba numbered 153,429 in that year (Herrera/Castillo (2003: 141).

7 When Chinese names are cited in Pinyin, the family name is written first, without separation by comma. Wong was an immigrant from Guangdong province, China (cp. Baltar 1997b: 22; Historia de la Alianza Socialista China de Cuba 2003: 1).

8 Though never reaching the importance of other established associations and institutions like the Casino Chung Wah (cp. Kenley 2011: 14–15).

Cuba was under the political and economic influence of its North American neighbor, and a directive from Washington to support the new Chinese government never came" (2013: 222). Consequently, Cuba did not recognize the PRC, but maintained diplomatic and commercial ties with the government of the Republic of China in Taiwan formed by the Kuomintang. In 1950, the Cuban Communists' main daily newspaper *Hoy* (Today) was shut down by the Cuban government. When leftist Chinese Cubans protested, their communist newspaper *Kwong Wah Po* (Bright China) was also forbidden; their press was destroyed, and 13 Chinese were detained and accused of being 'Communist spies' among them the newspaper's director, Juan Mok (Mo You-Ping) (ibid: 223).

The Chinese community in Cuba was experiencing an increased politicization and polarization (Herrera/Castillo 2003: 143–144). The first political clash between followers of the Kuomintang (now politically represented through Taiwan) and followers of the PRC took place on October 10, 1949, (a meaningful patriotic date for both Chinese and Cubans), when *Alianza* members hung the flag of Communist China at the Kuomintang headquarters in Havana, just days after its president, Enrique León, declared the solidarity of the 'Chinese patriots' in Cuba with the PRC (Álvarez Ríos 1995: 81; Herrera/Castillo 2003: 143; López 2013: 222). Though it had lost its monopolistic political position in Cuba after 1949, the Kuomintang still dominated the principal political and social institution of Havana's Chinatown, the *Casino Chung Wah* (García Triana 2003: 20), and maintained an ideologically leading position (Herrera/Castillo 2003: 149).

Conflicts between different groups in Cuba's Chinese community were being shaped by Cuba's political climate, which ultimately favored anti-communists and the Chinese merchant class.[9] This was accentuated under President Fulgencio Batista, who installed a pro-U.S. dictatorship through a coup d'état in 1952. Also under Batista, "[u]pper-class Chinese merchants enjoyed a mutually beneficial relationship with Cuban politicians [...]" (López 2013: 223). The *Alianza* had already been dissolved in 1951 due to economic problems; in 1955 its official registration was canceled. On the other hand, towards the end of the 1950s, the Cold War ideology endorsed by the Batista regime also had a coalescing impact on the leadership of the Chinese community in Havana. After purging leftist elements and uniting the nationalist forces under the banner of anticommunism, it reached an "ethnic-communitarian cohesion of great strength" (Herrera/Castillo 2003: 156)[10] that covered political divisions for some time.

---

9 This had not always been the case, as Herrera and Castillo have shown (2003: 81, 82, 117).
10 All translations are mine, unless noted otherwise.

CHINESE IN REVOLUTIONARY CUBA: FROM HONEYMOON TO INTERNAL SPLIT

When the Cuban revolution led by Fidel Castro triumphed in 1959, the situation changed. In its first year, the political climate stood for a turn towards more equality and distributive politics, and the revolutionary leadership promoted a nationalist course within a capitalist system, rather than socialism. The revolution opened possibilities for many kinds of organizations to participate in public life, among them previously banned leftist ones like the *Alianza* in Havana's Chinatown. Former members re-established this association in early 1959 as *Alianza Cultural China* (Chinese Cultural Alliance), soon renamed *Alianza Nueva Democracia China en Cuba* (Chinese New Democracy Alliance of Cuba), alluding to Mao Zedong's concept of "New Democracy" (López 2013: 226).[11] Taiwan's embassy in Cuba observed this development with mistrust, reporting to the Cuban revolutionary government any 'suspicious' movement of Chinese in Cuba, and trying to block any kind of influence of the PRC (García Triana 2003: 42–43). The ideological position of the Cuban government was unclear at that time. Even so, it was a revolution in course that tried to introduce rapid changes in the economic and social structure of the country (Díaz Castañón 2004; Martínez Heredia 2005: 199–220).

In the beginning, the leaders of Havana's Chinatown joined in what Herrera and Castillo appropriately call a "revolutionary consensus" (2003: 157) for a democratic and liberal Cuba. But this "honeymoon" (ibid.) would not last long. In view of the radical changes, many better-off Chinese were frightened to lose their property, and some started conspiring against the revolutionary government (García Triana 2003: 40). But there was no ethnically marked formation of an opposition group at that moment.

THE FORMATION OF A CHINESE MILITIA FOR THE DEFENSE OF THE REVOLUTION

In the summer and autumn of 1959, the revolution came under attack from a counter-revolutionary invasion attempt by the Dominican Republic and the

---

11 When Fidel Castro proclaimed the socialist character of the revolution on April 16, 1961, the *Alianza* changed its name to *Alianza Socialista China de Cuba* (Chinese Socialist Alliance of Cuba), the name it still bears today (cp. History of the Alianza Socialista China de Cuba 2003: 2).

bombing of cane fields with the acquiescence of U.S. authorities (Zaldívar/ Etcheverry 2009). Gradually, the political conflict escalated into an ideological confrontation, and the revolution started to radicalize. As the country was not prepared to confront an external invasion or a large-scale internal destabilization campaign, many civilians began to ask for arms and military training, and popular militias were founded in all provinces. Around 90 percent of all Cubans supported the revolution in 1959, and this support developed into a mass movement to defend both country and revolution (Manke 2014a: 101–149).[12]

At this early stage, militias were mainly organized in a decentralized way, but there was no militia organized for or by members of any specific ethnic group. From August 1959 mobilization was particularly high in the labor unions of the gastronomy and retail sectors in Havana.[13] Many Chinese of Central Havana were organized in this sector (García Triana 2003: 176), some of them in the union of *Víveres al Detalle* (supplies for retail traders). In this union, a key person in the organization of the support of Chinese was Pedro Eng Herrera. Pedro Eng was born in 1933 in Havana; his father was from Guangdong province, China, and his mother from Spain. According to his memoirs, he had been active against the Batista dictatorship in the labor sector together with another Chinese Cuban, Rufino Alay Chang.[14] After the triumph of the revolution, the revolutionaries took over the labor unions, and many founded militias to defend the revolution against external aggressions and internal resistance. Pedro Eng organized the militia in his union, in his position as *subresponsable* (second in charge).[15] He passed a short intensive military training course in Havana's Fifth Military District, which was under the direction of Captain Miguel Galán, chief commander of all militias in Havana province (Manke 2014a: 204–207). He then became the military and political instructor of this militia, and soon several Chinese employees of the gastronomy sector asked him to admit them for training in this militia.

But the course of the revolution was still not clearly leftist. After an accusation of alleged leftist political agitation initiated by Adolfo Rodríguez, the union's secretary general, Eng was dismissed from his position by the National Direction of Revolutionary Militias in early 1960. Eng left the militia, and about 20 Chinese that had been trained by him also resigned. Then he, Rufino Alay

---

12 For quantitative details of support for the revolution cp. Gutiérrez Serrano (1959).
13 Cp. *"Reiteran Apoyo los Camareros"* ("Waiters Renew Their Support"). In: *Revolución* (August 11, 1959: 2).
14 Interview with Pedro Eng Herrera, November 25, 2006, Havana.
15 Interview with Pedro Eng Herrera, November 25, 2006, Havana. For the role of the responsables (local leaders) in the militias cp. Manke (2014a: 208–211).

and Jesús Eng Guerra had the idea of founding a militia whose members would be Chinese residents and descendants of Chinese like himself. They contacted the *Alianza Cultural China* asking for support, but the *Alianza*'s leadership did not immediately approve of their plans. So they contacted Juan Mok, the former editor of the newspaper *Kwong Wah Po*, who led a leftist branch of the *Alianza*. He and Luis Li, both elderly communists and comrades of José Wong in the 1930s, helped the men around Pedro Eng to found the *Milicia Popular China Brigada José Wong* (Chinese Popular Militia José Wong Brigade), as it was named in Wong's honor. After approval by Captain Miguel Galán and the new labor union leader Narciso Sautié Socorrás, this Chinese militia was founded on February 17, 1960, with 54 founding members (among them Guillermo Chiu) who were soon joined by more leftist Chinese.[16]

THE SHIFT OF POWER IN HAVANA'S CHINATOWN

In the summer of 1960, due to both U.S. economic aggression and low-intensity warfare against Cuba and to the radicalization of the revolution, the political climate shifted decisively and Cuba turned towards the socialist bloc, including the PRC (Manke 2014a: 223–224, 266–273, 300). On September 2, 1960, Castro made his first 'Declaration of Havana', which underscored Cuba's right to self-determination against the United States' attempts to strangle it economically and politically. In this speech, he also announced the establishment of diplomatic relations with the PRC, and declared the rupture of those with Taiwan. With this move, Cuba would become the first country in Latin America to establish diplomatic relations with Beijing – an act which formally took place on September 28 (Álvarez Ríos 1995: 99; García Triana 2003: 49–51, 56; Benton 2009: xx). In Havana's Chinatown, power relations now changed with increasing pace, and Taiwan could no longer interfere. On October 1, 1960, the Chinese militia and members of the *Alianza* participated in a public festival to commemorate the 11th anniversary of the PRC (García Triana 2003: 175; López 2013: 227). Shortly afterwards, the revolutionary tide also hit the traditional institutions of the Chinese community. On October 10, the Chinese militia invaded both the *Casino Chung Wah* and the Kuomintang headquarters, including its newspaper *Man Sen Yat Po*, and raised the red flag of the PRC on the Casino's premises for the first time in history (Herrera/Castillo 2003: 159; García/Eng 2009: 40; López 2013: 227).

---

16 Interview with Pedro Eng Herrera, November 25, 2006, Havana (cp. also García Triana 2003: 174).

According to Herrera and Castillo (2003: 159), in the political conflict in the Casino the militia backed the leftist faction in Havana's Chinatown, which reflected the loss of power of the conservative faction. On October 10, a new Casino leadership took power: *Alianza* leader Manuel Luis became the president, and Enrique León became his secretary. Three days later, through bill no. 891, all foreign banks that had not yet been subject to such intervention – with the exception of the Canadian ones – were nationalized by the Cuban government, including the Cuban branch of the Bank of China (López 2013: 227). Furthermore, the takeover of the Casino was made officially effective; the Kuomintang building, the *Man Sen Yat Po*, and several establishments and private property of Chinese who had cooperated with Batista were confiscated. Though the new communist leadership of the Casino did not have a significant social basis in the Chinese Cuban community, there were almost no protests against this move, which took place in an almost peaceful manner.[17]

WAS THIS AN ETHNICALLY MARKED MOBILIZATION? AN ANALYTIC APPROACH

How can we interpret the agency of Chinese Cubans in the Cuban revolution, and specifically of those who were members of the Chinese militia? Were they participating in a purely political conflict, or did ethnicity play a more relevant role? To approach these questions, it is necessary to clarify the concepts and terms in use. When writing about 'Chinese' in Cuba, one can observe that the term is used with a variety of connotations and intentions by different speakers. From the point of view of the Chinese community in Cuba, this was heavily influenced by the events in China. In 19th-century China, nationalist tendencies had set in motion the buildup of a Chinese national identity. This led to a weakening of the relevance of ethnic differentiations in terms of identity formation – especially among Chinese outside of China, as Ford observes:

"The spread of nationalism through the Overseas Chinese community in the late nineteenth and early 20th centuries can be conceived as the beginning of a breakdown of 'ethnic' boundaries within Chinese society." (Ford 2014: 243)

---

17 López speaks of a "transition relatively free of violence" (2013: 227; cp. also Herrera/Castillo 2003: 160–161).

In Cuba, according to Martín (1939: 17), ethnic in-fighting (mostly between *hakka* and *punti*) eased off towards the 1920s, also influenced by nationalist and centralist agendas. In the 20th century, migrants from China to Cuba mostly used this generalizing term to refer to their country of origin when talking to persons outside the Chinese community in Cuba.

Inside the communities, the local origin and family ties of Overseas Chinese remained strong markers. José Baltar Rodríguez (1997b) pointed to the importance of patrilineal clan associations in Cuba, whose members were grouped and admitted according to their family name and their location of origin. Herrera and Castillo agree with this, adding that the wave of immigration in the 1920s, "played the role of an ethnic adhesive" (2003: 74) in that community. These authors also highlight the role of clan associations in the (re)construction of the migrants' cultural identity (ibid: 73). During the next decades, the conflicts between ethnic groups within the Chinese community in Cuba gradually decreased. At the same time, political conflicts between Kuomintang followers and communists became increasingly relevant, particularly during the Chinese Civil War and after the establishment of the PRC. So, inside Havana's Chinatown, the clash of 1960 seemed to be a more politically than ethnically marked conflict.

If we look at the conceptual placement of Cuban Chinese in the context of the whole Cuban population through the writings of Cuban intellectuals, there has been a tradition of identifying Chinese in Cuba as a minority group not belonging to the core of what was considered Cuban national identity. The egalitarian principles developed by José Martí at the end of the 19th century advocated an inclusive Cuba to which all Cubans belonged, no matter what color their skin. In contrast to discriminatory politics during the Spanish Empire, he emphasized that all Cubans were part of the same human race (Martí 1991). Scholars have argued that the idea of a "raceless nation" (Benton 2009: xii) could not take hold completely, in part due to the U.S. intervention in 1898 and the consecutive reinforcement of already existing segregationist and supremacist thinking. Instead, the long-standing idea of *blanqueamiento* (whitening) prevailed again (Santamaría/Naranjo 1999: 13), leading to the planned attraction of hundreds of thousands of Spanish immigrants in the first decades of the 20th century, and the "election of the white population of the island as the transporter of national identity" (Naranjo Orovio 2003: 517, footnote 17). Cuban society continued to experience strong racial tensions similar to those evident in the 19th century, and ethnic groups of non-white descent were considered a menace to the stability and integrity of the nation well into the 1920s (ibid: 525, 527), even by prominent historians like Ramiro Guerra and Emilio Roig de Leuchsenring. Roig de Leuchsenring argued that Chinese, Haitians, and Jamaicans were undesired immigrants, and that they were in competition with white Cuban laborers and desired immigrants (e.g. Spaniards), thus facilitating the expansion of U.S. trusts and companies through cheap labor (ibid: 532–533). In his early writings, the eminent anthropologist and historian Fernando Ortiz argued along the same lines, establishing parallelisms between a person's ethnic origin and his/her social behavior. He assumed that especially people of African and – to a lesser extent – Asian descent were more inclined towards criminal activities (ibid: 526).

Though Ortiz's racial prejudices reduced over the years, he still relegated the Chinese to a place of low importance inside the Cuban *ajiaco* (a metaphor for 'melting pot' in his concept of transculturation).[18] Equating the Chinese with other people of "yellow descent" (Ortiz 2008: 14) in general, in 1939 he did not appraise the Asian influence in Cuba as very remarkable, and situated the Chinese among other groups he considered of minor importance. Interestingly, Jesús Guanche Pérez further developed and expanded this line of argumentation, now (under the impact of the Cuban revolution) advocating the concept of a large "intraethnic consolidation" (1997: 52) that took place in Cuba since the end of the large waves of migration in the 1950s. Forty years after the revolution of 1959, he saw that an "etnos cubano" (ibid.) had formed in Cuba as a result of this consolidation. He identified a majoritarian group (98 percent) of the total population including white, black, and mulatto Cubans. He seems not to have included Chinese in this kind of Cuban melting-pot, though their heritage was significant. Counting merely the number of Chinese still living in Cuba, he said they belonged to the remaining two percent of minorities, along with Spaniards, Catalans, Canarians, Galicians, Basques, Haitians, Jamaicans, and others, who he interestingly also lists as ethnic groups. As he mingles notions of ethnic and national origins, 'conceptual meddling'[19] seems to surface here. Furthermore, we can observe the above-mentioned tendency to minimize the impact of the Chinese (with around 124,000 immigrants arriving in Cuba during the 19th century alone)[20] on the formation of Cuban national identity and the opposition

---

18 Céspedes gives a good resume of the concept of *ajiaco*: "[…] a traditional Cuban stew of ameridian origin that is cooked over a long period by continuously adding new ingredients to the simmering mixture. Like the ingredients of mixed race and culture, additions to the dish maintain their identities to varying degrees; some dissolve fully or evaporate, while others remain more distinct. This Ortiz described as 'transculturation' […]" (Céspedes 2007: 71). For his definition of transculturation, cp. also Ortiz 2001.

19 For this concept cp. Wolfgang Gabbert's contribution in this volume.

20 Of around 141,000 coolies that embarked (cp. Hu-Dehart 2004: 17) (table).

to their inclusion in a majoritarian we-group. In more recent publications, Herrera and Castillo (2003), Benton (2009), López (2013) and others are trying to reverse this trend by adding various strands of academic knowledge to the subject. And on a local level, for about 20 years now, descendants of Chinese immigrants have invoked a renaissance of the consciousness of the Chinese heritage in Cuban society, thus contributing to a redefinition of Chinese Cuban identity from an individual perspective (Benton 2009: xiv-xix; xx).[21] In general, in the late 20th century one can observe that little effort was made to draw distinctions between different ethnic groups from China; they were usually subsumed under the common marker 'Chinese' or 'Chinese Cubans', thus ethnicizing a nationality.

Against this background, for the present case it is important to consider in which conjunctures the marker 'Chinese' became relevant, and to whom. To disentangle these issues, it is useful to look at the intentions tied to the use of this marker. When the Cuban revolution triumphed in 1959, the Cuban government did not particularly emphasize the issue of 'race', beyond stressing the efforts that were being made toward the creation of an egalitarian society. But when the issue did become relevant, Fidel Castro usually did not mention Asians (Benton 2009: xix). On the other hand, the application of egalitarian policies and their effects was a process that would endure for decades, even if the government tried to declare Cuba to be a color-blind society from the beginning. In early 1959, in the Chinese community there were groups (like the *Alianza*) whose political activity can be interpreted as ethnically marked political activism (López 2013: 226). Now, was this also the case for Pedro Eng and the militia he co-founded? In the beginning it was certainly not: Eng was integrated into a workers' militia whose membership was not defined by ethnic markers but by affiliation to his trade union and by personal commitment to the revolution.[22] But when he and Rufino Alay started to organize a militia whose members should be Chinese and descendants of Chinese, they began to use the marker 'Chinese' to gather pro-revolutionary men for the defense of the revolution. From inside the Chinese community, this meant a formation of a new pressure group to influence the political balance in Havana's Chinatown in favor of the Cuban *and* the Chinese revolutions at that moment (February 1960), trying to strengthen leftist

---

21 This can also occur in the opposite direction (Ang 2001: 21-25).
22 This is also visible in a photo of him with four other members of this militia posing in the workers' militia uniform (cp. the image in García/Eng 2009, photo spread between pages 140 and 141).

groups like the *Alianza*.[23] Only after Castro officially announced Cuba's turn towards the PRC on September 2, 1960, were they able to effectively question the power balance in Havana's Chinatown. According to López, the militia members "[...] merged their Chinese ethnic identifications with political support of both the Chinese and Cuban revolutions" (2013: 226). Still, we have to observe that though the Chinese militia had been playing a key role in the execution of that political change, the Revolutionary Armed Forces did not officially approve it until November 1, 1960, weeks after the shift in powers in Havana's Chinatown.[24] Furthermore, it was dissolved only months later, in the process of integration of the militias organized by sectors into regular, ethnically mixed units of the armed forces, the police, and the secret services.[25] Returning to the personal experience of Guillermo Chiu, he saw his participation in that militia as a patriotic duty, like his integration into the police after its dissolution. Although he really wanted to work as a typesetter (as he finally did at the *Kwong Wah Po*), he also simply wanted to do something to help the security and success of the revolution. For him, the militia was but one of several possibilities to do this.[26]

CONCLUSION

In retrospect, on the one hand we can interpret the formation and development of the Chinese militia in line with the overall process of popular mobilization for the defense of the revolution. However, though this process was a common phenomenon, that militia clearly stood out among others, as it seems to have been the only revolutionary militia organized on the basis of an ethnic marker (Manke 2014a: 18). The revolutionary leadership considered it opportune to tolerate the mobilization of a single ethnic group in this exceptional case, but maintained a position of 'watching and waiting' before it extended official recognition. The strategy was to let the leftist and progressive forces in the

---

23 At this point, Cuba was on an ideological ground that still remained relatively open to future developments. For an analysis of the changing ideological development in Cuba in 1959 and 1960, cp. Martínez Heredia (2005); Manke (2015).

24 Cp. a copy of the official document signed by Rogelio Acevedo González, chief of the *National Direction of Revolutionary Militias* in García/Eng (2009, photo spread between pages 140 and 141).

25 Interview with Pedro Eng Herrera, November 25, 2006, Havana.

26 Cp. Interview with Guillermo Chiu, August 1, 2014, Havana.

various sectors carry out ideological disputes on a local level and support them only if necessary. In that way, the government did not interfere directly in the affairs of the Chinese community, but rather created favorable conditions for the success of these forces. In addition, from a transnational perspective, the leftist Chinese Cubans who got involved in the revolution in this or other ways were unique in the context of the Cold War on a global level, as Benton emphasizes (2009: xx).

Getting back to the question of the instrumentalization or even construction of ethnicity, one can partly agree with the processual concept of ethnicization elaborated upon by Frederik Holst in this volume. Nevertheless, in the present case study at no point were we able to state that ethnicity did not play a role for the individuals. In consequence, we think that it is appropriate to speak of ethnicity as one of several markers that can have relevance at certain points in time and space. As Thomas Widlok also stresses in his contribution to this volume, the relevance of ethnicity in comparison to other forms of reference depends on other situational settings and on the varying intentions of those who use or even exploit it.

REFERENCES

Álvarez Ríos, Baldomero (1995): La inmigración china en la Cuba colonial/El Barrio Chino de La Habana, La Habana: Publicigraf.
Ang, Ien (2001): On not speaking Chinese: Living between Asia and the West, London/New York: Routledge.
Baltar Rodríguez, José (1997a): Los Chinos de Cuba. Apuntes Etnográficos, La Habana: Fundación Fernando Ortiz.
—— (1997b): "La sociedad-clan y el proceso de asimilación étnica de los chinos en Cuba." In: Temas 7, pp. 13–27.
Benton, Gregor (2009): "Editor's Introduction." In: Mauro García Triana/Pedro Eng Herrera (eds.), The Chinese in Cuba, 1847-Now. Edited and translated by Gregor Benton, Lanham: Lexington Books, pp. 11–32.
Céspedes, Karina L. (2007): "Spam in the Cuban *Ajiaco*: An Interview with Alaen Pérez." In: Callaloo 30/1, pp. 71–74.
Chong Martínez, María Isabel (1986): La Migración China hacia Cuba (1850-1930). Tesis de Licenciatura, México: UNAM.
Díaz Castañón, María del Pilar (2004): Ideología y Revolución. Cuba, 1959-1962, (Filosofía) La Habana: Ciencias Sociales, 2nd ed.

Eng Herrera, Pedro J./García Triana, Mauro G. (2003): Martí en los Chinos. Los Chinos en Martí, La Habana: Grupo Promotor del Barrio Chino de La Habana.

Ford, Caleb (2014): "*Guiqiao* (Returned Overseas Chinese) Identity in the PRC." In: Journal of Chinese Overseas 10, pp. 239–262.

García Triana, Mauro (2003): Los chinos de Cuba y los nexos entre las naciones. Vol. II. Boletín "Problemas Filosóficos", Serie: Avances de Investigación 2, La Habana: Sociedad Cubana de Estudios e Investigaciones Filosóficas.

García Triana, Mauro/Eng Herrera, Pedro (2009): The Chinese in Cuba, 1847-Now. Edited and translated by Gregor Benton, Lanham: Lexington Books.

Guanche Pérez, Jesús (1997): "Etnicidad y racialidad en la Cuba actual." In: Temas 7, pp. 51–57.

Gutiérrez Serrano, Raúl (1959): "El pueblo opina sobre el gobierno revolucionario y la reforma agrarian." In: Bohemia, pp. 8–13.

Herrera Jerez, Miriam/Castillo Santana, Mario (2003): De la memoria a la vida pública. Identidades, espacios y jerarquías de los chinos en La Habana republicana (1902–1968), La Habana: Centro de Investigación y Desarrollo de la Cultura Cubana Juan Marinello.

Historia de la Alianza Socialista China de Cuba (2003): manuscript, courtesy of Mirta Sam, La Habana, Cuba.

Ho, Elaine Lynn-Ee/Madokoro, Laura/Peterson, Glen (2014): "Global Displacements and Emplacement. The Forced Exile and Resettlement Experiences of Ethnic Chinese Refugees." In: Journal of Chinese Overseas 10, pp. 131–136.

Hu-Dehart, Evelyn (2004): "El Caribe. Los culíes, los tenderos y sus descendientes." In: Banco Interamericano de Desarrollo (ed.), Cuando Oriente llegó a América. Contribuciones de inmigrantes chinos, japoneses y coreanos. Washington: Banco Interamericano de Desarrollo, pp. 13–34.

Kenley, David (2011): "The Chinese Diaspora in Cuba: Wielding the Tools of Overseas Identity." Paper for the 2011 American Association for Chinese Studies Conference, January 9, 2015 (http://aacs.ccny.cuny.edu/2011conference/Papers/Kenley,David.pdf).

López, Kathleen (2004): "'One brings another'. The formation of early-twentieth-century Chinese migrant communities in Cuba." In: Andrew R. Wilson (ed.), The Chinese in the Caribbean, Princeton: Markus Wiener, pp. 93–127.

—— (2013): Chinese Cubans. A transnational history, (Envisioning Cuba) Chapel Hill: University of North Carolina Press.

Manke, Albert (2014a): *El pueblo cubano en armas*. Die Revolutionären Nationalmilizen und die Verteidigung der kubanischen Revolution von 1959, Stuttgart: Heinz.

—— (2014b): "In defense of the Cuban revolution. Mobilization and popular support for revolutionary change, 1959-1961." In: Mauricio A. Font/Araceli Tinajero (eds.), Handbook on Cuban history, literature, and the arts. New perspectives on historical and contemporary social change, Boulder: Paradigm, pp. 25–36.

—— (forthcoming): "La reformulación de los conceptos de ciudadanía, patriotismo y cubanidad a principios de la revolución cubana de 1959." In: Vanessa Höse/Katharina Motzkau/Antonio Sáez-Arance (eds.), Identidades nacionales en América Latina. Discursos, saberes, representaciones, (Tiempo Emulado. Historia de América y España), Madrid/Frankfurt: Iberoamericana/Vervuert.

Martí, José (1991): "Mi raza." In: Patria, New York, April 16, 1893. In: José Martí: Obras completas, vol. II, La Habana: Editorial de Ciencias Sociales, pp. 298–300.

Martín, Juan Luis (1939): De dónde vinieron los chinos de Cuba. Los jaca, los joló, los puntí y los amoyanos, en la vida cubana. con un apéndice sobre las ideas morales de Cuba, La Habana: Atalaya.

Martínez Heredia, Fernando (2005): "El mundo ideológico cubano de 1959 a marzo de 1960." In: Eduardo Torres-Cuevas (ed.), Sartre-Cuba-Sartre. Huracán, surco, semillas, La Habana: Imagen Contemporánea, pp. 199–220.

Meagher, Arnold J. (2008): The coolie trade. The traffic in Chinese laborers to Latin America 1847-1874. Revised edition, [Bloomington]: Xlibris.

Naranjo Orovio, Consuelo (2003): "Creando imágenes, fabricando historia. Cuba en los inicios del siglo XX." In: Historia Mexicana 53/2, pp. 511-540.

Ortiz, Fernando (2001): Cuban Counterpoint. Tobacco and Sugar, Translated by Harriet de Onís, originally published by Alfred A. Knopf, 1947, Durham/London: Duke University Press 1995, third printing.

—— (2008): "Los factores humanos de la cubanidad." In: Perfiles de la cultura cubana 2, Arsenal, pp. 1-15, January 29, 2015 (http://www.perfiles.cult.cu/articulos/factores_cubanidad.pdf). (Conference to students of the fraternity Iota-Eta at the University of Havana, November 28, 1939. First published by Revista Bimestre Cubana V, XLV, no. 2 (1940), pp. 161–86).

Santamaría García, Antonio/Naranjo Orovio, Consuelo (1999): "La historia social de Cuba, 1868–1914. Aportaciones recientes y perspectivas." In: Historia Social 33, pp. 133–158.

Vellinga, M. L. (1976): "The Military and the Dynamics of the Cuban Revolutionary Process." In: Comparative Politics 8/2, pp. 245–271.

Waters, Mary-Alice (ed.) (2005): Our history is still being written. The story of three Chinese-Cuban generals in the Cuban revolution: Armando Choy, Gustavo Chui, Moisés Sío Wong, New York: Pathfinder.

Yun, Lisa (2008): The coolie speaks. Chinese indentured laborers and African slaves in Cuba, Philadelphia: Temple University Press.

Zaldívar Diéguez, Andrés/Etcheverry Vázquez, Pedro (2009): Una fascinante historia. La conspiración trujillista, La Habana: Editorial Capitán San Luis.

Authors

Albiez-Wieck, Sarah, studied Latin American Studies in Cologne, Lisbon and Mexico-City. She holds a Phd in Anthropology of the Americas by the University of Bonn. From 2010–2013 she was the Managing Director of the Research Network for Latin America 'Ethnicity, Citizenship, Belonging'. Since 2014 she is Senior Researcher at the Department for Iberian and Latin American History at the University of Cologne. Her research interests include colonial and precolonial Mexico and Peru and questions of colonialism, belonging, ethnicity and other social categorisations. Her publications include her contribution *Social categorisations in the Tarascan State. Debates about the existence of Ethnicity in Prehispanic West Mexico* (In Célleri/Schwarz/Wittger (eds.), Interdependencies of Social Categorisations, Frankfurt a.M/Madrid: Vervuert, 2013.
Email: sarahalbiez-wieck@hotmail.com

Antweiler, Christoph, is Cultural Anthropologist and Professor of Southeast Asian Studies at the Institute for Oriental and Asian Studies (IOA), University of Bonn, Germany. He is board member of the Bonn Center for Asian Studies (BAZ) and member of the Academia Europea (London). His fields of Research are urbanity, decision-making, cognition, local knowledge, ethnicity, societal evolution, human universals. He is interested in applied anthropology and his fieldwork area is Southeast Asia, especially Indonesia. Book publications include: *Was ist den Menschen gemeinsam? Über Kultur und Kulturen*, ²2009; *Inclusive Humanism. Anthropological Basics for a Realistic Cosmopolitanism*, 2012 and *Environmental Uncertainty and Local Knowledge. Southeast Asia as a Laboratory of Global Change*, (co-editor), 2012.
Email: antweile@gmx.de

Becker, Anja Katharina, is Researcher and lecturer at the Department of Social and Cultural Anthropology at the University of Cologne. She is currently writing her dissertation on female agencies and normative conflict in a sedentarizing society in Kenya where she focuses on the changing gender relations and ethnic identities among the Pokot. She has presented and published articles on Pokot division of labor, resilience and social change, and the relationship between the state and ethnic identities. Her regional expertise is southern and eastern Africa. Her latest publications include *Indigenous Women as Agents of Change in a transforming pastoral Society in Kenya* (Center for African Studies, Spring Issue: Rutgers University, 2013).
Email: beckeranjakatharina@gmail.com

Büschges, Christian, is Professor of Iberian and Latin American History at Bern University, Switzerland. His research interests focus on ethnicity and nationalism in Latin America in a comparative and global perspective (16th century to the present), the vice-regal courts of the Spanish Monarchy (17th century), and the transformation of Latin American social and political elites (18th and 19th centuries). His main publications include *Aristocratic Revolutionaries: The Nobility during the Independence Period of Spanish America and Brazil* (Journal of Modern European History, 11, 2013/4), *Demokratie und Völkermord* (2012), and *Culturas políticas en la región andina*, ed. with O. Kaltmeier and S. Thies (2011).
Email: christian.bueschges@hist.unibe.ch

Feyissa, Dereje, holds a PhD in Social Anthropology from Martin Luther University. He was a Post-doctoral Fellow at the Max Planck Institute for Social Anthropology and the 21st Centre of Excellence at Osaka University. Currently he is the Africa Research Director at the International Law and Policy Institute; Adjunct Professor at Addis Ababa University and Experienced Research Fellow of the Alexander von Humboldt Foundation. His research interest and key competence ares are ethnicity and conflict; religion and politics; borders and the political economy of development. He is the author of the book *Playing different games: The paradox of the identification strategies of the Anywaa and the Nuer in the Gambella region, Ethiopia* (Berghahn, 2011) and co-editor of *Borders and Borderlands as resources in the Horn of Africa* (James Curey, 2010).
Email: derejefdori2011@googlemail.com

Gabbert, Wolfgang, is Professor of Development Sociology and Cultural Anthropology at the Leibniz University of Hannover. His main research areas are historical anthropology, legal anthropology, conflict and violence, ethnicity and social inequality, colonialism, Christian missions in Latin America and Africa. His dissertation is the first book-length treatment of Nicaragua's African American Creoles (*Creoles - Afroamerikaner im karibischen Tiefland von Nicaragua*. Münster: Lit 1992). His book *Becoming Maya? Ethnicity and Social Inequality in Yucatán since 1500* (Tucson: University of Arizona Press 2004) is the first English-language study that examines the role of ethnicity and social inequality in the history of Yucatan, Mexico.
Email: w.gabbert@ish.uni-hannover.de

Holst, Frederik, is Senior Research Fellow at Humboldt-Universität zu Berlin. He studied communication studies, political science and psychology at Freie Universität Berlin as well as Universiti Sains Malaysia, and obtained a PhD in Southeast Asian Studies from Humboldt-Universität zu Berlin in 2010. His research interests focus on identity construction as well as the role and impact of media and technology in postcolonial societies. In his habilitation project he analyzes the ethnicization of religious identitites in Malaysia and Germany. His latest publications include *Ethnicization and Identity Construction in Malaysia* (London.: Routledge, 2012) and *Religiosity as a 'Currency' of Authenticity – Islam and Group Identity Formation in Malaysia* (In: Lee/Ferrarese (eds.), Authenticity in Southeast Asia: The Popular, The Pious, and the Practical, Lanham: Rowman and Littlefield, forthcoming 2015).
Email: frederik.holst@staff.hu-berlin.de

Krämer, Mario, is Postdoctoral Researcher and lecturer at the Institute of Social and Cultural Anthropology, University of Cologne. His main fields of research are political anthropology; chieftaincy and democratisation in Africa; war, (violent) conflict and order; and anthropology of sports. In his PhD thesis *Violence as Routine. Transformations of Local-Level Politics and the Disjunction between Centre and Periphery in KwaZulu-Natal, South Africa*, (Köppe: Köln, 2007) he examined local politics and violent conflict in the democratic transition. His latest publications include *Democratisation between violent conflict and the resurgence of chieftaincy. Local transformations of a travelling model in KwaZulu-Natal, South Africa*. (Andrea Behrends/Sung-Joon Park/Richard Rottenburg (eds.), Travelling Models in African Conflict Management. Translating Technologies of Social Ordering. Leiden: Brill, 2014).
Email: mario.kraemer@netcologne.de

Manke, Albert, is Senior Researcher at the Department of Iberian and Latin American History of the University of Cologne in Germany. During and after his PhD in Iberian and Latin American History he has worked on popular mobilization in revolutionary Cuba during the Cold War, on social movements, migration, and ethnicity. His current research project deals with Chinese migration to the Americas since Spanish colonial times, focusing on processes of exclusion, resilience, and the dynamics of ethnic conflict. He is one of two directors of the University of Cologne Forum 'Ethnicity as a Political Resource: Perspectives from Africa, Latina America, Asia, and Europe'. His latest publications include his monograph *El pueblo cubano en armas: Die Revolutionären Nationalmilizen und die Verteidigung der kubanischen Re-volution von 1959* (Historamericana 35, Stuttgart: Heinz, 2014). Email: amanke@uni-koeln.de

O'Toole, Rachel Sarah, is Associate Professor in the Department of History at the University of California, Irvine where she teaches classes on sex and conquest, race and empire, and the Atlantic and Pacific worlds. Her monograph, *Bound Lives: Africans, Indians, and the Making of Race in Colonial Peru* received the 2013 Latin American Studies Association Peru Section Flora Tristán book prize. With Sherwin Bryant and Ben Vinson III, she co-edited *Africans to Spanish America: Expanding the Diaspora*. She has published articles on the construction of whiteness, masculinity within slavery, African diaspora identities, indigenous politics, and gender influences on racial constructions in edited collections as well as in *Radical History Review*, *Secuencia*, *Social Text*, *The Americas*, and the *Journal of Colonialism and Colonial History*. Email: rotoole@uci.edu

Pelican, Michaela, is Junior Professor of Cultural and Social Anthropology at the University of Cologne. She is also the Co-Director of the University of Cologne Forum 'Ethnicity as a Political Resource: Perspectives from Africa, Latin America, Asia, and Europe'. Her current focus on indigeneity in Africa emerged from her previous research on interethnic relations and identity politics in Cameroon. Concurrently, she is working on South-South/East mobility, focusing on transnational migration from Cameroon to Gabon, South Africa, the United Arab Emirates and China. Her latest publications include her monograph *Masks and Staffs: Identity Politics in the Cameroon Grassfield* (Berghahn 2015) as well as two special issues on *Indigenous Identities and Ethnic Co-existence in Africa* (African Studies Monographs 2015, 36/1, co-edited with Junko Maruyama) and on *Global African Entrepreneurs* (Urban Anthropology 2014, 43, co-edited with Mahir Saul). Email: mpelican@uni-koeln.de

Pohl, Walter, is Professor of History of the Middle Ages and Historical Subsidiary Sciences at the Historical-Culture-Scientific Faculty at the University of Vienna. Since 2004 he is Director of the Institut für Mittelalterforschung of the Austrian Academy of Sciences and member of the Austrian Academy of Sciences. In summer 2002 he became an Austrian representative in the Committee for the Humanities of the European Science Foundation (ESF) as well as delegate in the general assembly of the ESF. In 2004 he was awarded the Wittgenstein-Preis, in 2010 the ERC Advanced Grant. His reaserch interests are the transformation of the Roman world and early medieval history, the role of ethnicity, migration and identity formation, the history of Eastern Central Europe and of the Eurasian steppe peoples, Italian cultural and political history and early medieval historiography and its manuscript transmission.
Email: Walter.Pohl@oeaw.ac.at

Sáez-Arance, Antonio, is Senior Researcher at the Institute for Iberian and Latin American History at the University of Cologne. Drawing on twenty years of teaching and research on the social and cultural history of the Spanish Monarchy and Latin America, he has published on such topics as humanism, confessionalization, nationalism, commemorative culture and politics of history. His book *Simón Bolívar. El Libertador y su mito* (Madrid, Marcial Pons Historia, 2013) deals with the sustained impact of 'heroic' Independence narratives on the Latin American political culture. He is currently writing a monograph on proto-national and national identity discourses in Chile between 1780 and 1870.
Email: saez.pikor@t-online.de

Schwarz, Tobias, is Senior Researcher at the 'Global South Studies Center Cologne' at the University of Cologne. He holds a PhD in 'Europäische Ethnologie' from Humboldt-University in Berlin, where he studied Cultural Studies and Sociology with an emphasis on immigration policies, the administration of foreigners, and the contemporary German discourse of expulsion. His current research project focuses on naturalization ceremonies in the Global South. His regional expertise is Germany, the European Union, and Latin America. His latest publications include *Regímenes de pertenencia nacional en Venezuela y la República Dominicana contemporanea* (Tabula Rasa 20, 2014) and *National belonging in the Dominican Republic. The legal position as an interdependent social categorisation* (In: Célleri et al. (eds.), Interdependencies of Social Categorisations, Frankfurt a.M/Madrid: Vervuert, 2013).
Email: t.schwarz@uni-koeln.de

Takezawa, Yasuko, is Professor of Cultural Anthropology at the Institute for Research in the Humanities of Kyoto University in Japan. Her fields of interest include race, ethnicity, and immigration. She has been leading an international collaborative research project on race and racism from Asian experiences with a large grant-in-aid from the Japanese government. Her publications in English include *Transpacific Japanese American Studies: Conversations on Race and Racializations* (Yasuko Takezawa/Gary Okihiro (eds.), University of Hawaii Press, in press); Japanese Studies, 35/1, Special Issue: *Rethinking Race/Racism from Asian Experiences* (Koichi Iwabuchi/Yasuko Takezawa (eds.), in press); *Racial Representations in Asia* (Yasuko Takezawa ed., Kyoto University Press, 2011).
Email: yasuko.takezawa@gmail.com

Widlok, Thomas, is Professor for the Anthropology of Africa at the University of Cologne. He holds a PhD in Anthropology from the London School of Economics and Political Science and has previously worked the universities of London, Heidelberg, Durham, and Nijmegen. He has also been involved with the Max Planck Institute for Psycholinguistics and the Max Planck Institute for Social Anthropology. His regional expertise is southern Africa and Australia. He has co-edited a two-volume book on *Property and Equality* (New York: Berghahn, 2005) and his recent contributions include *Sharing. Allowing others to take what is valued* (In: HAU. Journal of Ethnographic Theory 3/2, pp. 11–31, 2013).
Email: thomas.widlok@uni-koeln.de

Li Xi Yuan is Professor at the Department of Sociology at the Centre for the studies of Hong Kong, Macao and Pearl River Delta, Sun Yat-SenUniversity, China. She holds a PhD in Anthropology from the Sun Yat-SenUniversity. 2003 to 2004 she was visiting scholar at the dDepartment of Sociology of the University of California Los Angeles. Her research interests and areas of expertise include ethnicity, identity, social mobility in China, Hong Kong and Macao. Her publications in English include *Mobility and Trans-territorial Identity: Strategies of Adaptation of Mainland Professionals in Hong Kong* (In: Hong Kong Journal of Social Sciences 43, 2012) and *The Transformation and Reconstruction of Urban Community in China* (Beijing: The Commercial Press, 2011).
Email: puslxy@mail.sysu.edu.cn

Zeleke, Meron, is postdoctoral fellow of the Volkswagen foundation postdoctoral fellowship programme in the humanities in sub Saharan and northern Africa. She is a social anthropologist and adjunct assistant professor of Anthropology at the center for human rights in Addis Ababa University. She holds a PhD in Social Anthropology from the Bayreuth International Graduate School of African Studies. She is the chair of Eastern African chapter of African Good Governance Network (AGGN) and has previously worked as a researcher such as DFID and the World Bank. Her research interest and areas of expertise include ethnicity, religious based conflicts, religion and peace, youth and religious activism, Customary Conflict Resolution and gender.
Email: eressokiyya@gmail.com